This book is dedicated to the ladies of the Ph
whose friendship, inspiration, and guidance made t.

About the Author

Teresa Michelsen is a tarot reader and instructor with more than twenty-five years of experience reading tarot. She is well-known on the tarot e-mail lists under her reading name of Thrysse, and has published many articles on tarot on the worldwide web and in American Tarot Association publications. Teresa teaches on-line tarot courses for beginning and intermediate readers, and her first book, *Designing Your Own Tarot Spreads*, was published in 2002. Her award-winning tarot website, www.tarotmoon.com, is a favorite destination of tarot readers who come for her lessons and articles on tarot, her examples of completed tarot readings, and the beautifully laid-out pages on tarot cards and readings. Teresa lives near Seattle, Washington, and in addition to her tarot work, has home-based businesses in environmental consulting and mediation.

To Write to the Author

If you wish to contact the author or would like more information about this book, please write to the author in care of Llewellyn Worldwide and we will forward your request. Both the author and publisher appreciate hearing from you and learning of your enjoyment of this book and how it has helped you. Llewellyn Worldwide cannot guarantee that every letter written to the author can be answered, but all will be forwarded. Please write to:

Teresa C. Michelsen
℅ Llewellyn Worldwide
P.O. Box 64383, Dept. 0-7387-0434-2
St. Paul, MN 55164-0383, U.S.A.

Please enclose a self-addressed stamped envelope for reply,
or $1.00 to cover costs. If outside U.S.A., enclose
international postal reply coupon.

Many of Llewellyn's authors have websites with additional information
and resources. For more information, please visit our website at
http://www.llewellyn.com

the complete TAROT reader

Everything You Need to Know
From Start to Finish

Teresa C.
Michelsen

Llewellyn Publications
Saint Paul, Minnesota

First Edition
First Printing, 2005

Cover design by Gavin Dayton Duffy
Edited by Andrea Neff

Llewellyn is a registered trademark of Llewellyn Worldwide, Ltd.

Cards from the *Universal Tarot* © Roberto De Angelis, the *Tarot Art Nouveau* © Antonella Castelli, the *Avalon Tarot* © Joseph Viglioglia, the *Visconti Tarots* © Atanas A. Atanassov, the *Esoteric Ancient Tarots* © Etteilla, and *The Fey Tarot* © Mara Aghem are all reprinted with permission from Lo Scarabeo.

Cards from *The Gilded Tarot* © Ciro Marchetti, *Medieval Enchantment: The Nigel Jackson Tarot* © Nigel Jackson, *Legend: The Arthurian Tarot* © Anna-Marie Ferguson, the *Victoria Regina Tarot* © Sarah Ovenall, *The World Spirit Tarot* © Lauren O'Leary, and *The Robin Wood Tarot* © Robin Wood used with permission from Llewellyn Worldwide.

The card from Ffiona Morgan's *Daughters of the Moon Tarot* © Daughters of the Moon is used with permission.

Library of Congress Cataloging-in-Publication Data

Michelsen, Teresa.
    The complete tarot reader : everything you need to know from start to finish / Teresa Michelsen.—1st ed.
        p.   cm.
    Includes bibliographical references.
    ISBN 0-7387-0434-2
    1. Tarot. I. Title.

    BF1879.T2M53 2005
    133.3'2424—dc22   2004063311

Llewellyn Worldwide does not participate in, endorse, or have any authority or responsibility concerning private business transactions between our authors and the public.
    All mail addressed to the author is forwarded but the publisher cannot, unless specifically instructed by the author, give out an address or phone number.
    Any Internet references contained in this work are current at publication time, but the publisher cannot guarantee that a specific location will continue to be maintained. Please refer to the publisher's website for links to authors' websites and other sources.

Llewellyn Publications
A Division of Llewellyn Worldwide, Ltd.
P.O. Box 64383, Dept. 0-7387-0434-2
St. Paul, MN 55164-0383, U.S.A.
www.llewellyn.com

Printed in the United States of America

Other Books by Teresa C. Michelsen

Designing Your Own Tarot Spreads
Llewellyn Publications, 2003

Acknowledgments

I would first like to thank the tarot acquisitions editor at Llewellyn, Barbara Moore, for encouraging me to write this book and actively working with the tarot community in so many different ways. She deserves a lot of credit and acknowledgment for her creative ideas and friendly personality. Thanks, Barbara!

Most of the material in this book is adapted from a series of on-line courses originally taught through my tarot sites, *Tarot Adventures* and *Tarot Explorations* on YahooGroups.com, and which are now part of the American Tarot Association curriculum. I would like to thank the ComparativeTarot on-line discussion group and the ATA for giving me the encouragement to teach, and especially all the students, tarot readers, and teachers who joined me on this journey of mutual learning—without you, this book wouldn't be what it is. I received much useful feedback and many suggestions from these early courses. Personal thanks to Patty, Janet, Vasiliki, Batia, Rhys, Diana, Sheila, Valerie, Arielle, Diane, Sandra, and Mary—all of you have been special contributors to this journey, in different ways.

In addition, I would like to thank many of the members of the TarotL on-line discussion list for their assistance with the historical material in this book, and for the great deal that I have learned from them over the years. Any remaining historical errors are my sole responsibility.

And always, my thanks to my husband and family—some are interested in tarot and some not, but no matter what, they are always loving and supportive of my interests and activities. It's wonderful to know you have a family you can count on, and the thought is never far from my mind.

Contents

Part Five: Intermediate Reading Techniques

one

Introduction

Welcome to the world of tarot! Tarot reading is a blend of artistry, intuition, self-taught education, communication, and practical skills, and no one part is more important than the others. In this book, I hope to share with you some of the techniques that helped me become a better reader, which blend these different approaches.

There are three main ways to learn tarot, and this book will focus mostly on two of them. These include (1) learning traditional keywords and meanings for the cards, (2) learning a more intuitive approach to tarot reading, and (3) learning about the underlying structures and patterns in the tarot, including the associations of various cards to other disciplines such as astrology, numerology, psychology, and myth. Most beginning readers start by learning the traditional meanings of the cards, and branch out into the other two areas with time. As a result, there are many books available to help you learn the basic meanings of the cards. Most decks come with a "little white book" or, preferably, a larger, deck-specific book that lists the meanings of the cards and may also provide some information on the symbolism and design of the cards.

Temperance
Medieval Enchantment: The Nigel Jackson Tarot

This book focuses on the other two areas: developing the intuitive side of reading, and learning the underlying structures and symbolic associations of the cards. You should already have a deck and a book that goes with it, which you can use to look up and learn the cards. You may use any deck you like with this book. Tarot decks are not all alike, and some of them are quite different from one another, which is one good reason to get a book that is specifically intended to go with your deck. And, it is one reason that I generally do not give card meanings in this book—because card meanings can vary from deck to deck. What I will do is help you strengthen your understanding of the meanings given for your deck, and help you expand on those meanings to personalize them, as well as explain some of the underlying ideas behind why tarot deck authors choose the meanings they do.

Choosing a Tarot Deck

Many beginning readers ask for advice on which deck to buy. This turns out to be a very difficult question to answer. Some readers suggest that beginning readers should start with the most widely used decks, which are generally thought of as the *Rider-Waite-*

Smith group of decks (named after the publisher, the author, and the artist, respectively, of a widely popular tarot deck published in 1909). You could choose the *Rider-Waite, Universal Waite, Hanson-Roberts, Robin Wood,* or any number of similar decks in this family. However, some people find that these decks don't resonate with them, and there are many other good choices. Whatever traditional decks you may have for historical and study purposes, it is important to have at least one whose imagery evokes strong responses in you so that it will engage your subconscious in the reading process.

There are older decks, such as the fifteenth-century *Visconti-Sforza* and the eighteenth-century *Tarot de Marseille,* which have an entirely different feel to them (but normally have minor cards that have only suit symbols—like a deck of playing cards). The *Thoth* deck was developed by the magician Aleister Crowley and artist Frieda Harris, and has become one of the standards among tarot decks, although it is not one of the easier ones to learn because of its strong esoteric and magickal content. Finally, there is a huge range of modern decks, developed with every possible interest in mind, such as herbs, shamanism, Wicca, feminism, animals, faeries, gemstones, Arthurian legends, various cultures of the world, and Greek mythology, just to name a very few.

I would suggest getting one of the traditional decks, for study if nothing else, and another deck that appeals strongly to your visual/artistic sense and personal interests. The comparison between them will be interesting, and you may learn a lot from both the differences and the similarities between them.

Creating a Tarot Journal

The other thing you should have before you begin your study of the tarot is a tarot journal. For those not inclined to write, don't worry! This is not a journal in the sense that you'll have to write 500 words about each card. Instead, just find yourself a nice book with empty pages, and set aside at least two pages for each of the 78 cards in the deck. Also, leave some space to write down ideas about the suits, numbers, and court cards, since we will be looking at each of these systematically.

Your journal is a place where you can do almost anything you want: jot down notes, keep track of ideas, draw or color, make lists and charts of keywords and associations, write down dreams or visualizations, do collage, impress herbs or plants—the list is endless. If you'd like, you could even write essays or stories. No matter how much you think you're not into journaling, you'll find it to be a useful tool. There is so much to learn about tarot, from so many different sources, that it helps to have it all organized in one place so you can look things up easily. You can use your computer for this purpose also, if you'd prefer.

How to Use This Book

Modern tarot decks generally have 78 cards, and are divided into the 22 Major Arcana cards (also called the trumps) and the 56 Minor Arcana cards, composed of the pips (Ace–Ten cards) and the court cards. Like a standard playing deck, there are four suits in the Minor Arcana, each of which has ten numbered cards and four court cards. The Major Arcana are a separate series of cards that are usually numbered 0 through 21.

The first three parts of this book follow the structure of a tarot deck and systematically explore the pips, court cards, and Major Arcana. After that, there are chapters designed to help you begin reading for yourself and others. Following this are chapters on more advanced reading techniques, including reversals, dignities, timing readings, and large-scale interpretations. Finally, there is a wealth of supplemental information in the appendices for your reference, including how to play the game of *tarocchi*—for which tarot cards were originally designed. When you use this book, feel free to jump around and work with whatever areas interest you most. There is no need to read everything in order if you don't want to. The keyword self-test in appendix A will help highlight areas you might want to focus on, or you may already know what you want to work on first.

To guide your studies, each chapter contains study goals at the beginning of the chapter as well as a section at the end called "Evaluating Your Progress." Also included throughout the chapters are exercises to do as you read along. The study goals summarize the main points of the chapter and what you will focus on learning, while the section at the end contains tools you can use to see how well you have met those goals. Keep in mind that tarot reading is a process of continual learning, and is something you will develop at deeper and deeper levels with time. Most importantly, it takes practice. So don't be surprised if all your study goals are not met the first time you read a chapter.

One good approach for working with the section titled "Evaluating Your Progress" is to try it for the first time once you have finished reading the chapter and have completed all the exercises. This will let you know which goals you have fully met, through working with this book and any previous experience you may have with tarot. Check these off as being completed. You will also identify areas where more work is needed. Practice over time is especially important. You may wish to continue on through the book, keeping these areas in mind and remembering to focus on them when you do readings. You can also repeat some of the exercises in the chapter until you become more confident and comfortable with these areas. Then come back later, perhaps in a few months or even a year, and try these evaluations again. In this way, you can see your progress over time.

Welcome to the journey that is tarot! May it lead you to endless vistas of knowledge and fascination.

The Fool
The Gilded Tarot

two

Intuitive Tarot Reading

Study Goals

1. Become familiar with the appearance of each card in the deck.

2. Identify important symbols on the cards that contribute to their meanings.

3. Develop concepts and keywords for each card using your intuition.

Once you have become acquainted with the basic meanings for the tarot cards, it is helpful to go deeper into the cards and personalize your understanding of them according to your own intuition and life experiences. It is one thing to read and memorize a list of keywords, and another to firmly root these ideas into your subconscious so that you don't have to struggle to remember them during a reading. Also, some of the meanings you find in books may not work for you, and you will want to add ideas of your own. Each person is unique, and in a sense, our minds act like translators. Information is being conveyed through the tarot reading, using the tools, or the cards, that we have available. Because this information is presented to us in the form of symbols, both our conscious and subconscious minds are involved in interpreting the information. Therefore, our own personal associations are important in how we read our cards.

Every tarot reader does not need to learn the same card meanings or use the same decks or spreads. Three tarot readers could ask the same question, and might choose different spreads and receive different cards in the reading, and still get the same answer. The cards that each reader receives will be appropriate for his or her own personal associations and, with experience and practice, will lead to the right answer. The tarot itself will also teach you over time what its symbols represent—you will notice that certain cards appear in certain circumstances, and your list of associations and meanings will expand as you begin to see these patterns.

One of the most basic rules in tarot reading is to have confidence in your own associations with the cards. Do not let anyone else tell you that you have to interpret a card a certain way. Use your own ideas, along with everything else you learn from others, and you can feel certain that you will receive the right cards for your own mind to draw the appropriate interpretations. In working through the exercises in this chapter, try not to be concerned about whether your thoughts are wrong or right. There is no "wrong." Even if you later decide to use a different set of meanings for a card, it is important to know what your subconscious mind spontaneously associates with the images you see on the cards, to know what "filters" you may be applying to your interpretations. One of the reasons this chapter comes before the other chapters that provide more systematic information, is that intuitive associations come from the subconscious and are easily overridden by conscious learning. In order to hear your inner voice more clearly, it is better to try this while you are still relatively free of what you think the cards "should" mean.

Also, it's a good idea to remain flexible as you learn more and more. It is okay to leave behind previous ideas if you decide they no longer fit your understanding of the cards. You will also encounter new ideas from time to time that you will want to incorporate into your interpretation. As you continue exploring the tarot, you will discover many interesting related areas, like astrology, numerology, psychology, alchemy, mythology . . . there is a never-ending realm of ideas to encounter and new things to add to your understanding. Keep things simple as you get started, but never limit yourself to just a few keywords for each card, or you will be missing out on much that the tarot has to offer. You may also find that your ideas and keywords for each card vary from deck to deck.

This chapter provides some ideas on how to develop intuitive card meanings. The rest of this book will give you a great deal of information on the underlying structure of the cards, such as the meanings of the numbers, suits, cycles represented by the suits and trumps, symbols you may see in the cards, astrological and elemental associations, and other things that provide you with a deeper understanding of the cards and the relationships between them. However, most experienced tarot readers agree that the first step in learning a new deck is to put away your books and look closely at the images—so we'll start there.

Free Association

For the exercises that follow, clear your mind of whatever you have already learned and set aside your books and notes. There are no right answers, and you will have plenty of time later to study what others have to say about the cards. Use the cards only in their upright positions. Since the reversed meanings of the cards generally follow from their upright positions, we will discuss those once the upright positions have been mastered. Use your tarot journal to record your observations.

EXERCISE 1: GETTING TO KNOW THE CARDS

Shuffle your deck thoroughly, and then take the cards out and look at them one by one, always in an upright position. Without thinking too much about it, write down your first impressions of each card. What thoughts or emotions does the card immediately evoke?

Next, look closely at each card. Notice all the details in the card—the background, any people in the card, or any animals, plants, buildings, symbols, colors, and expressions. How do you think they relate to the meaning of the card? Do they support or change your first impressions? You may want to take note of any unfamiliar symbols, or anything in the card whose meaning is unclear, so you can look them up later (see appendix E for some ideas).

Imagine that you have stepped into the card. Look around you. What do you see, feel, smell, and hear? If there is a person in the card, imagine that you have become that person. What are you doing and why? If the person in the card could speak to you, what do you think he or she would say?

Try to associate this card with some event or period in your own life, and write it down. If the card doesn't seem to fit your own life, does it remind you of anyone you know? How about a scene in a book or movie? Whatever it most reminds you of, write that down. If you can think of this event or person every time you look at this card, it will be much easier to remember what it means.

Now add to your journal any words or ideas that you associate with these experiences. Continue writing things down until you can't think of any more. It is fine if you use some of the same words for more than one card. For now, don't worry about which keyword or idea is most important or most represents the card. ✪

Once you have done this exercise, go back and read through the book that accompanies your deck, or another resource you have chosen to provide basic meanings for the cards. Compare each page of your journal with the meanings given for the associated card. At first, some of them may not seem to be very much alike. Is there a way you can expand on what is in the book or what you have written to help integrate them? Try putting the two sets of ideas together and see what happens. If it doesn't work out right away, don't worry. It will come with time. Later chapters in this book will help explain some of the traditional meanings for the cards, and you may eventually find some of your initial ideas changing as you read more and work more with the tarot. Just remember that your own impressions are important because they reflect what your mind thinks and feels when it sees those particular images or symbols on the cards. This is the personal, intuitive part of tarot that cannot be found in any book except the journal you create for yourself.

Storytelling

One fun way to get in touch with your intuitive ideas about the cards is to tell stories with them. You could lay them all out in order and make up a story that follows the numerological cycle (we will do that in later chapters). But for now, a random approach may be better for tapping into your subconscious associations with the cards. If you have children in the house, get them involved in playing this as a game—kids are really good at this (just don't fall into the trap of "correcting" their meanings, because this is meant as an imaginative exercise).

EXERCISE 2: TELLING A STORY
Shuffle your deck and choose three cards, or however many you like, and place them on the table. Move them around into any order you want, and then tell a story about the people and actions in the cards as if you were looking at a picture book. ✪

Aside from getting more familiar with the cards and learning your own associations with them, another good reason for doing this is to practice the storytelling that is an essential part of tarot reading. By this I do not mean making up things, but rather weaving the individual cards together into a coherent whole. The cards in a layout interact with one another, but it takes some practice to learn how to take the individual card meanings you know and integrate them into an overall reading. Getting used to working with the cards in groups, as part of an overall situation or story, will help you get comfortable doing this.

Developing a Range of Meanings

Each card in the tarot deck has many different meanings, depending on the question that is asked, the position of the card in the spread, the cards around it, and any ways of modifying the meanings of the cards, such as reversals or dignities, that the reader is using. At a minimum, all the cards in the deck can be read on at least three levels: spiritual, psychological, and everyday or mundane. In addition, there are times when the cards are more positive and other times when they are more negative, even when read upright. For these reasons, it is a good idea to learn a range of ideas, keywords, and phrases for each card, as there will be many times when any particular keyword you might have learned does not fit the situation.

One of the most important ideas you can learn about tarot is that every card contains duality within it, just as we all do. No card is inherently positive or negative—all cards reflect the cycles of life and the activities and lessons we have to learn from life. However, many tarot books (especially the little white books—or LWBs) tend to treat some cards as solely positive and others as very negative. While it is true that some tend more toward the positive or negative, each has ways in which it can be read that are positive, neutral, or negative, depending on the situation. Learning the inherent qualities of the card, both good and bad, will be very helpful later on when learning about reversals and dignities, and will also help you understand how to read the cards in different positions in a spread.

As an example, let's look at the Eight of Wands. Neutral descriptions of this card might include rapid change, messages coming, or strong energies being released. All these things can be good or bad, depending on the situation and what the client wants or needs. Positive meanings might be good news, a fresh start, spring thaw, or feeling enthusiastic and revitalized. Negative meanings could include unexpected or unwelcome change, feeling overwhelmed by events, or angry messages (or worse) coming your way.

Eight of Wands
Lo Scarabeo's *Universal Tarot*

EXERCISE 3: LOOKING AT THE CARDS IN DIFFERENT LIGHTS

For this exercise, shuffle your deck once again, and then take out the cards one by one. You may refer to the keywords and phrases you wrote in your journal during the first exercise. Now imagine a three-card spread where the positions are as follows:

Card 1: The situation.

Card 2: Problems or challenges to be overcome; negative influences.

Card 3: Strengths and resources that will help; positive influences.

Now take your card and rotate it through each of these three positions. How does the meaning change? The first position is purely descriptive, and should be relatively neutral. The next two positions are designed to look at the card in a more negative and more positive light, respectively. Notice any cards that are particularly hard to fit into the positive or negative positions. Add any new insights that you receive from this exercise to your tarot journal. ✪

Evaluating Your Progress

Study Goal 1

Shuffle your deck and turn the cards over one by one, hiding the name or title of the card if possible. Quickly say out loud the name of the card, identifying from its picture. Place any card you have to think about or can't identify into a separate pile from the ones you know well. Now study the ones that were difficult to recognize. Do this exercise until you can quickly identify all your cards.

Study Goal 2

Shuffle your deck and turn the cards over one by one. For each card, identify at least three visual cues that are important to developing and remembering the meanings you have associated with that card. These may be symbols, colors, expressions, things the people are doing, or just the overall ambience and feel of the card. Consciously explain to yourself or another person what the symbols mean to you (it is also helpful to record them in your journal).

Study Goal 3

Complete the keyword self-test in appendix A. The ultimate goal of this exercise is to have all your cards fall into category A (cards you know well and can use fluently). Remember that it is highly unlikely that you will meet this goal at this point in the book. However, doing this exercise now will give you a good sense of what your strengths and weaknesses are in terms of feeling familiar and comfortable with each card, and will help you focus your energies on the areas that need the most attention. The coming chapters will give you much more information to work with, and by the time you finish this book, you should find that your score has dramatically improved.

part one

The Pips (Ace–Ten)

three

Suit Correspondences and Elemental Associations

Study Goals

1. Develop elemental associations for each suit.
2. Associate other symbols and aspects of life with the suits and elements.
3. Learn how the elements interact with each other.

In this section, we will begin exploring the underlying structure of the pip cards, numbered Ace through Ten, which are part of the Minor Arcana. The cards in the Minor Arcana are often thought of as representing scenes from everyday life, while the Major Arcana cards are more spiritual in nature. This chapter focuses on the unique attributes of each suit, along with their elemental associations, while the following chapter focuses on the meanings of the numbers. Used together, these two aspects can easily be cross-referenced to give at least one possible meaning for each card, and deepen your understanding of the relationships between cards. For example, if the suit of Cups represents emotions and relationships, and Threes represent expansion and abundance, then one aspect of the Three of Cups is an abundance or expansion of social relationships.

Three of Cups
Medieval Enchantment: The Nigel Jackson Tarot

For this chapter, separate out the Ace through Ten of each suit, and set the rest of the deck aside. Lay these cards out in four rows of ten, with each suit in sequential order, so that you can see all the cards at once. For all the exercises in this chapter, including the example readings, use only the Ace through Ten cards of the four suits. In later chapters we will learn and apply elemental associations to the court and trump cards.

EXERCISE 1: DEVELOPING SUIT ASSOCIATIONS

Look at all the cards in one of the suit rows. On a piece of paper or your computer, make a heading for each suit, and under each heading, write down every word you can think of that seems to represent the cards in that suit. What aspect of everyday life does each suit represent? What common themes do you see in the cards for that suit? Choose two or three keywords that seem to best represent the suit. You will use these later, along with your numerological associations, to develop new meanings for each of the pip cards.

Each of the suits is also associated with one of the four elements: earth, air, fire, and water. Decide which of these elements goes with each suit and write it under the appropriate heading. Which suits seem active and which seem passive to you? Various authors have also ascribed one of the four seasons of the year to the various suits. Which season do you think goes with each suit and why? Write those associations down as well. ✪

Associating seasons with the cards is not absolutely necessary. Its main use is for timing questions, which we will discuss later on in the book, although it can also be used in a more abstract sense to represent new growth and beginnings (spring), fullness and abundance (summer), harvesting and preparing (fall), and dormancy and conservation of energy (winter).

Now study the table at the very end of this chapter (no peeking until you are done with this exercise!). It provides associations that others have developed for the suits. How similar are these to yours? Are there any that surprise you? Remember that your choices do not have to match those of others. Each deck may be unique in its associations, or you may choose to use associations that are personally meaningful to you.

Using Suit Associations in Tarot Spreads

There are many ways in which the suit associations are used in tarot readings. First of all, you can look at all the cards drawn together. Are most of them from one or two suits? This will tell you something about what is on the mind of the client or the approach they are taking to their problem. A completely balanced situation should have all four elements present (if the spread is large enough), but often a reading will be dominated by one or two suits. Next look to see if there are any suits missing. These may represent areas that the client needs to focus on or energies that need to be added to the situation.

Finally, check to see if the suits that come up are appropriate to the question. For example, it is common for Cups to come up for relationship questions, and for Pentacles and Wands to come up with respect to jobs and careers. If a person asks about her career, and all of her cards are Cups, this may suggest that what is really important to her in her career is being emotionally and spiritually satisfied. Or if reversed, it could indicate that she is taking an emotional approach to her career, but a little more planning (Swords), action (Wands), and practicality (Pentacles) might be beneficial.

EXERCISE 2: USING SUIT ASSOCIATIONS

Do a three-card reading on the following question: "I am so depressed lately, and I don't even know why. Can you help me figure out what is going on?" Use a three-card spread, as shown below. Use the suit associations in the reading to help explain where this problem comes from and how to solve it.

Card 1: Why she is so depressed.

Card 2: What she can do about it.

Card 3: Where she can look for help. ✪

Another way of looking at readings is to see how many active (Swords and Wands) and passive (Cups and Pentacles) cards come up. If your client wants to make a major change in his life, but receives only passive cards, this could suggest that he is holding back, and doing more planning and thinking about it than really taking action. He may be afraid to let go of something stable (Pentacles). A passive set of cards may also represent an internal focus to a problem, and active cards an external focus.

Exploring Elemental Interactions

The elemental associations of earth, air, fire, and water are often used to design and interpret tarot spreads. Elemental associations are one of the ways in which we look at interactions between cards, and can be used instead of reversals (this is called using elemental dignities). Compatible elements strengthen each other, while opposing elements weaken each other.

In Greek philosophy, and later in alchemy, the four elements were associated with combinations of certain qualities. They are considered hot or cold, wet or dry, as follows:

Earth: Cold and dry.

Water: Cold and wet.

Fire: Hot and dry.

Air: Hot and wet.

Elements that belong together and are compatible with each other are those that have a primary feature in common—they are both cold (or passive/feminine) or both hot (active/masculine). These elements can be easily mixed and combined in nature. Elements that have a secondary characteristic in common (both dry or both wet) are neutral toward each other. They can be mixed with some difficulty (think of glowing ashes or air bubbles in water). Elements that have no characteristics in common are incompatible and weaken each other. These elements cannot be mixed together and are not found together in nature. The following table of elemental compatibilities, also known as elemental dignities, is based on these concepts. We will take a much more detailed look at elemental dignities in chapter 16, but for now it is just helpful to be aware of how the elements are associated with the suits and how they naturally interact with one another.

Compatible	*Neutral*	*Incompatible*
Fire and air	Fire and earth	Fire and water
Earth and water	Water and air	Earth and air

One way to use elemental associations is to use a spread that is designed to bring out these aspects of the situation. A widely used spread is known as Mind-Body-Spirit, and there are other similar spreads, such as Mental-Physical-Emotional or Health-Wealth-Happiness. These are very useful spreads that can be used to explore several different levels of a situation. The natural suit and elemental affinities with these card positions could be thought of as Mind = Swords, Body/Health/Finances = Pentacles, Emotion/Relationships = Cups, and Will/Career = Wands (Spirit can be either Cups or Wands, or is sometimes thought of as a fifth element represented by the trumps). Any one of these suits in its corresponding position would be considered to be strengthened by that association, and other suits would be neutral or weakened. If cards are in their "natural" positions according to suit, then those energies in the situation are expected to flow more freely. If some positions contain opposing suits, then those energies might be blocked or the client may feel frustrated and ineffective.

EXERCISE 3: ELEMENTAL SPREADS
Do a three-card Mental-Emotional-Financial reading on the question "I am thinking of becoming an architect. How will this career change work out for me?" Comment on the elemental affinities of the cards you receive with the card positions in the spread. ✪

Although all the cards of one suit are normally considered to be associated with the element corresponding to that suit, several elements may also interact within a single card.

For example, look at the Two of Swords. In most decks, the swords and wind-swept sky do invoke the element of air, and the posture of the woman, along with her blindfold, indicate retreat into the mind or contemplation. However, water is almost always a significant part of this card, and there is often a moon shining above her, which is also associated with water. Depending on the deck, the water may be stormy or calm. This is also true of other cards, such as the Six of Swords and the Two of Pentacles. In each of these cards, the water may reflect the emotional state of the person in the card, and indicates that emotional responses may be important to the situation depicted by the card along with its usual elemental and suit associations.

Two of Swords
Lo Scarabeo's *Universal Tarot*

EXERCISE 4: ELEMENTAL INTERACTIONS

Look through your deck for several cards that seem to have more than one element interacting in the picture. Describe how this could influence your interpretation of the card or add to its traditional meanings. ✪

Colors

Colors are used by some deck artists as a way of indicating the elemental qualities of a card. Traditional color associations for the elements are air = yellow, fire = red, water = blue, and earth = green. Not everyone follows this system; for example, an artist could choose to use blue for air, yellow for fire, green for water, and brown for earth—or any other system they choose. If the colors are used consistently in your deck to illustrate the elements, you should be able to quickly determine which colors are associated with which elements. Sometimes elemental colors are used along the borders of the card to identify the suit, and sometimes in the main artwork of the card.

Aside from the overall elemental association of the card, the colors may be used for individual aspects within the drawing. For example, in the *Universal Waite* version of the Magician, there is an overall yellow glow to the card associated with the element of air, which the Magician represents. He also wears a red robe to indicate his active, passionate masculine nature, over a white tunic of purity. As you can see from this example, there are many other meanings to the colors other than elemental associations, and it is worth taking a look through your deck to see how the colors are used and what they might represent. Some authors, such as Robin Wood, provide a detailed explanation of the colors they chose in the companion book to their deck. Some traditional meanings of the colors are provided in appendix E, along with a wide variety of other symbols you may find in your cards.

EXERCISE 5: COLORS AND SYMBOLS

Lay out the Ace through Ten cards of each suit in order, in four rows of ten. Looking at the cards, decide whether any of the colors used are likely to have elemental associations in your deck. Also notice whether there are any other suit-related color patterns that appear when you compare the different rows, or any other drawing elements or symbols that frequently appear in the cards of one suit. ✪

Table of Suit Correspondences

Suit	Areas of Life	Part of Self	Qualities	Element	Season
Cups	Relationships, love, creativity	Spirit/ emotions	Passive, feminine	Water	Spring
Wands	Career, initiative, activities, inspiration	Will/ actions	Active, masculine	Fire	Summer
Swords	Plans, intellectual activities, solving problems	Mind/ thoughts	Active, masculine	Air	Fall
Pentacles	Money, possessions, family, health	Body/ foundation	Passive, feminine	Earth	Winter

Please note that the seasons, especially, are subject to interpretation and vary in different decks. There are also some decks in which the elemental and suit attributions shown here are altered—the most frequent change is attributing fire to Swords and air to Wands.

Evaluating Your Progress

Study Goals 1 and 2

Write the names of the four suits across the top of a sheet of paper. Underneath the suit names, write down the element you associate with each suit. Below this, add at least four additional words describing associations you make with that suit or element that could be used in your tarot readings.

Study Goal 3

Using only the Ace through Ten cards of each suit, shuffle your deck. Draw cards two at a time, and place them upright in front of you. For each pair, identify the elements associated with each card and whether the two elements are compatible, neutral, or incompatible with each other. Do this without reference to your notes or journal, and continue until you can quickly recognize the elements and their relationships to each other. As a further exercise, identify any cards that seem to contain another element in addition to their primary one, and indicate how that might modify the interaction of the two cards you draw.

———— **four** ————

Numerological Associations

Study Goals

1. Develop numerological associations for the Ace through Ten cards (pips).

2. Combine these with suit associations to provide one set of meanings for the pips.

3. Learn to recognize and use numerological cycles in readings.

Combining suit and numerological associations provides structure and consistency to your card meanings that you can add to whatever other card meanings you may have learned. Systematic associations are easier to learn and remember than forty seemingly unrelated sets of keywords. It is also very helpful to use a system like this when using decks that have no illustrations on the Minor cards, since you will have no other visual cues to work from.

In this chapter, you will become familiar with the numerological associations of the pip cards, Ace through Ten of each suit, as well as additional uses of numerology in conducting tarot readings. For the following exercises, separate out the Ace through Ten of each suit, and set the rest of the deck aside. Just like in the previous chapter, use only the Ace through Ten cards of the four suits for readings and exercises. To start with, lay these cards out in the same four rows of ten, with each suit in sequential order.

EXERCISE 1: DEVELOPING NUMEROLOGICAL ASSOCIATIONS

Look at each column, starting with the Aces. What aspects or properties do all the Aces seem to have in common? Write down as many keywords for Aces as you can think of. Then do the same for each number Two through Ten, focusing only on the traits that the cards sharing the same number seem to have in common. List the keywords that are shared by all four of the cards of that number, and then describe how each card modifies those keywords in its own way. ✵

After you have developed your own keywords and phrases, take a look at the next section, "Keywords for Aces Through Tens." While this may provide additional information for you, remember that your own keywords are the most important—don't try to use ones that don't make sense for you.

EXERCISE 2: TRUMP ASSOCIATIONS

Now take out the trumps that have the numbers 1 through 10, and place them above the columns with that number. What associations can you form between the trumps and the Minor cards of the same number? Write these new insights down in your journal. If you want to take this exercise even further, take the rest of the trumps and place them in the appropriate column as follows: Add the two digits of the trumps together until they reduce to a single number. For example, trump 14, Temperance, would work like this: 1 + 4 = 5. Place this card above the Fives. These cards are considered "higher-order" versions of the basic numbers and have associations with the primary card. Thus, Justice is associated with the High Priestess, the Moon is associated with the Hermit, etc. Technically, in numerology, 10 is not a basic number and should be reduced to 1, although for this exercise, you may choose to put both the Wheel of Fortune (10) and the Sun (19) in the 10 position for comparison to the Minor Arcana. What does this tell you about the associations between the Tens and Aces of each suit? ✵

We will explore the relationships between the trumps and the Minor Arcana further when we study the trumps, so don't worry if not all the trumps seem to fall into place at this time. As with all the patterns in the tarot, not all the cards will seem to "fit." There are various possible reasons for this. The earliest decks did not have pictures on the cards at all—these were added later and may not have been originally designed to follow clear numerological patterns. The meanings traditionally ascribed to the individual cards may have come from an older card-reading tradition (no one is really sure where the first divinatory meanings came from). Some of the newer decks may be more consistent in this regard, since their authors may have had astrological, numerological, and qabalistic patterns in mind when the deck was designed.

EXERCISE 3: COMBINING SUIT AND NUMEROLOGICAL ASSOCIATIONS

As you know from the previous chapter, each of the suits is also associated with one of the four elements, and with particular areas of life. Looking at the keywords for the suits that you developed earlier, combine your keywords for the suits with your keywords for the numbers. For example, if your keyword for Swords is *thoughts* and your keyword for Sixes is *harmony,* then one possible meaning of the Six of Cups is "harmonious thoughts." Review these pairs for all ten cards of each suit, and compare these phrases with the intuitive meanings you developed for your cards in chapter 2, as well as any meanings listed in other reference books you may have. Do you notice any cards whose keywords don't seem to fit the suit/number pattern? For the cards that don't fit, is there any way to expand either set of meanings so that they work together? ✪

Keywords for Aces Through Tens

Here are some keywords I have compiled for the Ace through Ten tarot cards. These won't necessarily match the ones you develop or use, but they are provided here as an added resource.

Aces: Beginnings, potential, elemental energy, unity, perfection.

Twos: Duality, choices, decisions, partnerships, division, balance, complementary energies.

Threes: Expansion, growth, expression, creativity.

Fours: Foundation, stability, consolidation, safety, rest.

Fives: Fives have very different meanings in different decks and traditions. The keywords here are divided into traditional *Rider-Waite-Smith* meanings and nontraditional meanings derived from feminist, Wiccan, or pagan traditions. Some of these earlier, more negative meanings may reflect early attitudes of society toward women and their spirituality.

- *Rider-Waite-Smith:* Conflict, instability, danger, sorrow, intemperance.
- *Alternative:* Spirit, magick, ritual, female energy, nurturing.

Sixes: Harmony, success, generosity, symmetry, balanced flow of energy.

Sevens: Challenges, rites of passage, ingenuity, flexibility.

Eights: Maturity, ability, resilience, self-directed movement.

Nines: Abundance, accumulation, living in the now, completion.

Tens: Worldly manifestation, long-term cycles, endings, transitions.

A detailed discussion of the numbers one through ten is provided in appendix B for those who want to explore the numbers in greater depth, and some additional meanings of numbers that are found in tarot-specific symbolism are included in appendix E, the glossary of symbols.

Numerological Cycle

In numerology, the numbers one through nine are considered to be part of a repeating cycle representing stages of life that we all go through. These numerological associations, described here, can be helpful in understanding the meanings of the Minor Arcana, and can be added to your list of keywords for the numbers. More importantly, numerology introduces the concept of sequences and flow from one card to the next—a complete cycle progressing from one to nine, and starting over again.

1: Beginnings, potential, spark or idea.

2: Emotional and practical investment.

3: Expansion, growth.

4: Foundations, consolidation.

5: Change, communication.

6: Rewards, creativity.

7: Unexpected challenges, upheaval.

8: Maturity, peak of ability.

9: Endings, preparing for the next cycle.

In this system, tens are not represented—all two-digit or higher numbers are reduced to single numbers. Therefore, Tens in the tarot may be considered to have an additional meaning of transitions between cycles, or situations that are in the process of ending or are overdue to end.

EXERCISE 4: SUIT STORIES

Lay out the Ace through Ten cards of one of the four suits (you can do this exercise for all four suits, if you wish). Make up a story that moves sequentially through all ten cards, from beginning to end. Imagine that the people and places in the cards are your characters and setting. The story can be about anything, but should be true to the suit and the numerological cycle, and should use the symbols and depictions on the cards to inspire your "plot." One example of a suit story appears at the end of this chapter. ✪

Using Numerology in Tarot Spreads

Numerological associations may be used in a variety of ways in tarot readings. You may find situations where the numerological/suit combination of meanings makes more sense than the keywords or traditional meanings of the card. It is also very significant if a particular number appears several times in a reading—for example, a five-card reading in which three Twos show up. The interpretation of this spread should discuss the general meaning of Twos in addition to the specific meanings of each of the individual cards. In looking at repeated occurrences of numbers in readings, one should also keep in mind the numbers associated with any trump cards received in the reading. For example, the High Priestess in combination with several Twos would reinforce the two energy of the reading, since her number is also two.

EXERCISE 5: USING NUMEROLOGICAL KEYWORDS

Do a reading on the following question: "Is this the right time for me to quit my job and start a home business selling real estate?" Use any spread of your choice, from one to five cards. Instead of using your normal keywords for the cards, use the combination of number and suit keywords to interpret the cards, paying particular attention to any number that appears more than once in the reading. Comment on the numbers that appear with respect to the numerological cycle to determine whether this is a good time for the client to make changes in his work situation. ✪

Another way to use numerology in a tarot reading is to consider what comes before and after each card that is received in a spread. This can be especially helpful when reading a "difficult" card, such as any of the Fives. Especially when doing a one-card reading, this method provides insight into how and why the client probably got to this place, and what is likely to happen next. Fives have a purpose, which is to spur a person on from the stability and stagnation of the Fours, in order to reach the balanced and harmonious Sixes. This cannot occur without some difficult and trying life lessons, and letting go of the security of what you have in order to allow change. Each of the other cards can be read in a similar way, and you can use the stories you developed earlier to help provide inspiration for how these transitions might work as you move through the cards. Providing this larger perspective will be much appreciated by your clients when they are working through a difficult situation.

Five of Pentacles
The World Spirit Tarot

EXERCISE 6: USING NUMEROLOGICAL CYCLES TO PROVIDE PERSPECTIVE
Do a one-card reading on the question "My mother and I have a very difficult relationship that causes us both a lot of pain. What are we supposed to be learning from this

and how can we move to a better place?" Interpret your one card with respect to its place in the numerological cycle to identify how they likely got to this point, what the situation is now, and how they can transition into the next natural step in the cycle. This method is one way to get a tremendous amount of information out of smaller readings on difficult topics, and can also be used with the trumps, once we have studied their cycles in more depth. ✪

Numerology can be used in a more traditional manner to supplement tarot readings when the client's birth date is known, to identify which year of a nine-year cycle they are currently in. To find their "year" card, take the complete date of the person's most recent birthday and add the digits of the month, day, and year. Then add the digits of that number until it is reduced to a single digit. This shows what year of their current cycle they are in, and can help shed light on aspects of the tarot reading. For example, my birthday is December 31. My last birthday (at the time of this writing) was in the year 2003, so the cycle I am currently in can be determined as follows: 12 (the month) + 31 (the day) + 2003 (the year) = 1 + 2 + 3 + 1 + 2 + 0 + 0 + 3 = 12. This number is further reduced as follows: 1 + 2 = 3. This is a good year for me to expand and creatively manifest something I have been thinking about and planning for the last couple years. If I were in a 9 year, I would be thinking about finishing up an old cycle and getting ready for a new one.

To tie this back to the tarot, this method can be associated with the trump card of the same number to show the overall energy for the current year, or can be used with the birth date and year to identify the "destiny" card, or trump card, that best represents this lifetime. To use the tarot in this way, reduce the birth date or most recent birthday until it corresponds with any number from 1 to 22 (22 = 0, the Fool). In my case above, my number 12, associated with the Hanged Man, might mean that whatever I am busy creating is an internal change rather than a more worldly project, which might be associated with 3, the Empress.

EXERCISE 7: USING BIRTH DATES

For your own birth date, determine your year card and your destiny card using the method just described. Reflect on what this means to you in terms of your life path and the energy you feel in your life this year. What part of the numerological cycle are you in, and what are you doing during this time of your life? ✪

A Swords Story

As an alternative to the traditional "doom and gloom" feeling of the Swords suit, this story provides an example of how numeric keywords and suit concepts can be combined to give a different and more balanced feel to the suit of Swords, while still remaining true to the core concepts. In this case, Swords are used to represent ideas, academic research, and technology, and the numeric keywords I used are shown in parentheses. This story comes from my own experience as a graduate student in a scientific field, and shows how even the most modern of our personal experiences can be illustrated through tarot cards.

Ace—Initiation

One day a graduate student (we'll call him Ryan) is working away in his advisor's laboratory, getting a series of experiments ready to run. It's a tedious job, and his mind wanders off into other areas. Suddenly he has an idea, one so exciting and unusual that he has to stop what he is doing and think about it. He goes to his computer and writes it down so he won't forget it. Later that night, he has a hard time getting to sleep because he is thinking about this concept, which blazes and crackles with energy in his mind. Up until now, he has pretty much been following along on his advisor's research, but for the first time, he feels like he has had a unique brainstorm that could be the start of his own research career.

Two—Balancing, Planning

For the next week, he can barely keep his mind on his daily work as he turns this idea over and over, looking at it from all possible angles. He doesn't do anything or say anything to anyone yet because he is worried that maybe it's not such a great idea, or maybe someone has already thought of it. He spends his evenings doing internet research and poring over journals at the library to firm up his ideas. One of the other graduate students in the lab, Susan, notices that he seems preoccupied and, when she runs into him at the library, asks him what's up. Feeling like he has a little more grounding for his idea now, he shares it with her. The two of them talk it over late into the night. They agree to spend the next few weeks writing a research proposal, just to see what it would look like.

Three—Expansion

They finish the proposal, and decide to go ahead and present it to their advisor, who is a tenured professor with access to funding and who has the respect of scientists in their field. He listens carefully, adds a few ideas of his own, and finds some weak spots that they need to work on. He asks them to rewrite the proposal, taking his comments into account, and then promises to look at it again. After this review, they are in turmoil. They are excited by his apparent support and his new ideas, and alternately dismayed by the things they missed and worried that he might try to take over their idea and use it as his own. They rewrite the proposal, adding some new ideas of their own, and make it clear in the author line that Ryan is the lead investigator and Susan is the second author. They take it back to the professor, who meanwhile has made a list of possible funding sources and grant institutions. He pronounces their proposal ready for submission, and gives them the go-ahead to apply. He agrees to serve as third author on the proposal, lending it credibility.

Four—Stability, Foundation

Now they wait. This is the first time they have ever submitted a proposal to a granting institution, and it's a scary process. For months and months they don't hear anything. Their graduate advisor assures them that this is normal—grants often take six to nine months to process. They do their best to be patient, and work diligently on the lab's day-to-day experiments, knowing that if they win their grant they had better be caught up on their work, or even ahead. They pass the time studying and planning, imagining how they would set up the experiments, and praying that they will get their funding. Ryan feels like his whole academic life hangs on this decision, since it was his idea and he has invested a lot of mental energy into it.

Five—Instability, Change

One day their advisor calls them into his office and gives them the bad news. The National Science Foundation budget has been cut as part of a secret deal during a congressional budget committee negotiation. As a result, the grant application was not approved, since the NSF could only fund a few projects this year, and they have been directed to focus on research of immediate application, rather than basic science. Through political maneuvering, their project has been killed. He tries to give them some perspective—research funding goes in long-term cycles, many other people lost their grants this year, etc., but of course they are devastated anyway. They go back to work, half-heartedly, wondering if they have what it takes to be researchers and if they can stand living through this kind of grant application process repeatedly throughout their careers. They suddenly realize why their professor does not spend that much time in the lab—he has to spend a lot of his time writing proposals in order to ensure funding for his lab and students. They start to think about "selling out" and going to work for industry, rather than following their dream of becoming researchers at a university.

Six—Harmony, Flow

After a few months, they begin to get a little perspective on the situation. They realize that this is a normal part of research, and that they need to just go with the flow a little more, remain flexible, and not invest so many hopes in a single grant application. They realize that they need their PhDs to get a good job regardless of what they eventually choose, so they renew their efforts and regain some of their enthusiasm. Meanwhile, the professor has been looking around for other sources of funding to replace the NSF money—these students are not the only ones who did not get their grants approved. Having a larger perspective on this field of science, he is able to locate a corporate sponsor who is interested in the application of basic research to computer technologies.

The professor approaches the graduate students about rewriting their proposal with this new application in mind. This time they are successful—although there is an element of compromise in that they are now looking at a particular application in addition to the basic research they originally had in mind, it is still a chance to follow through on their ideas. For the next two years, they design and run their first real research project, with modestly positive results. Excited at their successful collaboration, they publish several papers and prepare to write their dissertations, each of them choosing a different facet of what they have been working on as their thesis topic.

Seven—Challenge

Now comes the real test—pleasing sponsors and writing a few papers for publication is nothing compared to writing a dissertation and defending it in front of a group of tenured professors. Not only must they show that their research was well designed, carried through, and had results, they must also be able to show that it is fully original and contributes materially to the body of science in their field. On the dissertation committee are the head of the department and several prominent professors who are known to be tough critics and who have reduced previous graduate students with less-than-perfect dissertations to tears during the exam. These people hold their future in their hands, and so Ryan and Susan spend the next six months writing and rewriting their dissertations, keeping up on all the latest research in the field, imagining every possible argument, question, and criticism, and practicing with each other and their advisor. They each present their research at a lunch-time seminar for their fellow graduate students as a practice run, a critical but friendlier audience. The big day comes, and they both pass their oral exams, and are notified that their dissertations have been accepted. Woohoo!!! Of course, after the jubilation wears off, they realize that they have taken what is only the first step of a long and promising career, and there is much hard work ahead.

Eight—Maturity

After graduation, Ryan takes a job at the computer corporation and continues his original research, and Susan takes a postdoctoral fellowship at MIT. They stay in touch over the years. After a decade of research, Ryan works his way up to Head of Research and Susan gains tenure. He funds some of the work of her graduate students, and they continue their successful collaboration in addition to their own individual areas of research. Both become well respected in their field. Susan continues her daily struggle with getting enough funding for her students, and Ryan has to continually fight battles to keep his basic research budget in a corporate environment, but both survive and learn to work the system to support their initiatives.

Nine—Abundance

Ryan's research pays off with a lucrative innovation in hard drives that positions his company to be the leader in its field. Ryan is offered the position of VP of Engineering and Research, and he accepts, as there are many young hotshots rising in the company whose research will be the next wave of innovation. He wins a major technology prize and is interviewed by design magazines and journalists. He begins to spend more time on strategic planning and industry-level design conferences. However, he has a large department to oversee, and while he is gratified at the recognition being given to his life's work, he soon realizes that there are many headaches and worries that this position brings, such as personnel and manufacturing issues, that he never had to deal with before. Meanwhile, Susan has become chair of her department at MIT, and is the editor of a prestigious research journal. She has been nominated for the National Academy of

Sciences, and has won a variety of other awards over the years. She too has new responsibilities that are a recognition of her work, but are time-consuming, and at times, the academic bickering among her colleagues in the department becomes tedious, since it is now her job to resolve disputes. She begins to wonder how and when her life shifted from the research she loved to performing administrative functions, and suddenly realizes that her most original and interesting work is probably behind her.

Ten—Transition, Completion

Ryan tires of the stresses of corporate life and, when his company is bought out, takes an early retirement. This is a bittersweet decision since he was forced out by the new owners, who wanted to install their own VPs, but he also realizes that he has been chafing for some time in that position. His severance package is generous, and he realizes that he has a lot of options, which he begins to explore. A few months later, he calls up Susan and they go out to dinner, face to face for the first time in years. They talk over their life's work and the trials and tribulations, joys and excitement, of the work they have done, and comment on how their paths diverged and what each of them has accomplished. Then he springs the big one: Would she be interested in joining him in a small research and technology start-up? He asks her not to answer right away, but to just think about it. He will be providing most of the capital through his private funds and industry connections, and has already identified some of the most promising young men and women in his former company who are interested in joining up. He suggests that she think about retiring from academic life and join him as a partner (and maybe bring along a few of her former graduate students). With their combined expertise and prestige in the industry, they will lend this new company instant credibility in both academic and corporate circles, and will have more autonomy and freedom to pursue their own interests. He plans to keep this company small, and recruit only the best and the brightest. Is she interested? Susan goes home and thinks it over. Suddenly she realizes that she, too, has options. Could this be the next new adventure?

Measuring Your Progress

Study Goal 1

Without looking at the cards or your notes, write down at least three meanings or associations for each of the numbers Ace through Ten, as they are used in tarot.

Study Goal 2

Shuffle the Ace through Ten cards of your deck and turn them over one by one. For each card, state a keyword associated with the suit and one associated with the number, which combine to provide a meaning for that card. The keywords you use from card to card need not be the same for each suit or number, as long they represent one of the core concepts associated with that suit and number.

Study Goal 3

Identify three different situations in your life, or those of people you know, that are still in the process of being resolved. Draw one card for each situation. In each case, visualize in your mind the cards that come before and after the card you drew (don't look—you will need to be able to do this mentally during a reading). Now think about how that sequence of three cards represents the situation—where it has been, where it is now, and where it could go next following the natural progression of the numerological cycle. Consider that every Ten is followed by an Ace—a new beginning. Once this type of interpretation feels comfortable to you, then you will be able to integrate numerology fluently into your readings.

part two

The Court Cards

———————————— five ————————————

Developing
Personality Profiles

Study Goals

1. Develop keyword associations for the court card ranks.

2. Combine these with suit associations to develop one set of meanings for the court cards.

3. Add intuitive associations to round out the court card personality profiles.

In this chapter, you will get to know the court cards of each suit. These cards most often represent people in readings, either aspects of one's own mind and personality, or other people that affect the situation. By far the largest percentage of readings have to do with other people—love relationships, spouses, children, family, and coworkers—yet many readers find the court cards to be the hardest to interpret. This series of exercises is designed to make the court cards much more accessible and easy to understand.

You will begin by developing your own personality portraits for each court card, independent of what you may have learned from books or other study. In later chapters we will look in detail at the structure and symbology of the court cards, but your connection to these cards will be much deeper if you have built your own relationships with them.

Court Cards and Their Variations

Nearly all tarot decks have four court cards for each suit, but they are not always called the same thing from deck to deck. Traditionally, there are Pages, Knights, Queens, and Kings. Sometimes you will see Princesses rather than Pages, and even Princes instead of Knights. Occasionally you will see Knights in place of Kings, which can be very confusing the first time you see it. Regardless of the specific terms used, the Queens and Kings or their equivalents are traditionally used to represent mature adult men and women, while the Knights, Pages, and Princesses or the equivalent are used to represent younger men and women, teenagers, and children. However, this is not a hard and fast rule, it's just tradition. Queens and Kings may represent a mature and experienced approach to a situation, while Pages and Knights may represent a youthful or innocent approach, or a new life experience for the client. Both youthful and mature qualities can coexist in any one person, in different areas of their life.

Court cards have three major uses in tarot readings. They may represent:

- Actual people, including the client, that are affecting the situation.
- Aspects of the client's mind or personality that are coming into play.
- Activities associated with the court cards, such as starting out on a quest or new activity (Knights), receiving a message (Page of Wands or Cups), beginning a new area of study (Page of Pentacles), or taking on a position of leadership (King of Wands).

It is best not to limit yourself to any one of these meanings, as which one applies will almost certainly vary from reading to reading. In this chapter, however, we will be focusing on the innate personalities represented by the cards, whether associated with the client or someone else involved in the situation.

EXERCISE 1: IDENTIFYING WITH THE COURT CARDS

Remove all the court cards from one or more decks and set the rest of the deck(s) aside. Become familiar with the names used for the court cards in your decks and whether there are any differences in the names between your decks. Lay out the court cards for one of these decks in four rows of four, by suit and rank, and look them over. Which court card do you feel intuitively represents you? Think about whether you might be represented by different court cards in different areas of your life or in different moods. What additional card or cards might you pick for these situations? Now look at the rest of the cards. Which person would you choose as an ideal spouse and why? How about if you were starting a new business and needed a business partner? Choose one card to represent each of your family members and then notice what attributes of these cards reminded you of them. ✪

Developing Personality Portraits for the Court Cards

In the previous exercise, you began the process of developing intuitive associations of personalities with each court card. Although you may read descriptions of card personalities in books, they do vary strongly from deck to deck. Here are some images of Pages of Swords from three different decks. Notice how different they are from one another—one may appear defensive or protective, another daring and adventuresome, another imaginative and idealistic, and so on.

Page of Swords
The World Spirit Tarot, Tarot Art Nouveau, Avalon Tarot

When learning to read court cards, it is most helpful if you develop your own personalities for your cards based on what the images in your specific deck suggest to you. Each of the Pages shown here share certain traits or attributes—all are Pages, so they represent youth, inexperience, and idealism. Each is in the suit of Swords, so each shares an affinity for thoughts or ideas rather than emotions or practicality. However, within these shared qualities each approaches their thoughts (Swords) very differently—some with imagination and enthusiasm, some with protectiveness or even obsession, and some with curiosity or confusion. The deck you choose for your readings may strongly influence your interpretation of the court cards (some decks even use animals!).

EXERCISE 2: VARIATIONS AMONG DECKS

If you have more than one deck, take out the court cards of various decks and compare them. Notice how the personalities you might assign to each card change with the deck. Pick out two or three of the court cards that appear most different to you from deck to deck. For each set of cards, determine what attributes all the cards share and what changes from deck to deck. Write down at least one keyword that is unique to each card. Now pick one set and imagine that you are doing a reading to answer the question "What kind of person should I look for in hiring a new manager at work?" Imagine how your answers might change depending on which of these decks you were working with, drawing the same card from each deck. ✪

EXERCISE 3: SUIT QUALITIES

Using your layout of four rows of four, start developing keywords for the cards by reminding yourself of the qualities of each suit. All the court cards in the suit of Cups will share personality traits related to emotions, relationships, creativity, spirituality, etc. Now develop some keywords for each rank: Pages, Knights, Queens, and Kings (or whatever ranks your deck uses). When you are done, combine the keywords for the suits with the keywords for the ranks as a starting place for identifying the basic attributes of each court card. ✪

You will find as you work with different decks that the court cards may be a key factor that attracts you or turns you away from a particular deck. For example, many readers find the court cards in the *Rider-Waite-Smith* deck to be somewhat unapproachable because their faces are fairly expressionless. One way to become more comfortable with reading court cards is to choose a deck in which you can relate to the court cards as real people. Similarly, most readers have specific court cards that they intuitively like or dislike more than others. This may be due to an association you have between the cards and people in your life, or due to a basic affinity or clash with your own personality type.

EXERCISE 4: PERSONAL BIASES

Working with the deck you use most often for readings, lay the sixteen court cards out in front of you. Think of several people in your life that you are closest to and most enjoy being around. Pick out the court cards that most remind you of them and set them to one side. Now think of some people that you dislike or have difficulty working with or being around. Pick out the court cards that most remind you of them and put them in another group. Describe what specific personality traits or attributes of these people led you to choose their cards. Now look at the remaining court cards. Are there any that really appeal to you, or that you particularly dislike, just in general? Pick these out and put them in the groups with other liked and disliked cards. Look over these cards carefully, and make a mental note of the ones that you instinctively like or dislike. ✪

The main purpose of this exercise is to realize that we all have a conscious or unconscious preference for some court cards, and a dislike for others, because of who we associate these cards with or simply the way they look. It is important to be consciously aware of these potential biases and take care to be impartial when doing readings for others. Each card has positive and negative attributes, and may be helpful or harmful in a given situation. Just as we try not to judge people by their appearances, we need to exercise the same degree of care when reading court cards for others. Try not to fall into the trap of thinking of some court cards as always bad or always good—look instead at the position the card is in, whether it is upright or reversed (or well or poorly dignified), and what association the card seems to have with the client. (We will discuss reversals and elemental dignities in detail in part 5.)

However, when reading for ourselves, it is fine to use these associations in the reading since they are appropriate for our own personal lives. This is also a valuable exercise to work through with clients that you will be working with a lot, especially when using a counseling or interactive approach. By doing this exercise together, you can learn a great deal about people who influence your client's life, and whom certain court cards may represent when they appear in her readings.

_____

EXERCISE 5: PERSONALITY TRAITS

Choosing the deck you use most often, lay out the court cards one by one, and write down some keywords describing their personalities in a journal or notebook based only on their visual appearance and what you know about the suit and rank. On the first pass through, limit yourself only to positive character traits. Try to think of at least two or three positives for each card (some can be the same from card to card). Now look at them again and think of several keywords that represent the negative potential attributes of that personality type and write these down. Try to make sure that the overall personality you are developing for each card is evenly balanced between positive and negative qualities. For example, keywords for the King of Wands could include leadership and, on the flip side, domineering.

It is also a good idea to write down any neutral qualities you can think of that are not necessarily either positive or negative. If you have difficulty with any of the court cards, don't worry. Most readers resonate better with some court cards than others. Simply leave those areas blank and come back to them later in these lessons. As you learn more associations with the court cards, such as astrological, elemental, and psychological types, you should be able to fill in the blanks and round out your personality portraits. ✵

Evaluating Your Progress

Study Goals 1 and 2

Take the court cards out of your deck and shuffle them. Turn them over one by one. For each card, write down at least two personality characteristics associated with the suit, and two associated with the rank, without looking at your notes. Make sure that your personality characteristics are neutral or evenly balanced between positive and negative qualities.

Study Goal 3

For each card, add three additional personality characteristics that come from other sources, without looking at your notes. These may be drawn from the visual characteristics of the card, keywords you have learned in books, or people you know that might be represented by these cards.

six

Elemental and Astrological Associations

Study Goals

1. Learn astrological associations for each of the court cards.

2. Learn elemental associations for each of the court cards.

3. Use these associations to further develop personalities for the court cards.

4. Explore interactions between the court cards based on their elemental natures.

This chapter focuses on rounding out the personalities of the court cards using elemental and astrological associations. As with the Minor Arcana, developing these associations will help provide an underlying structure and framework to the court cards, and broaden your range of personality attributes for each card. They also provide ways to look at how court cards, and the people they represent, may interact with one another.

Elemental Associations

Each suit is associated with one of the four elements, usually (but not always) as follows:

Wands: Fire

Swords: Air

Cups: Water

Pentacles: Earth

While these elemental/suit associations also apply to the court cards of these suits, court cards have an added elemental dimension since each rank is also associated with an element, again usually, but not always, as follows:

Kings: Fire

Queens: Water

Knights: Air

Pages/Princesses: Earth

In each case, you should feel free to follow the elemental associations of the deck you are using if it is different from the above, or develop your own. Using these associations as an example, the King of Cups could be thought of as water combined with fire, and the Page of Swords as air combined with earth. There are several ways in which these ideas can be used in your readings. The first step is to assign personality characteristics to each element and combine them to represent various court cards. Here are some examples of personality traits for each element:

Fire: Active, intuitive, assertive, passionate.

Water: Emotional, empathetic, romantic, caring.

Air: Intelligent, rational, logical, clear-sighted.

Earth: Practical, down-to-earth, honest, hard-working.

EXERCISE 1: ELEMENTAL PERSONALITIES

Develop your own keywords representing personality traits associated with each element. For each court card, combine these traits according to the elemental system just presented. For example, the Knight of Wands would have primary personality traits associated with fire, but modified by personality traits associated with air. ✪

As discussed in chapter 3, certain elements reinforce each other, while others are antagonistic or neutral. These relationships can give valuable insights into personality types and the court cards. Here is the table of elemental relationships for reference in the next set of exercises.

Compatible	*Neutral*	*Opposing*
Fire and air	Fire and earth	Fire and water
Earth and water	Water and air	Earth and air

EXERCISE 2: BLENDING ELEMENTS

Individual court cards or personality types can be balanced and well-rounded, or unbalanced in various ways. Take out the sixteen court cards, and find the eight cards that represent combinations of compatible or neutral elements. These are personality types that have more than one set of strengths and abilities to draw on, and in which the personality does not contain internal conflicts. Now find the four cards that have all their energy in one element, such as the Queen of Cups (water combined with water). These are personality types that are very strongly directed toward one set of traits and abilities, and these people may find it difficult to deal with other types of energies. These personality types may be especially prone to both the strengths and weaknesses of their suit, and may have difficulty adapting to situations that require other abilities. Finally, find the four court cards that are made up of opposing combinations. These personality types may have internal conflicts that are difficult to balance and resolve. ✪

These elemental associations can also be used to look at relationships between two people. In relationship readings, it may become apparent which court card represents the querent and which a love interest, family member, or coworker. From the associations given here, you can determine whether the two personality types are likely to be a good match, work well together, and have complementary or opposing characteristics.

EXERCISE 3: PERSONALITY COMPARISONS

Sort the court cards into pairs of opposites; for example, the Queen of Pentacles (water of earth) and the King of Swords (fire of air). These are personality types that are likely to have little or nothing in common. On the other hand, if they can learn to work together, they will have the complete range of abilities to draw from. Now make some pairs that share only one common element. These pairs have enough similarity that they are likely to be able to find common interests and lifestyles, yet bring other different qualities to the relationship that may complement each other's abilities. Now sort your court cards into a third type of pair in which the two people have the same two elements reversed, such as the Knight of Cups (air of water) and the Queen of Swords (water of air). These pairs may be very strongly attracted to one another and may feel like mirror images or soul mates, but may also share certain strengths and weaknesses and be limited to only two types of energy. For example, two people with no earth energy between them may lack practical common sense and money management abilities. ✸

EXERCISE 4: RELATIONSHIP READING

Using only the sixteen court cards, do a two-card reading in which the two cards drawn represent a couple who are considering getting married. Using your elemental associations and the personality profiles you developed in the previous chapter, write out a reading in which you describe their areas of compatibility, areas where they may experience conflict, their combined strengths as a couple, and any areas where they may need to pay special attention to during their marriage. If you wish, try this exercise again, choosing cards to represent an actual couple you know and conduct this reading for them. There are various options for doing this—either choose court cards to use based on what you know of the couple's characteristics or personalities, ask them to choose their own cards, or shuffle the court cards and let the tarot provide a card for each person. ✸

Astrological Associations

Many decks relate astrological signs to the court cards, either on an elemental basis or more specifically to each card. On an elemental basis, the court cards can be assigned as follows:

Wands: Fire signs, including Aries, Leo, and Sagittarius.

Pentacles: Earth signs, including Taurus, Virgo, and Capricorn.

Swords: Air signs, including Gemini, Libra, and Aquarius.

Cups: Water signs, including Cancer, Scorpio, and Pisces.

This is one good reason to ask for the birth date of your clients before doing a reading, as then you can determine their astrological sign and age. With this information, you can select a likely court card to represent them (using the age and/or sex of the person to choose a court card in the appropriate suit) or recognize their significator if it comes up in a reading. Obtaining the birth date of any other person the client is asking about (such as a love interest or spouse) is also a good idea.

If you know a lot about a person's astrological chart, you can be even more focused in your choices. For example, if your client is a Taurus Sun with a Cancer Moon or rising sign, then you could choose the Queen of Pentacles (water + earth) as her significator. Different court cards may be appropriate for different aspects of a person's life. If your client is a middle-aged woman who has Cancer as her Sun sign, she may be represented by the Queen of Cups. However, if she has a lot of fire energy in her tenth house of career and responsibilities in her chart, her approach to these activities may be better represented by a court card that combines water and fire energy, such as the Queen of Wands or the King of Cups.

Queen of Cups
The Gilded Tarot

EXERCISE 5: LOOKING AT RELATIONSHIPS

Using your birth date and the birth date of someone important to you, select appropriate court cards to represent each of you, using any additional information you choose (age, gender, astrological chart, etc.). Place these court cards to the left and right, shuffle the rest of the deck, and choose one card to place between the two cards you have chosen. Do a reading in which this third card provides insight into the current relationship you have with this person (read a reversed card as an area that needs work). Use the personality profiles and/or elemental relationships of the court cards to each other and to the third card in between to provide added insight into the relationship. ✪

Some decks associate specific court cards with each of the twelve astrological signs, using only the Knights, Queens, and Kings. In this system, Pages or Princesses are assigned the pure elemental energy (earth, air, water, or fire), without any further defining characteristics. There are three types of astrological signs: cardinal, fixed, and mutable. These can be assigned to the three ranks in order to determine which astrological sign goes with which card. For example, fixed may be assigned to Kings, cardinal to Queens, and mutable to Knights. This results in the following assignments:

Aries (cardinal fire)—Queen of Wands

Taurus (fixed earth)—King of Pentacles

Gemini (mutable air)—Knight of Swords

Cancer (cardinal water)—Queen of Cups

Leo (fixed fire)—King of Wands

Virgo (mutable earth)—Knight of Pentacles

Libra (cardinal air)—Queen of Swords

Scorpio (fixed water)—King of Cups

Sagittarius (mutable fire)—Knight of Wands

Capricorn (cardinal earth)—Queen of Pentacles

Aquarius (fixed air)—King of Swords

Pisces (mutable water)—Knight of Cups

In other decks, each card, including the court cards, is assigned to a specific month and/or day of the year, in which case you may find your significator following the specific timing system chosen by the author of that deck. Whatever system you use is entirely up to you, and should also be compatible with the underlying system on which your deck is based.

EXERCISE 6: ANIMAL PERSONALITIES

Some tarot decks use animals for court cards (sometimes for all court cards, sometimes only for the Pages), using the habits and traits of the animals to suggest personalities and strengths of individuals. Using what you have learned of the personalities of each card, choose an animal that you would use to represent each court card. ✪

Page of Cups
Legend: The Arthurian Tarot

Evaluating Your Progress

Study Goals 1 and 2

Remove the sixteen court cards from the deck and shuffle them. Turn them over one at a time and write down or say out loud the elemental and astrological correspondences you have developed for these cards. Practice this until the associations come easily.

Study Goal 3

Explain how the elemental and astrological associations of each card relate to the personality of that card. You may wish to do this with a friend, until you both understand the overall system that you are using. Choose some examples from people you both know to help illustrate your ideas.

Study Goal 4

Explore how the elements (and the suits they are commonly associated with) may be reflected in the life of a person represented by each court card. For example, how might they be related to the person's interests, activities, and careers? Write down three attributes like this for each card. Pretend that your court cards are actual, unique people and feel free to be creative with the interests you assign to each one.

Study Goal 5

Draw two court cards at random and imagine they're having an argument. What are they most likely to disagree about? How do they express their anger or unhappiness? Now draw a third card as the conciliator. What strategies is this person likely to use to resolve this argument? Try this exercise again, changing the scene (for example, workplace, family, neighbors, car accident). If you prefer, choose other kinds of conversations for your court cards to have. Practice this until you can easily imagine each of your court cards "speaking" in various situations.

seven

Using Court Cards in Readings

Study Goals

1. Learn to use court cards as significators in readings.

2. Learn to use court cards to represent oneself and other people in readings.

3. Learn to use court cards to represent aspects of one's own personality or mind.

4. Become familiar with other possible meanings for court cards.

5. Become aware of clothing, body language, and expressions in the cards.

In this chapter, we will practice a variety of ways to use court cards in readings, including as significators, as persons influencing the situation, as aspects of the mind or personality, and as activities or approaches. In addition, we will discuss how to handle reversed court cards and deal with gender issues in readings.

Court Cards as Significators

A significator is a card that is used to represent the querent in a reading. It can be added to any reading, but is never required. A significator can be used to tell you something about the client's personality or lifestyle, making it easier to interpret the reading. It may also tell you how the client feels or sees herself in the situation being asked about. A significator provides a sense that the client is an integral part of the reading, and can even provide a physical presence for the client when the reading is done over the phone or by e-mail. Significators are typically placed as the first card in the reading, either in the center of the layout or above and off to one side, as if observing. Alternatively, a significator can be chosen and then shuffled into the deck, to see if it turns up in the reading.

Court cards are the most common cards chosen as significators for tarot readings, as they are the cards that can most easily be used to represent a person. However, it is worth keeping in mind that any card in the deck can be used as a significator, and it is sometimes valuable to allow the significator to be drawn as part of the reading. If you choose to use a court card as a significator and select it out of the deck in advance of the reading, here are some methods to use in determining which court card is appropriate.

- *Client choice:* If the client is present during the reading, spread out the court cards and allow her to choose the card that she most strongly identifies with. Let her know that she does not have to choose a card that matches her gender or one that physically resembles her. Instead she may choose any card that she is drawn to, or that best represents her personality, or even the issue she is asking about. Which card she chooses may tell you a lot about her approach to the issue, as well as what strengths or insecurities she may be bringing to the situation.

- *Astrological:* Using the birth date of the client, choose a significator as described in the previous chapter, based on her astrological sign, age, and/or gender.

- *Personality:* If you know the client well, you can select a significator for the client based on her personality once you have developed personality profiles for your court cards. Try to think beyond traditional gender roles in selecting significators using this method.

- *Question or situation:* If none of the above methods are available to you or appropriate, you can choose a significator based on the situation or question. For example, if the client is a young man just starting out in a new career, you might choose the Knight of Wands. Or if the client is a woman with a large family who is concerned about issues of inheritance, you might choose the Queen of Pentacles.

- *Physical resemblance:* Traditionally, court cards were associated with physical attributes: Cups with blond hair and fair skin, Pentacles with dark hair and dark skin, etc. However, this is something of a holdover from when tarot was largely a European pastime. The physical attributes shown on traditional decks are largely European in nature and inappropriate to other world cultures and races. As such, they are irrelevant to many of our clients today. When doing e-mail readings, we may not know the physical appearance of our clients. Finally, physical appearance is not likely to have anything to do with personality traits, as it would be silly to imagine that all fair-haired people are emotional and all dark-haired people are practical. Therefore, I do not recommend this method, although it may factor into a client's own choice of a significator to represent herself.

EXERCISE 1: CHOOSING SIGNIFICATORS 1

A middle-aged woman comes to your booth at a tarot fair and asks you to do a traditional Celtic Cross reading for her. She prefers not to give her age, and asks you a question about how to handle her relationship with her teenage daughter. She is trying to be strict in order to keep her daughter out of trouble, but her daughter is breaking the rules and they are having many arguments as a result. What significator do you choose for her reading and why? ✪

EXERCISE 2: CHOOSING SIGNIFICATORS 2

A reading is automatically assigned to you by an on-line tarot network. Your client gives his birth date as November 17, 1938, and wants to know if he will ever have another serious relationship after being widowed for five years. What significator would you choose for him and why? ✪

Court Cards as People

One traditional interpretation of court cards is as people involved in the question or situation, which can be the client or anyone else, including someone he has not met yet. Later we will discuss situations in which court cards may represent aspects of the client's self or personality, and it can sometimes be difficult to distinguish between these two situations. If you can, it is best to decide ahead of time how you will handle this. Try to avoid always using one method or the other—allow the question and situation to influence your approach.

For example, if a person asks about a relationship or situation in which other people are involved, then it is very likely that a court card may represent another person, particularly if it is clearly not one that would be used to represent the client. Alternatively, if the question is about the client's own personal development, or is worded more personally, such as "How can I . . .?" or "What would be the best way for me to . . .?" then it is much more likely that court cards that appear in the reading reflect the client's own state of mind or a recommended approach to the situation. One way to avoid confusion is to carefully define the position of each card in the reading so that there is no ambiguity. For example, one card could represent other people involved in a situation and another card could represent the client's own approach and thoughts.

In reading court cards as people, it is helpful if you have in mind a clear sense of what court card(s) you believe would represent the client if they appeared in the reading, so that you can tell if a court card you receive represents her or another person. For the same reason, it is helpful to know as much as you can about other people that may be involved in the reading, so that you recognize them when you see them. However, in many or most situations, you will not know who the person is. It is best to avoid guessing, or describing the person in terms of physical attributes. Instead, use the personality traits you have developed that go along with each card, and let the client decide who this reminds her of.

For example, if Julie asks, "Should I marry John or Brian?" you may want to rephrase the question to "What type of husband would make Julie the happiest?" Then if you get a court card in the reading (or any card), you can simply describe the personality of the person that would make her happiest and she can decide which one best fits the description (if either). Often when you describe a court card the client will come back to you with comments like, "Oh, that's my grandmother you're describing" and proceed to tell you all about it. This is helpful if there is any chance she will be coming back to you for repeat readings, because then you will have a sense of which court cards represent important people in her life.

EXERCISE 3: COURT CARDS AS OTHER PEOPLE

Do a three- to five-card reading on any topic of your choice that is externally focused and includes interactions with other people. First, choose a significator to represent yourself in the reading, and place it above the other cards in the reading. Determine ahead of time that any court cards that appear will represent other people. Lay out the reading, and pay particular attention to any court cards you receive—decide who each court card represents, and how that person relates to the card position. Think about what you can learn about that person from the court card that represents him or her, and how you can use that information to improve or positively influence the situation you asked about. ✪

Court Cards as Aspects of Self

There are many occasions in which court cards do not represent other people, but instead aspects of oneself or the client's mind or personality. This is most likely when the question is one that is internally focused, or when the position in the reading in which the card appears is about inner issues. When a client asks a question that is ambiguous, it is best to deal with this by designing the layout so that there can be no confusion. For example, if the client asks, "What is the biggest obstacle toward finishing my master's degree?" there could be many answers that involve his own attitude or approach, or involve other people, such as his spouse, children, or advisor (of course, there may be non-people factors as well). For this type of question, design the spread so that the card positions distinguish between self and other influences on the situation. Reversed or negative cards will then point out the main areas of concern.

When reading cards as aspects of self, remember that each of us has many different sides to our personality that come out at different times—some aspects may be more masculine and some more feminine, some may be rational and some emotional, etc. It is helpful to realize that each person may be represented by a variety of cards at different times. Over time you will learn which cards most often represent you or another person, but any given situation could surprise you. Particularly in card positions that represent hidden or subconscious influences, court cards can also represent people or influences in your past that you have internalized as an inner voice, which can be either helpful or harmful. Court cards may represent attitudes we have developed, approaches to problems, or inner strengths or weaknesses that affect our lives. I often think of Princesses or Pages as our inner child, who may pop up from time to time with messages for our adult self.

Princess of Cups
Victoria Regina Tarot

Here are some possible associations for court cards that represent ourselves:

- *Kings:* Areas of our lives and ourselves that we are in firm control of and confident about. Areas where we feel strong and mature, experienced and decisive.

- *Queens:* Areas where we feel mature and loving, nurturing and creative. Areas that are productive and fulfilling.

- *Knights:* Areas where we feel daring and courageous, in which we want to start something new or be adventurous. Areas in which we have a particular quest or goal that drives us.

- *Pages/Princesses:* Areas that are largely undeveloped or exist as unrealized potentials. Areas in which we have childlike or idealistic dreams and desires. Starting completely over in some area of life, as a student or beginner.

EXERCISE 4: COURT CARDS AS SELF

Do a three-card reading on a particular goal you wish to achieve in your life. Use the following spread, using only the sixteen court cards in the first two positions and a card from the rest of the deck in the third position:

Card 1: What aspect of my personality, approach, or attitude will most help in achieving this goal?

Card 2: Who outside myself can help me achieve my goal?

Card 3: What is the most important action for me to take in getting started? ✪

EXERCISE 5: WORKING ON RELATIONSHIPS

Using only the court cards, do a three-card reading for a client who is having a long-standing argument with a supervisor at work:

Card 1: What internal strengths will help me in this situation?

Card 2: Which of my attitudes or approaches are unhelpful or contributing to the problem?

Card 3: What approach should I take to reach a positive resolution of this situation? ✪

Gender Issues

Regardless of what method you are using to interpret court cards, gender issues can be confusing. Frequently you will receive questions about a client's ideal or actual partner, or about when she will meet her soul mate or have a serious relationship. It is not a good idea to assume that the client is wishing for or involved in an opposite-sex relationship, particularly new clients about whom you know little or nothing. Clients may share with you desires and situations that they would not feel comfortable disclosing to their family or friends, especially when you are communicating via e-mail. The safest approach is either to ask directly or to give gender-neutral descriptions, but this can get uncomfortable or awkward at some point. If you routinely read court cards as the genders they appear to be, this may give you a clue when someone is asking about a gay or lesbian relationship, although if you are wrong, you risk giving offense. Nevertheless, I have been in this situation often enough not to discount the experience.

However, court cards can truly be genderless, and this is particularly true when they represent aspects of oneself or of a client's own personality. Each of us has both feminine and masculine energies and attributes that come out in different situations to different degrees. Whether reading the cards as the self or others, it is important to always keep in mind that the gender cannot always be read literally, and not let it lead you astray from the appropriate interpretation.

Other Meanings for Court Cards

Court cards don't always represent people, and conversely, non-court cards may represent people in your readings. It is helpful to be open to these other possible interpretations and be flexible. The most important indicator is the card position—if the position is defined as a person, then it represents a person regardless of what card is drawn to fill it. For example, an Eight of Pentacles may represent a master craftsman, who is dedicated and skilled at his work. If a position is defined as an action or approach, then even a court card can be read that way. Below are some examples of alternative ways in which court cards can be read. These are just a few examples, and other associations will occur to you as you become more familiar with these cards.

- *Activities or actions:* Court cards can be read as activities that the people in the cards seem to be engaging in. For example, Knights may represent starting something new, pursuing a goal, or exploring the world. Kings could represent taking on a position of leadership, or making decisions. Queens could represent nurturing or starting a creative project. The Page of Pentacles could represent the need to study something before taking action.

- *Abstract concepts:* Kings may represent an entire bureaucracy or establishment, decision-making body, or business community. Queens may represent a more nurturing community, agency, or social group. The Knight of Swords and Knight of Wands are sometimes associated with war, terrorism, or destructive influences or events, mainly when reversed.

- *Roles or professions:* Certain court cards are often associated with certain professions or roles, and can sometimes appear in readings in that capacity. For example, the King of Swords could be a doctor, lawyer, or judge (as can the Queen) who is influencing the situation. Pages might represent students. The King or Queen of

Cups could represent a counselor or psychic. These may not represent the client or anyone he personally knows, but they may appear as a possible resource for help, decision-maker, or other influence on the situation.

- *Messages:* Pages have often been interpreted as messengers or messages related to the activities or areas represented by the suit. These messages may come from inside yourself or outside from the external world.

- *Changes or initiations:* Knights may be interpreted as major life changes, crossing thresholds of life, initiations, or graduations.

EXERCISE 6: COURT CARDS AS ACTIVITIES

Do a one-card reading using only the court cards to answer the question "What action should I take to improve the quality of my life and my personal satisfaction with it?" Interpret this card as a specific action rather than an area of your personality. ✪

EXERCISE 7: USING OTHER CARDS TO REPRESENT PEOPLE

Using the entire deck, choose a question involving your whole family. Then draw one card to represent each person in your family and their attitude or approach to the question. ✪

Clothing

Clothing is an interesting thing to look at in your deck, since it can reveal a lot about the designer's intentions and philosophy in creating the deck. There are two main things to look for: the first is whether the people in the deck are wearing any clothing, and if so what kind, and the second is the colors that are in their clothing. Start by taking the deck out that you normally use, and see if you notice any patterns associated with clothing. This relates to the court cards, but also to all the people in the cards, both Major and Minor Arcana.

It is very interesting to look at the issue of clothing in the *Rider-Waite-Smith* deck, although this is one area that varies greatly from deck to deck. In this deck, all the people in the Minor Arcana are wearing clothing, signifying the mundane or worldly aspect of these cards. Also, all the people in the trumps are wearing clothing, until we reach the Devil—with the one exception to this rule being the Lovers in the Garden of Eden, presumably before the fall and their knowledge of good and evil. Even the Fool, who is the closest to being spiritually pure, has taken on some clothing—a reference to incarnation in the physical body and a willingness to live on earth.

After we pass through the Tower, there are no trumps in which people are wearing clothing—everyone is naked. So there is a kind of transition point around the Devil/Tower cards. If we think about the psychological or spiritual journey associated with the trumps, we can see that there might be a reason for this. In the Devil card, our ego is dissolved and laid bare. From this point on, we have completely left the mundane world and are working on transforming ourselves into our higher selves. Once we pass through the Tower, there is no longer a place for false modesty, hiding anything from ourselves or other people, or any protection from the forces and processes we encounter—we must face each step honestly and openly in order to complete the process of integration and transformation. Therefore, no clothing.

The other thing to look at is the colors of the clothing. In most *Rider-Waite-Smith* decks, the colors are highly significant, at least in the Major Arcana. For example, place the Magician and High Priestess side by side. Here you will see that they are both wearing undertunics of white, symbolizing their purity of intent and innocence of heart. The Magician, however, wears an outer robe of red, symbolizing his more active, masculine nature, and the High Priestess wears an outer robe of blue, symbolizing her passive, feminine, intuitive nature. The Empress has pomegranates on her dress, symbolizing fertility. The Emperor's clothing is a deep red, with almost no other colors, showing him as a man of action. A bit of his blue undergarment is showing through, which along with the thin stream in the background shows that he has not completely lost his connection to the feminine Empress and his own intuition.

In the Minor cards, we see less direct evidence of color in clothing being significant, but it is still worth looking through the cards with this in mind to see what we can find. For example, in the Five of Wands, the five sparring figures are all wearing tunics of different colors, showing that they have five different points of view and conflicting agendas. However, several of them have undergarments of yellow, suggesting the possibility of at least some kind of compromise, if any of them were willing to stop fighting long enough to listen. The man in the Five of Cups wears a cloak of deep black, symbolizing his depression and the gloomy void he has cast himself into. However, it is only a cloak, and if he cast it off, he could move on with his life. In the Five of Swords, the central grinning figure has undergarments of red, symbolizing anger, war, and aggression, but his overtunic is green. This could be a reference to the opportunity for growth that inevitably follows destruction (especially in nature), and provides a possible positive note to the card.

Aside from color, many of the people in the court cards are wearing symbols of their energy; for example, the Knight of Cups has fishes on his tunic, and the Knight of Wands has salamanders. In some decks, you will find the astrological signs associated with the court cards woven into the design of their clothing. In other cards, such as the Six of Pentacles and the Eight of Pentacles, the clothing seems designed more to give the impression of a certain profession or standing in society, such as a wealthy merchant or a tradesman.

Body Language

Body language is fun to look at in the tarot and, if you are very visually oriented, can become an important part of your tarot readings. The people in the *Rider-Waite-Smith* deck tend to be a bit stiff compared to those in many other decks, so sometimes you really have to look to find the body language, but it is there. Also, body language is something that varies a lot from deck to deck, so it is important not to become overly attached to meanings associated with certain postures, but rather to interpret body language as it appears to you in each reading. This provides a unique way of looking at how the cards are interacting with each other in the particular circumstance or question you are working with.

One thing to notice is where the people in the card are looking. If you place the Empress and the Emperor side by side, you will notice that the Empress is sitting facing the Emperor and the Emperor is looking toward the Empress, even though he is facing forward. This is an indication that on the earthly plane, these two work hand in hand, and one cannot rule without the other. In contrast, the Magician and the High Priestess, which represent the more heavenly archetypal forces of masculine and feminine, look straight out from their cards and don't seem to acknowledge the other. Most of the trumps look right out of the card at you, making their point in a very direct way. However, a few are looking downward, such as Strength, the Hermit, and the Star. These are cards where the energy is directed more inward in a passive, meditative way. Much has been made of the fact that in the Lovers card, the man is usually looking at the woman, while the woman is looking up at the heavens—I will leave that meaning to your interpretation!

Seven of Swords
The Robin Wood Tarot

Among the court cards, it is interesting to note what the people in the cards are looking at. The Pages, for example, are typically looking at the symbols of their suit, as if studying them or trying to understand them. Knights usually hold the symbol of their suit, but are looking off into the distance at a particular goal. The Kings and Queens of Wands and Swords tend to be looking directly out at something, as if surveying their realm, while the Queens of the more passive suits are studying or nurturing their Cups and Pentacles. In any reading of more than a few cards, it is very helpful to look at what is going on between cards—who is looking at whom and why. For example, if you had the Seven of Swords in the Robin Wood deck (a thief stealing over the wall with his swords) and a Queen of Swords or King of Wands looking directly at the thief, you could interpret that someone was engaged in dishonest activity but was about to be caught or exposed by someone in authority. If, on the other hand, the person in authority was looking the other direction, or gazing into their cup, then the thief is more likely to get away with it.

Other forms of body language are interesting too. If you take out all the Knights, it is easy to place them in order of how fast their horses are moving—the Knight of Swords is galloping, the Knight of Wands is cantering, the Knight of Cups is trotting or walking, and the Knight of Pentacles is standing still. This clearly shows which suits have the most energy, and is one way to decide which suits are fast or slow for a timing system (see chapter 17). The Hanged Man has an interesting posture, with his legs crossed in an up-side-down or reversed 4. To me, this means that part of what he is reversing or undoing is the rigid thinking of the Fours and the aggressive, more outward and active lifestyle of the Emperor (who also crosses his legs in exactly the same way, in many decks).

Other things to notice are the open and upward-facing posture of the Fool, showing that he is still connected to the universal energies, and the similar posture of the little child in the Sun, who after a long journey has once again reached wholeness. Contrast this with the bent back of the Ten of Wands or the Seven of Pentacles, and you can see where their attention is focused. All in all, it is always very helpful to place yourself in the card and see what the body language is telling you—and it may vary greatly from deck to deck, even in the same card. This is part of what gives us deck-specific nuances, so allow yourself to go with the flow and the suggestions of the specific visual images on the cards.

EXERCISE 8: BODY LANGUAGE

Do a three-card reading to answer the question "How can I get along better with my coworkers?" Pay attention to the clothing, eye contact, and body language of all the figures in the cards and work these observations into your reading. ✪

Evaluating Your Progress

Study Goal 1

Describe two different situations in which you might use a significator in your readings. Identify at least three possible ways of choosing significators (which may or may not be court cards) and when you might use each one.

Study Goal 2

Assume you are doing a reading on a situation that involves a variety of other people along with your client, and you receive several court cards in the spread. Explain how you would help your client figure out which cards might represent herself or other people in the situation. What attributes of the cards would be most important in identifying the people involved? Would you use the ranks and genders of the cards to help determine age and gender, or not? (There is no one right answer to this, but it is helpful to have your own system figured out ahead of time.)

Study Goal 3

Make a list of the different roles you play in your life: parent, spouse, lover, sibling, child, friend, volunteer, career, teacher, reader, artist, musician, athlete . . . as many different aspects of yourself as you can think of. Choose one or more of the sixteen court cards that best represent you in each role or your approach to that role or task. Notice how the cards change from one area of your life to the next. Now pick out one or two of the cards that you did not include as an aspect of yourself. Is there any part of your life where the approach suggested by that card would be useful to apply, even if it is not one you are normally comfortable with?

Study Goal 4

Think about the main activities you are doing today or in the week ahead and list them on a sheet of paper. Choose one court card that best represents each activity you plan to do (as opposed to what might be your approach to that activity). Now think about some of the organizations and institutions you will be dealing with in the coming week (for example, school, church, workplace, library, bank. etc.). Choose one court card to represent each of these institutions and the types of people and activities you are likely to encounter there.

Study Goal 5

Shuffle all the Minor cards (pips plus courts) from your deck and draw several groups of two to three cards (discard any card that does not include people and draw another card). For each group, set the cards upright next to each other and imagine you had come across this group of people standing on the street or another public place. What might this situation be and what does it look like they're doing? What do their clothing, expressions, and body language tell you about how they are interacting with each other, if at all? If you could imagine a conversation between the people in the cards, what would they be saying? Try to bring the scene to life in your mind and draw clues from the clothing, colors, postures, expressions, and small details of the scene in the cards. Now take one group of three cards and explain how your observations would help enhance a reading based on the meanings you have learned for these cards.

—— part three ——

The Major Arcana

eight

Journeys through the Major Arcana

Study Goals

1. Become familiar with various ways of looking at the Major Arcana as a continuous progression or cycle.

2. Recognize themes and archetypes that occur in major spiritual, philosophical, and mythological traditions.

3. Learn astrological and elemental correspondences for the Major Arcana.

4. Practice applying the Major Arcana to real-life situations.

In this chapter, we begin our work with the Major Arcana. Unlike the Minor Arcana, which were most likely derived from already existing packs of playing cards, the Major Arcana are unique, and constitute the heart and soul of tarot. Tarot cards were developed during the Italian Renaissance, at a time when art, religion, mysticism, mythology, and science were much more intertwined than they are today. Even simple parlor games and nearly all works of art tended to have religious or mythological themes. It is not really known whether the Major Arcana were intended to be anything other than a series of trumps for the game of tarocchi, but it is relatively certain that they drew from and represent popular views of religious and mystical concepts that permeated Renaissance art and philosophy at the time. As such, they represent powerful archetypes that can be read on many different levels.

Central to nearly every way of viewing the Major Arcana as a whole is the concept of a cyclical journey, beginning with the Fool, progressing through the trumps, ending with the World, and then starting over again. In this chapter, we will explore this journey at five different levels: spiritual, psychological, mythological, astrological, and mundane. There are other more esoteric approaches to the Major Arcana as well, involving religion, mysticism, alchemy, and magick, which can be explored once a basic understanding of the trumps is gained.

Spiritual Aspects of the Journey

A spiritual understanding of the trumps involves a journey of the soul—from the moment it first incarnated on earth throughout its struggle to return to its higher source. The endpoint of this journey may vary according to your religious or philosophical beliefs—it is a highly personal journey that is understood differently by each person. Along the way, the Fool is provided with various tools and teachers, learns lessons and undertakes tasks, and finally learns how to reach his or her goal.

The basic concepts of the Major Arcana are discussed in every tarot book, and there is no real substitute for reading about them and studying them. Although insights into the Minor Arcana can be gained solely through intuition and a basic understanding of numerological and elemental concepts, the Major Arcana are more complex and should be studied in depth. Here are some basic concepts and keywords to get you started:

0. The Fool: Creation from nothingness, incarnation, being.

1. The Magician: Self-awareness, consciousness, will, male/yang life force.

2. The High Priestess: Subconscious, memory, intuition, female/yin life force.

3. The Empress: Creativity, growth, fertility, nature, earthly mother.

4. The Emperor: Order, logic, rules, boundaries, civilization, earthly father.

5. The Hierophant: Spiritual link to God/dess, mentor, morality, institutions, church.

6. The Lovers: Choices, discrimination between good and evil, self versus other.

7. The Chariot: Will, initiation, breakthrough to adulthood, direction, movement.

8. Strength: Inner strength, controlling one's animal nature, productive use of passions.

9. The Hermit: Self-knowledge, seeking wisdom and maturity, teaching.

10. The Wheel of Fortune: Understanding of cycles, living with change, turning point.

11. Justice: Karma, universal (not personal) justice, balance, fairness, clear sight.

12. The Hanged Man: Reversal of thinking, inner work, suspension to allow inner growth.

13. Death: Transformation, major changes as a result of inner work, rebirth.

14. Temperance: Balance of mind and body, alchemy, integration of energies.

15. The Devil: Struggles with and liberation from the material world, self-imposed bondage.

16. The Tower: Bolt of inspiration, tearing down artificial constructs, revelations.

17. The Star: Inspiration, hope, blessings of the cosmos, rejuvenation.

18. The Moon: Facing your deepest inner self, integrating your subconscious.

19. The Sun: Becoming whole, ascending to the light, knowing and being yourself.

20. Judgment: Awakening, self-judgment, transition to a higher state.

21. The World: Rejoining the all, becoming one with the universe, dancing a cosmic dance.

In order to illustrate the cyclical nature of this journey, we can conceptualize the Fool's Journey in the context of a single lifetime, although the cycle may require many incarnations to actually complete and the process may not be entirely linear. Think of the following as a story of one man's travels through the Major Arcana during a lifetime, illustrating the major concepts associated with each trump:

0. The Fool: The soul incarnates into a physical body and is born. The baby experiences his new world in a rush, without conscious thought.

1. The Magician: The baby becomes aware of himself and others. The baby begins to form his first thoughts and mental impressions.

2. The High Priestess: The baby begins to remember what he has experienced and to draw mental connections between objects. He begins to make associations and to experience feelings, although he cannot articulate them yet.

3. The Empress: The baby begins to realize that he can make things happen by behaving in certain ways. He begins to explore his environment, drawing scribbles on the wall, turning over his food bowl, and banging on things just to see what happens. He develops an imagination and experiences new sensations. He becomes aware of nature and living things. He is attached to his mother and is nurtured by her.

4. The Emperor: The toddler learns that there are rules and that certain things are not allowed, although he doesn't always understand why. He begins to ask questions and to question the authority of his parents. He tests his limits by saying no and running away when called. He explores the boundaries of his world. His father provides a strong role model.

5. The Hierophant: The child begins to learn about right and wrong, and his parents try to instill in him a sense of morals and values. The child learns what is expected of him in society, and goes to school. The child first encounters the concept of religion, and goes to church. He begins to encounter authority figures and teachers other than his parents. He begins to form a value system, and for the first time realizes that there may be something more than the material world.

6. The Lovers: The teenager begins to have a mind of his own, and starts the process of separating from his parents. He faces tests of right and wrong, good and evil, and makes his own choices. He becomes interested in dating, love, and sex. He believes he can stand on his own, and rejects the philosophy and beliefs of his parent on the surface (while not realizing that they are firmly instilled inside).

7. The Chariot: The teenager leaves home, and goes to college or gets an apartment of his own. He believes he is invincible, and can do or be anything he wants. He travels and gains experience in the world, and tests the limits of his strengths and abilities.

8. Strength: The young adult faces many temptations, and may give in to some of them for a time. Eventually, he learns how to control his impulses without external guidance, and directs his passions and drives into productive use.

9. The Hermit: The young adult struggles to define himself and his chosen path in life. He finishes graduate school, chooses a career, becomes a parent, or otherwise determines the path he wants his life to take.

10. The Wheel of Fortune: He discovers that life does not always go as planned, and that he is not invincible after all. He develops coping tools and ways of dealing with disappointment, learns flexibility, and continues on his way.

11. Justice: He begins to realize that life is not random—things happen for a reason, and you get back what you put into life. He begins to take responsibility for his own life and his own actions, and sets out to right some past wrongs he has done others. He has a clearer sense of his own failings as well as his strengths and skills. He starts to deal more honestly and fairly with others.

12. The Hanged Man: As a middle-aged man, he faces a time of internal crisis. His career no longer seems meaningful and his marriage is facing difficulty. He wants to take some time out for internal processing, and decides to take a sabbatical. He spends quite a while soul-searching, evaluating his life so far and deciding where he wants to go next.

13. Death: As a result of this process, he realizes that he wants to make some major changes in his life. Not all of what has been in his life so far can be carried through this transition—he may lose his job, leave his marriage, change his residence, or make any number of other significant changes.

14. Temperance: He attempts to live a more balanced life, integrating work, family, personal interests, and spirituality into a whole life. He begins to have a sense of his mortality, and tries to exercise and watch his weight.

15. The Devil: In spite of his efforts, he becomes increasingly tied to material things— he has a big mortgage, he has to take out college loans for his kids, and he buys a fancy car so he won't feel middle-aged.

16. The Tower: His company gets bought out, and he is forced to take early retirement. Two months later, his daughter announces that she's leaving university to become an actress. His whole world seems to be falling apart—then he has a heart attack.

17. The Star: His brush with death seems to pull the whole family together. He and his wife go on a second honeymoon and renew their wedding vows. He decides to go to his daughter's plays and support her as best he can, even though he no longer has much of an income. He realizes that he was put on this earth for a reason, and for the first time, begins to seriously think about what that might be. He takes a renewed interest in spirituality and philosophy.

The Moon
The Fey Tarot

18. The Moon: Having lots of time to reflect, he begins to think back over his life and look at his actions in a new light. He starts to have frightening dreams, and thoughts begin to surface that have been buried for a long time. He faces these aspects of his life and self honestly, and begins a long process of coming to terms with himself and forgiving others.

19. The Sun: After long contemplation, he finds peace with himself, and begins to actively enjoy his retirement. He now has grandchildren to play with and gardening to keep him busy, and enjoys a pleasant and loving relationship with his wife. He is content. Many years later, he dies in his sleep.

20. Judgment: With the help of his spiritual guides, he reviews his earthly life and assesses what he has learned, and whether the soul has achieved its purpose for this lifetime. The soul selects its next set of tasks and lessons.

21. The World: The soul returns to the universal energy for rejuvenation and reintegration. For a brief period between lives, it exists in perfect harmony and light. Eventually, it will be reincarnated, and the cycle will begin again.

There may be things in this story, especially near the end, that may not fit with your personal spiritual beliefs. If so, change the story, and think about how your beliefs could be represented by the cards. Reflect on your own life, and see if you recognize these archetypes acting in the patterns of your life.

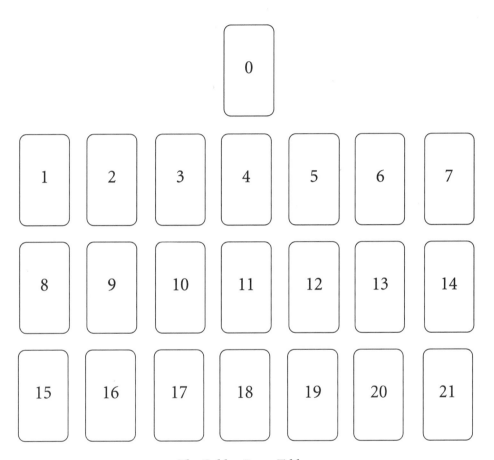

The Golden Dawn Tableau

EXERCISE 1: THE GOLDEN DAWN TABLEAU

One way to explore the Fool's Journey is to lay out the Major Arcana as follows: First, set the Fool aside. Place the rest of the Major Arcana in order into three rows of seven cards each. Then place the Fool above trump 4, the Emperor, above the center of the top row. Now arrange the Minor Arcana as follows: Pile the Aces underneath the Magician, the

Twos underneath the High Priestess, and so on. Once you have reached the Tens, continue placing the court cards under trumps 11–14. This arrangement is called the *Golden Dawn Tableau.*

In the first row of cards, the Fool is provided with teachers and guides, and learns the "rules and tools" of existence. These seven cards represent the early growth and development of the soul, a period in which he (or she) needs assistance and guidance. This can be considered the childhood of the Fool, and the seventh card, the Chariot, represents a "graduation" of sorts. In the next seven cards, the Fool struggles with earthly existence. He is now actively experiencing life, and learning lessons the hard way by doing—this can be considered the adulthood or middle age of the Fool. Notice that all the Minor Arcana are associated with these first two rows. Each set of Minor cards can be considered "lower vibrations" or mundane versions of the Major Arcana they are associated with. Once we reach the third row of cards, we leave the Minor Arcana behind altogether. The first two cards of the third row represent the final liberation of the soul from earthly concerns, and the remaining cards are purely a spiritual struggle for reintegration. This represents the wisdom and old age of the Fool.

There are various paths through the Tableau, all of which are read in threes. One may proceed in the "normal" manner, linearly across the rows from left to right. One may proceed downward from top to bottom, although this approach is more difficult. The "path of the adept" is diagonally, from upper left to lower right, and is even more difficult to achieve. Each of these paths has something to teach us about the spiritual journey and can be meditated on to gain insight into our own lives and journeys. Choose one card that seems to represent where you would like to go with your spiritual path. Now study the three-card paths that lead to and through this card. While it may not be obvious right away what these paths mean and how they might work, keep them in mind as you read through the following material, and at the end, see if you have gained some insight into your own spiritual path. This is one way that the Major Arcana are used—as personal spiritual guides. ✪

Psychological Aspects of the Journey

Many authors, particularly followers of Jung, see the Major Arcana in the light of Jungian archetypes and the development of the mind and personality. Archetypes are certain universal concepts that appear over and over in world religions, myths, and philosophies.

Jung introduced the idea that these archetypes are "hard-wired" into our minds and because of this, can be understood on a purely intuitive level, creating a sort of "collective unconscious" that we all share. The journey through the Major Arcana can be viewed in psychological terms as the development and integration of the personality over a lifetime. As part of this process, a "shadow self" is first created and separated from the conscious ego, and then later must be recognized and reintegrated into a whole personality.

In a psychological context, tarot cards become tools for projection of what is going on in our inner minds. Readers who approach tarot from a psychological standpoint differ in their beliefs on whether anything more is going on than a dialogue between the client's mind and archetypal symbols on the cards. Jung himself believed that something known as "synchronicity" occurred in the use of such tools as the I Ching and the tarot, in which the fall of the cards is not random, but rather a "meaningful coincidence." Others believe that even if nothing particularly mystical is occurring, tarot cards are useful in working with clients in an interactive approach, to bring out hidden issues and help explore psychological and emotional concerns. Because the Major Arcana are the cards in the tarot deck that typically have the most archetypal content, they may be the most useful for this type of work.

EXERCISE 2: INTEGRATION OF SELF

Before reading any further about the Major Arcana and psychology, first conduct this exercise. Shuffle and lay out all the trumps before you, upright, but in no particular order. Examine these cards and choose the one that appeals to you most, on a gut level. Then reexamine the cards and choose the one that you dislike the most. Put these two cards next to each other with a space in between. Now examine the trumps once again, and choose one card that you feel could form a bridge between these two cards in a positive or integrative way. Place it in the center space.

The first card represents your positive and conscious perception of yourself and what you aspire to—your ego. The second card represents your shadow self—those parts of yourself with which you are most uncomfortable. These aspects of yourself nevertheless exist in your subconscious, and you will eventually have to come to terms with them. The third and central card represents the path toward integration of these two aspects of yourself, to become whole. Read on to find out more about the archetypes and aspects of the mind that your chosen cards represent. ✪

Listed here are some of the major archetypes associated with each card, and the aspect of the mind or psychology that can be related to each card.[1] I am using the term *archetypes* broadly for purposes of illustration and study, though perhaps not strictly in the Jungian sense. In the list that follows, Justice and Strength are in their original order, with Justice as 8 and Strength as 11. If your deck has these cards reversed, simply switch the order of these cards and ignore their numbers for the purposes of this section.

0. The Fool
Archetypes: Wanderer, court jester, divine fool, joker, beggar, seeker, eternal youth.
Psychology: Essential self, egoless and eternal, inner child.

1. The Magician
Archetypes: Magician, miracle worker, trickster, alchemist, juggler, Adam, yang.
Psychology: Ego, will, self-consciousness, communication, synchronicity.

2. The High Priestess
Archetypes: Priestess, moon goddess, virgin, oracle, sybil, Eve, yin.
Psychology: Memory, subconscious, intuition, psyche.

3. The Empress
Archetypes: Mother, wife, queen, Madonna, Mother Nature, muse.
Psychology: Right brain, creative process, emotion, feeling, imagination, love, attachment to mother, anima.

4. The Emperor
Archetypes: Father, husband, king, protector, authority figure, civilization.
Psychology: Left brain, rational thought, logic, language, realism, weaning away from mother and attachment to or emulation of father and authority figures, animus.

5. The Hierophant
Archetypes: Religious teacher, wise man, pope.
Psychology: Conscience, morality, values, spiritual striving, transcendence, consciousness of self as part of a larger society, beyond the immediate family.

6. The Lovers

Archetypes: Lovers, Eros, Cupid, Adam and Eve, Garden of Eden.

Psychology: Free will, integration of conscious self with inner animus/anima, first step toward individuation, separation from parents, separation and suppression of the shadow self.

7. The Chariot

Archetypes: Hero, knight, warrior, sun god.

Psychology: Persona, will, initiation into society, strengthening of the ego, danger of ego trip/ego inflation.

8. Justice

Archetypes: Justice, balance, karma, equilibrium.

Psychology: Taking responsibility for actions, discrimination, insight, self-judgment resulting in further strengthening and suppression of the shadow self.

9. The Hermit

Archetypes: Wise old man, hermit, sage, philosopher, monk.

Psychology: Self-knowledge, search for inner wholeness, acceptance of self, the first attempt to seek the inner depths.

10. The Wheel of Fortune

Archetypes: Fate, destiny, fortune, cycles, reincarnation, evolution, sphinx.

Psychology: Humility, objectivity, flexibility, awareness of cycles and larger patterns, turning point in development of psyche from outward issues toward inner growth (integration of ego with the shadow self).

11. Strength

Archetypes: Inner strength, endurance, triumph of good over evil, beauty and the beast.

Psychology: Mediation between the conscious ego and primal instincts through the anima, acceptance and transformation of one's animal nature, healthy sexuality, positive channeling of anger, lust, violence, and other instinctual behaviors.

12. The Hanged Man

Archetypes: Sacrifice, initiation, crucifixion, suspension, reversal.

Psychology: Giving up ego-centered images of life, confronting the abyss, putting oneself in the hands of a higher power, connection with a transpersonal self.

13. Death

Archetypes: Death, change, transformation, rebirth.

Psychology: Acceptance of mortality, facing the moment of truth, reduction of self to the bare essentials, mourning and celebrating the transience of life.

14. Temperance

Archetypes: Angel, union of opposites, alchemy, healing.

Psychology: Beginnings of subconscious reintegration, a glimpse of inner wholeness, becoming aware of our inner guides or angels.

15. The Devil

Archetypes: Fallen angel, evil, materialism, vice, bondage, libido.

Psychology: The collective Shadow, ego indulgence, destructive instincts, refusal to acknowledge and thus unconsciously becoming a slave to our shadow selves, guilt and self-punishment, dehumanization, codependency.

16. The Tower

Archetypes: Tower of Babel, chaos, destruction, catastrophe, lightning bolt.

Psychology: Liberation from artificial constructs of the mind and rigid mental processes, breaking down the ego, illumination, truth.

17. The Star

Archetypes: Star, hope, inspiration.

Psychology: The soul, spirituality, meditation and contemplation, awareness of self as part of the cosmos, access to the collective unconscious, assimilation and understanding of Tower events, insight, a conscious vision of wholeness.

18. The Moon

Archetypes: Moon, dreams, instincts, dark night of the soul, descent into the underworld.

Psychology: Descending into the subconscious, facing, acknowledging, and eventually embracing the shadow self, coming to terms with instinctual wisdom and the primordial self, letting go of illusions.

19. The Sun

Archetypes: Sun, success, fulfillment, joy, return to the light.

Psychology: Spiritual illumination, inner harmony, spontaneous joy, the natural self, the inner child, awareness and consciousness.

20. Judgment

Archetypes: The Last Judgment, awakening, resurrection, ascension.

Psychology: Awareness of impending transformation, reunion between subconscious, conscious, and higher self, inner awakening, judgment and closure, rebirth, heeding a higher calling.

21. The World

Archetypes: Wholeness, synthesis, completion, universe.

Psychology: Integration, psychic wholeness and equilibrium, self-awareness, transcendence, self-actualization, one with the universe.

These ideas can be used in various ways in a reading. First, the trumps as a whole can be seen as a psychological journey that begins with an unformed personality at birth, through the development of that personality into the conscious ego and shadow self, the difficult process of self-knowledge and awareness, and finally to reintegration of the self and wholeness. Receiving a trump in a reading can indicate which stage of this journey the client may be in, particularly if the cards he tends to receive when asking about an issue are all in the beginning, middle, or near the end of the cycle. Also, very positive or negative reactions to certain cards may indicate archetypes with which the person either identifies, or responds to negatively because of projection of his shadow self onto the card. Conscious knowledge of the archetypes represented by each card also deepens our overall range of meanings for the card and the different ways in which it may be seen to act in readings.

Mythological Aspects of the Journey

In many mythical stories and fairy tales, there is a hero who goes on a quest. These heroes share many of the characteristics of the tarot Fool, and meet many of the Jungian archetypes on their journeys. This section explains how the tarot trumps reflect archetypes as expressed in myths and fairy tales.[2] Once you can see how the spiritual, psychological, and mythical journeys fit together and complement one another, you will have a much clearer vision of what the Major Arcana are all about.

0. The Fool

The hero (or heroine) of our myth (especially western European fairy tales) typically shares many characteristics of the tarot Fool. He is usually the youngest child, with no particular talent or distinguishing characteristics. He usually has brothers or sisters who are expected to complete the quest due to their superior equipment, beauty, or the favor of their parents, yet who invariably fail. The youngest child undertakes the task out of a spirit of adventure, and usually has little in the way of provisions, which he gladly shares with whomever he happens upon. This child has no sense of inflated self-worth (lack of ego), and happily converses with any person or animal he meets along the road, thus receiving valuable clues and help along the way. Without worrying about the future, he traipses along the road, going wherever his path may lead, but always keeping the goal in mind. In the end, he succeeds because of his Fool-ish attributes, not in spite of them.

1. The Magician

The Magician represents the hero's spiritual or magical guide, as opposed to an actual parent. In many fairy tales, the child's true parents are not known or are no longer living—he lives with his stepparents (Cinderella, Baba Yaga) and often has supernatural guardians. The Magician is a wizard who sets the stage for the story by creating the circumstances of and need for the quest, and who watches over the hero's progress throughout the story (like Gandalf in Tolkien's *The Lord of the Rings*). In the end, he may be revealed as the hero's true father, or he may simply stay behind the scenes and allow the hero to find and leave with the magical treasure. Sometimes he appears as a demonic or impish creature, such as Rumpelstiltskin, who nevertheless ends up benefiting the heroine in the end.

2. The High Priestess

The High Priestess represents the Magician's female counterpart, and may appear in the form of a fairy godmother (Cinderella) or a good witch (Glenda in *The Wizard of Oz*). She usually provides a valuable clue or assistance just when the heroine is in dire straits. She may turn out to be the heroine's real mother in the end, or takes the place of the real mother, who is dead. She usually cannot directly interfere, but provides assistance of a more indirect nature or magical items that later protect the heroine at key moments. This is in keeping with the High Priestess' essentially passive or receptive nature.

3. The Empress

In the Empress we find the hero's actual mother, or the one who appears to be his mother. This may be a loving mother, such as the poor mother who loves her youngest son the best and weeps to see him go with nothing but a crust of bread, or the cruel stepmother who features in so many European fairy tales. Here we have the Goddess in both her creative and violent aspects, a personification of the destructive powers of nature. She may secretly be a witch who uses the forces of nature against the hero or heroine and who stands in opposition to the High Priestess.

4. The Emperor

Here we have either the hero's father, or the King, who is often prominently featured in the story. Often it is the King who sets the nature of the quest (in response to the machinations of the Magician) and offers a reward to anyone who can solve the puzzle or retrieve a magical item. His reward is usually part of his kingdom and the hand of his daughter, and he fully expects a prince or knight to win the prize. Imagine his surprise when the lowly Fool is the one who succeeds!

Notice how in these four cards we have various magical or powerful worldly forces working in opposition to each other, with the Fool or hero as something of a pawn in between. This is very typical of Greek and Roman myths as well, and illustrates the nature of the formative influences on the hero, and his later struggle to complete the quest and at the same time free himself from these parental influences. At this point in the cards, the hero has not yet set out on his journey. These cards all represent the background of his childhood and development, the forces that surround him, often entirely without his knowledge. Notice the similarity of these archetypes to the child's early development, which we just discussed.

5. The Hierophant

The Hierophant appears as a teacher or educator for some heroes, particularly in Greek and Roman myths. This is someone who understands the potential of the hero and works to prepare him for the journey that he knows the hero must eventually undertake, even if the hero himself does not know it. An example might be Merlin in the King Arthur stories. The young hero often has a wise teacher in childhood who instills values of goodness and wisdom, and who blesses him when he sets out on his journey, but cannot accompany him any farther. The Hierophant can also be a personification of God, such as Aslan in the Narnia tales.

6. The Lovers

The Lovers represents the point at which the heroine learns about the quest and makes the decision to set out on the Journey. She may wait until many others have tried and failed, or may leap out on the road as soon as she hears of the magical quest to be undertaken. Either way, this represents a step toward maturity, a realization that one can leave one's parents and do something worthwhile. Here the heroine may gather together her few belongings and whatever items she wishes to carry with her, and make plans and preparations for the journey.

7. The Chariot

At this moment, our hero walks out onto the open road in broad daylight, not knowing what he will find, but certain of his task and his willingness to try. There is a kind of naive certainty that any obstacle he may meet can be overcome, and the quest will succeed. There may be a sense of invincibility or youthful indestructibility that carries with it some aspects of the Fool. Indeed, at this point our hero may fail if he tempts fate or hubris too strongly, such as Icarus flying too close to the sun. There may be some form of magical transportation, such as Cinderella's carriage, or something more mundane, like a horse.

8. Justice

Justice represents a series of tasks or tests that the hero must complete before he can begin his journey and find the help he needs; for example, agreeing to share the last of his food with a dirty old beggar woman (who is really a good witch in disguise), or Arthur pulling the sword out of the stone. Sometimes he finds the guide (Hermit) first, but is required to complete certain other tasks before learning what he needs to know to complete his quest. Often there is equipment he must gather, particularly swords for the more martial heroes. These tasks always require discernment, and often include tests of the hero's virtue, temper, quickness of mind, and ingenuity.

The Hermit
Medieval Enchantment: The Nigel Jackson Tarot

9. The Hermit

In nearly every one of these myths, the heroine cannot succeed alone. She meets or is told to seek out a wise man or woman, represented by the Hermit. This Hermit is in reality her inner wise voice, but in myths this voice is personified by a person. This person gives the heroine valuable advice or assistance in her quest, and oversees the tests represented by Justice that strengthen and prepare her for the rest of the journey. The Hermit knows where she has to go next, but usually does not reveal this information until the heroine is fully prepared. The Hermit may also reveal the heroine's true name and origins, or the true names of other people or creatures the heroine may meet in the coming journey. To use a modern example, this is Yoda's dark cave, where Luke Skywalker confronts his shadow self in the form of Darth Vader (which later makes him stronger, as he accepts his dark side). Learning one's true name is a metaphor for knowing oneself and one's true nature, and being in control of one's destiny.

10. The Wheel of Fortune

Now comes a turning point in the journey. Once our hero has gained the knowledge of his true self and has passed all the tests, he is ready to know the full nature of his task. Up until now, everything has passed in the light of day, yet now he must descend into the underworld in order to complete the task. The cards that follow chronicle this journey through the underworld, and final emergence back into the land of the Sun and completion of the task. This cycle of day and night is reflected in the turning of the Wheel, and also mirrors the psychological journey just described, where the conscious ego is first formed and strengthened, and then descends into the subconscious to come to terms with the shadow self. The last gift of the Hermit is knowledge of the task and travels ahead, but the hero must descend alone. Since in psychological terms this descent often entails finding the lost or neglected parts of yourself, so too must the hero rely on his hidden strengths and abilities to face the unknown dangers ahead. The sphinx sitting on top of the Wheel represents the guardian of the underworld, which the hero meets in the next step of the journey.

11. Strength

Guarding the entrance to the treasure, there is usually a beast that must be dealt with, and cannot simply be killed (or if it is killed, the hero will suffer later!). Those who fail in dealing with the beast are often turned into beasts themselves, and it is here that the youngest child may find his older brothers and sisters turned into animals. The beast is a metaphor for our own inner animal selves, which is what we first encounter when descending into our subconscious minds. This is a very frightening experience, and only the hero who approaches the beast with compassion, courage, respect, and love may succeed. The guardian beast is often tamed through an offering of food, love, or the knowledge of its name. The beast may then turn into a strong and protective companion, who fiercely guards the hero through the rest of his travels in the underworld.

12. The Hanged Man

In the Hanged Man we find the upside-down person reflecting the fact that our heroine's world has turned upside-down—answers to questions are to be found in the depths of the earth and not in the sunlight. The heroine is faced with making great sacrifices, and often turns away from the task. She may be afraid of becoming trapped in the underworld, never to return. She may repeatedly try to avoid or accomplish the task in another way, only to fail over and over. At this point, the heroine may be tempted to turn aside from her journey—for which she is punished by the gods and often becomes trapped in a form of limbo (e.g., Jonah in the belly of the whale) until she willingly chooses to continue her journey. Once the heroine finds the inner strength and sense of purpose to continue, she is released from purgatory and makes her final descent.

13. Death

Here the hero gives herself up to the underworld, without looking back. The descent into the depths is complete, and although she may despair of ever seeing the light again, she perseveres. This is akin to a conscious surrender of the ego in order to fully experience the subconscious. In this card the heroine faces death with open eyes, and may remain in the underworld for some time, in some cases even becoming the wife or consort of Hades. The heroine is often required to leave behind all her earthly possessions as a condition of entering. Note that the "underworld" described here is metaphorical—in myths or fairy tales it may appear in many forms, such as Aladdin's cave, Baba Yaga's hut, the Giant's castle, or a deep dark forest; but it always symbolizes entering the scary regions of the subconscious mind, in which one may find monsters, spirit guides, and treasures of great value, if one only dares to enter.

14. Temperance

Just as in the depths of the subconscious we find not only fears and terrors but also hope and the potential for wholeness, our hero, having dissolved his ego and given himself up to the underworld, finds a spirit guide there waiting. This spirit guide may come in the form of an angel, a fairy, an animal, a dream, or a voice. This is a messenger of hope from the gods that gives a glimpse of the path back to the light and gives the hero hope that he will indeed pass through the depths of hell intact and out the other side. The yellow irises in this card symbolize Iris, messenger of the gods, and the path leads to a crown, reminiscent of the King who started this whole journey off, and the earthly rewards that may await our hero should he succeed in his task.

15. The Devil

Now our hero descends to the lowest point, the central room of the castle, the darkest heart of the forest. Here is hidden the treasure or princess he must liberate from bondage, guarded by a terrible beast, giant, serpent, ogre, or dragon. Here we come face to face with our inner demons and see them for what they are. In the depths, the hero must recognize aspects of himself, or he will not be able to free the prisoner. For a male hero of the fairy tales, the object of the quest is almost always either a maiden or a treasure that will win him a maiden—Sleeping Beauty, or the king's daughter. This is represented by the two chained lovers in the Devil card—the unification of the sexes and their liberation from bondage. In a psychological sense, this represents the unification of the male and female halves of the psyche into a whole person, and reverses the process of differentiation begun in the Lovers.

16. The Tower

The Tower represents the moment when the heroine liberates the object of her quest, unlocks the door, frees the prisoner, and attempts to escape. However, this act is never without a price—often the castle comes crumbling down around them, the earth shakes, dragons fly up and begin terrorizing the village, demons are let loose, or angry djinns materialize and demand retribution. Here, with the help of our anima or animus, we are freeing ourselves from the constructs that hold us back, at the cost of our security structures. Often this involves slaying a guardian or an internalized shadow-mother or shadow-father image that has been keeping us enslaved—Hansel and Gretel stuffing the witch into her oven, for example, or Jack killing the giant. It is amazing how often wicked stepmothers meet their demise in children's fairy tales, without the slightest qualms on the part of the heroine! This can only be understood as a metaphor for what is going on in one's mind, rather than the killing of real people.

17. The Star

The hero feels joyful success, as he has gained what he came for, and can see the light at the end of the tunnel. There is hope and the promise of a bright future. Often, an omen is seen at this point, a shooting star, or a vision of hope. Yet, our hero still has a ways to go—this journey was a long and difficult one coming, and there is a long return yet to go. The Star represents a moment of rest and rejuvenation before the travels that await.

18. The Moon

Having gained the object of her quest, the heroine must now return and deliver it to the King. This return voyage is often fraught with difficulties, which are all the more unexpected because it seems that the hard part should be over. However, she is still deep in the underworld, and many tales are told of the lover lost at this point due to carelessness or not following the rules of the quest; Lot's wife turns into a pillar of salt, travelers are led astray by elves in the forest, a pomegranate seed is eaten, and Persephone must stay forever in the underworld. The shadow world is still a dark and dangerously inviting place, and great care must be taken to pass successfully through it and reach the light.

All that has been learned until now must be remembered and faithfully followed, or all will be lost and the heroine will lose her way. There are temptations on all sides, inviting us to stay in the underworld, and we must stay true to our goal and remember to stay on the path, even when it is faint and hard to see. In many myths, one can drink from the waters of forgetfulness and lose one's memory and even one's name, which had been previously bestowed by the Hermit. Often the heroine must pass over an abyss on a narrow bridge, or pass yet one more guardian (Cerberus, represented by the wolf in the Moon card) before she can emerge into the sunlight. Often she must follow a narrow trail—the thread leading out of the labyrinth or the bread crumbs in the forest—to escape.

19. The Sun

At last our hero has truly succeeded—he reaches the sunlight; Percival finds the Holy Grail, Dante emerges from Hell, and the lost children are joyfully reunited with their father. The two lovers are together and the two aspects of the self stand side by side in the sunlight. In another version of the story, brothers are reunited that were previously separated, or even fighting one another. In older tarot decks, this theme was represented by two children playing in the sun, rather than just one.

20. Judgment

This card represents the moment when the quest is fulfilled and the kingdom is won—a magic spell is lifted, the frog turns into a prince, Sleeping Beauty wakes up, and the Holy Grail is used to heal the king and the land. Those who are evil are revealed for what they are and banished forevermore, and those who are proven good receive the kingdom and the beautiful princess (or the handsome prince). This is an allusion to Judgment Day and the Kingdom of Heaven, but also represents our own self-judgment and healing that can come about when we are truly united and whole.

21. The World

And they lived happily ever after . . .

EXERCISE 3: FAIRY TALES

Reread your favorite fairy tale, myth, or children's story, and identify as many of the archetypes and characters just described as you can. List your correspondences for the group. Not every fairy tale will have all these aspects of the mythological journey, and they will not always appear in the same order. ✪

Astrological Correspondences

Many authors have drawn astrological correspondences with the tarot cards, and this set of archetypes will round out our initial study of the Major Arcana. While there are many methods of assigning the signs and planets to the trumps, we will focus in this chapter on the most widely used system, developed by the Golden Dawn (see chapter 9 for more information on tarot history and development). However, if you are using a pre-Golden Dawn deck, your deck will almost certainly work better with the associations derived from the Renaissance period, discussed in the next chapter. And if you are using a pagan deck or one that is based on a completely different set of cultural images (such as Chinese, Native American, or African), these systems may not work at all for you, and you will want to learn about the gods and goddesses portrayed in your deck instead.

The modern version of the Golden Dawn system draws its correspondences from the twelve astrological signs and the ten planets (in astrology, the term *planets* includes the Sun and the Moon)—perfectly corresponding to the 22 trumps. The planets and signs were assigned to the trumps according to a modern view of their astrological attributes, as well as which trumps most closely reflected those attributes, a system that, on the whole, works quite well. However, the Golden Dawn decided that the astrological signs should go in order through the trumps. This is almost certainly one of the reasons that Arthur Waite switched Justice and Strength, because Leo comes before Libra in the order. This results in one or two attributions that feel forced to many people, such as the assignment of the Chariot to Cancer. In addition, it should be recognized that at that time, three of the planets had not yet been discovered. These three trumps were originally assigned to the three primary elements of air, water, and fire, and were subsequently reassigned to Uranus, Neptune, and Pluto, respectively. The following list provides the astrological and elemental associations of the trumps, based on the Golden Dawn system:

0. **The Fool**—Uranus (air)

1. **The Magician**—Mercury (air)

2. **The High Priestess**—Moon (water)

3. **The Empress**—Venus (earth)

4. **The Emperor**—Aries (fire)

5. **The Hierophant**—Taurus (earth)

6. **The Lovers**—Gemini (air)

7. **The Chariot**—Cancer (water)

8. **Strength**—Leo (fire)

9. **The Hermit**—Virgo (earth)

10. **The Wheel of Fortune**—Jupiter (fire)

11. **Justice**—Libra (air)

12. **The Hanged Man**—Neptune (water)

13. **Death**—Scorpio (water)

14. **Temperance**—Sagittarius (fire)

15. **The Devil**—Capricorn (earth)

16. **The Tower**—Mars (fire)

17. **The Star**—Aquarius (air)

18. **The Moon**—Pisces (water)

19. **The Sun**—Sun (fire)

20. **Judgment**—Pluto (water/fire)

21. **The World**—Saturn (earth)

Note that Judgment was originally assigned to the element of fire, and later assigned to Pluto, a planet associated with water. This is the only card that has conflicting elemental associations, based on the new planetary assignments.

EXERCISE 4: YOUR ASTROLOGICAL SIGNS

Take a look at your astrological chart, if you have one. If you don't have one, but are interested in doing this, go to one of the many on-line sites that calculate free birth charts (you must know your birth date, exact time of birth, and place of birth)—Astrodienst (www.astro.com) is a great one. Write down the planet and astrological sign corresponding to your Sun sign, Moon sign, and rising sign (the sign on the cusp of the first house in your birth chart). If you don't know your exact time or place of birth, you can still use an ephemeris to look up your Sun and Moon signs.[3]

Now take out the trump cards that correspond to these three signs. For example, if you have your Sun in Aries, take the Sun card (for your Sun sign) and the Emperor (for Aries) and put them together. Do this for all three signs. Now study these cards, based on what you have learned in this lesson, and see if this gives you any insights into your basic personality. If you think of your Sun sign as your ego or conscious self, and your Moon sign as your unconscious or emotional self, what do these cards tell you about the interaction between the two? The rising sign is related to your outward personality and how you appear to others. How does your rising sign modify the picture? If you are really interested in astrology, you can do this for every planet in your chart, modified by the house that each planet/sign combination is in. ✪

Mundane Manifestations of the Trumps

Finally we come to real-life manifestations of the trumps, after exploring their spiritual, psychological, mythological, and astrological attributes. The trumps can appear as actual events in our lives, or these events may seem to mirror the trumps. We may experience different trumps or archetypes acting in different parts of our lives. By reflecting on the appearance of these archetypes in our lives, we can better understand them when they occur, and can help our clients recognize how they relate to their own lives. Although there are many deep concepts associated with each trump, as Freud said, sometimes a cigar is just a cigar, and sometimes the Chariot is just the family Volvo. So be prepared for the trumps to manifest not only when you are having a deep spiritual crisis, but when their imagery and concepts apply perfectly well to everyday aspects of your life.

EXERCISE 5: SEEING YOURSELF IN THE TRUMPS

Think about your life and divide it into different areas, such as work, relationships, kids, tarot reading, spirituality, other significant activities, or whatever is important to you. Look over the trumps and see if you can identify which trump seems to reflect where you are in each part of your life. What kind of energy do you see there? How long do you think you might stay in this particular trump? Might there be a transition coming any time soon, and if so, where might you be going next? ✪

We do not always experience the trumps in linear sequence. Sometimes we get them out of order, skip over some, or come back to others. Sometimes we repeat a minicycle many times over before getting beyond it. We may spend one area of our entire life in a single trump, while in other areas we may pass through several cards in rapid succession.

One very useful approach to using the trumps in real life is to identify and recognize cycles that typically occur, which can be represented by the tarot cards. We all have cycles in our lives—some good, some bad. The good ones are often ones that prompt us to make changes for our personal growth or to keep life interesting—that periodic urge that prompts us to change jobs, take up new hobbies, or do some deep thinking about our lives. These may be tied to astrological cycles, as well as the different types of energies that surround us on a periodic basis.

The not-so-good cycles are related to dysfunctional behaviors in ourselves and those close to us. We may go through cycles of losing and gaining weight, addiction or alcoholism interspersed with periods of sobriety, repeated attractions to inappropriate partners followed by eventual breakups, making and losing large amounts of money, etc. These cycles—and the ways out of them—can be found in the Major Arcana. Here is one example, relating to alcoholism:

The Devil: The cycle starts here, with the first descent into addiction or alcoholism. At this point, the behavior is firmly established and the person is in bondage to it, whether she realizes it or not. If she does realize it, she may feel powerless to change it, or uninterested in changing it. She may even believe it provides some benefit or pleasure. There may be others chained in here along with her—family members, spouses, friends—some of whom may be enablers or codependent, and others who may just be suffering due to the alcoholic's behavior.

The Tower: At some point, her world crashes down due to her drinking—she loses her job, gets in a car crash, hurts or kills someone accidentally, or develops a major health problem tied to the drinking. This brings her alcoholism out into the open where everyone can see it, along with the disastrous results. Hopefully, she experiences an illumination here—a realization that things cannot continue as before, although it may take several trips through the Tower to reinforce this.

The Star: Here she gives herself up into the hands of a higher power: her religion, a twelve-step program, her doctor, and/or friends and family who want to help. At this point, she may feel stripped bare, relatively helpless and naked, but with hope for a better future. In this card, there is no more room to hide. She must be honest with herself and everyone else, take responsibility for her actions, and provide restitution if possible. There is a positive outlook for the future, and humility for past behavior, as well as an acknowledgment that the road ahead may be difficult, and there is always the danger of recurrence.

Temperance: At this point in a repeating version of this cycle, she changes her behavior and begins to live a healthier life, without really facing the inner demons that prompted the alcoholic behavior in the first place. She returns to the Temperance card, in which she walks a fine line—controlling her urges, staying productive, going to AA meetings, and doing all the things she needs to do to stay sober. Life is looking up, she gets a new job, and her relationships with her friends, family, and coworkers improve. Plus, her health is much better. With luck, she could stay in this card indefinitely.

The Devil Through the Star: If and when such a person "falls off the wagon," we have a repeat of this entire cycle. Either slowly, through rationalization that she can handle it now, or suddenly, as a result of an emotionally traumatic event, she may begin drinking again. More often than not, this will be hidden at first from those around her. Yet inevitably, it leads once again to the Tower and beyond.

The Moon: The healthy way out of this cycle involves a trip through the Moon, and this is one reason that it is so hard to take this path. This is the emotional and psychological part of the recovery process, which is more than just creating good habits or following the doctor's orders. It involves a serious self-examination and gaining an understanding of the underlying reasons why she would be tempted by alcoholism and drawn to that kind of self-oblivion. It may require dealing with very painful issues from the past, involving parents and lovers. It can involve counseling to work through insecurity, self-love, and identity issues. Whatever the path, it is long and winding, and may take years and years. In the end, though, she will have gained an understanding of how she got to where she is, and how to move beyond it. Her level of self-knowledge is much greater, and with this knowledge, she might not even feel a need or urge to drink (other than a physical one).

The Sun: At last she emerges into the Sun, confident in herself and strong enough to prevent this behavior from recurring. This is a much happier state than the tightrope-walking one that occurs in Temperance. While Temperance represents significant progress from an alcoholic state, it is not the same as the full self-knowledge reached after passing through the Moon and Sun cards. Now she is truly free to live her life, having thrown off the self-created shackles of the Devil once and for all. Even if a physical craving remains, she is secure enough in her new self that she knows there is no need to give in to it.

EXERCISE 6: REPEATING CYCLES

Think about some of the "ruts" that we all get into in our lives, where we seem to repeat the same cycles over and over. Pick one, and try to identify what series of trumps seems to reflect this repeating cycle (you don't have to put them in the same order in which they appear in the deck). Based on what you have learned about these trumps and which trumps come next on the journey, what would be one possible way for you to break out of this cycle? ✪

Evaluating Your Progress

Study Goal 1

Without looking at your deck or notes, write down the names of the 22 Major Arcana in order. Repeat this until the sequence comes easily to mind. It does not have to match the sequence or names used in this chapter as long as it accurately matches the deck you use most often. Think about some area of your life in which you have traveled partway through what you expect to be a long journey of learning, study, or exploration. Imagine yourself as the Fool starting out on that journey, and explain how each of the Major Arcana you encounter represent real-life experiences and stages of your journey. What card do you think you are in at this point in your travels?

Study Goal 2

Lay out the Major Arcana in order. Thinking in terms of your spiritual or philosophical beliefs, work out in your mind how the sequence of the trumps could fit into these beliefs and help illustrate basic concepts from them. What symbols on the cards or archetypes help integrate the tarot with your spiritual beliefs?

Study Goal 3

List the trumps in order, and indicate for each any astrological and elemental correspondences you have chosen to go with the cards. Explain at least three different ways you might use these in readings.

Study Goal 4

Remove the Major Arcana from your deck, and shuffle them. Turn them over one by one, and for each card, name a real-world activity or situation that the card could represent. Try to choose everyday activities or situations rather than abstract spiritual or philosophical concepts. For example, the Chariot might represent a teenager leaving home for the first time to live on his own.

---

1. For further reading on psychology and the tarot, see *Tarot and Psychology: Spectrums of Possibility* by Arthur Rosengarten (St. Paul, MN: Paragon House, 2000); or *Jung and Tarot: An Archetypal Journey* by Sallie Nichols (York Beach, ME: Samuel Weiser, 1980).

2. For further reading on mythological archetypes and the tarot, see *Tarot and the Journey of the Hero* by Hajo Banzhaf (York Beach, ME: Samuel Weiser, 2000); or *Mastering the Tarot: An Advanced Personal Teaching Guide* by Juliet Sharman-Burke (New York: St. Martin's Griffin, 2000).

3. An ephemeris is a book of tables that list the locations of the Sun, Moon, and other planets throughout the year; for example, *The American Ephemeris* by Neil F. Michelsen (San Diego, CA: ACS Publications, Inc.).

nine

Historical Themes in the Major Arcana

Study Goals

1. Become familiar with the basics of tarot history.

2. Develop spiritual, mythological, and astrological associations for pre-twentieth-century decks appropriate to their period.

A Brief History of Tarot

Any student of tarot should know a little about the history of tarot, partly because it has been so romanticized and mythologized that much of what you read or hear may be inaccurate, but also because understanding its history helps explain why you see certain images on the trumps and what they might have meant to those who designed them. If you use pre-twentieth-century decks or a modern deck designed with a Renaissance theme, this may be much more relevant to how you would interpret your cards than what you may find in general tarot books that refer mainly to *Rider-Waite-Smith* decks. What follows is a brief summary of what can be found in the references at the end of this chapter, and is written from a historical, rather than metaphysical, perspective.[1]

To the best of our knowledge, tarot cards were invented in the early fifteenth century, almost certainly in northern Italy. They may have been created by a scholar or artist associated with or commissioned by one of the wealthy aristocratic houses, such as the Visconti-Sforzas of Milan or the d'Estes of Ferrara. Early references to tarot cards, *carte da trionfi* or *tarocchi* as they were then known, appear in various cities in northern Italy, including Milan, Ferrara, and Florence. The deck was created by adding the trump suit and the Fool to a deck of playing cards. Playing cards had already been introduced to Europe from Islamic countries about fifty years prior, with suit symbols very similar to those seen on modern-day European tarot cards.

Temperance
Visconti Tarots

The 21 of Trumps
Tarocco Francese

Tarocchi was originally invented as a trick-taking card game similar to bridge, but with a fifth permanent trump suit. Variations of the game of tarocchi, or *tarock,* are still played in European countries today, particularly in Italy, France, Hungary, Austria, and Switzerland (rules for one of the most widely played modern variants are included in appendix F). Decks used for tarocchi may be quite different from what we may be used to thinking of as tarot decks; they may have pictures of historical or social scenes, animals, royalty, hunting scenes, landscapes, ships, or any subject imaginable, not necessarily with any esoteric content.

As far as we know, tarot was not invented for the purpose of divination, although what specifically was in the mind of the inventor is unknown, as we are not really certain who that person was. Nevertheless, the time of the Italian Renaissance was fertile with religious, philosophical, and metaphysical themes that found their way into the symbolism of the trumps (at this time, the Minor suits of most decks were illustrated only with embellished suit symbols, with the notable exception of the Sola Busca deck). Regardless of their original purpose or use, this rich symbolism provided a foundation for divinatory and metaphysical uses of the tarot cards.

As with regular playing cards, tarot cards eventually became associated with divination and fortunetelling. In the late 1700s, we find the first complete discussions of divinatory meanings associated with playing cards and tarot cards, as well as the first tarot deck designed with esoteric and metaphysical concepts in mind, published by the French occultist Etteilla. Many romantic notions about tarot cards were first popularized during this time and throughout the nineteenth century, such as their claimed origins in ancient Egypt or with the gypsies, none of which are accurate. In the mid-nineteenth century, the French magician Eliphas Lévi drew new associations between the tarot, the Hebrew language and Jewish qabala, and the four elements. The systemization of tarot and development of correspondences between tarot and astrology, alchemy, and other aspects of the Western mystical tradition were later taken up by others active in magick and Freemasonry, including Papus in France, and the Hermetic Order of the Golden Dawn and Aleister Crowley in England.

Tarot card 5
Esoteric Ancient Tarots

In 1909, the *Rider* tarot deck (or *Rider-Waite-Smith*, as it is popularly called today and is referred to throughout this book) was created by Arthur Edward Waite (author) and Pamela Colman Smith (artist), and published by Rider & Co. in London. This deck was the first modern deck to include illustrations on all the Minor cards. Designed to reflect the Western mystical tradition, its symbolism was heavily influenced by the Hermetic Order of the Golden Dawn, to which A. E. Waite and Pamela Colman Smith both belonged. This deck was one of the few published in the United States for decades, and along with the *Thoth* deck, designed by Aleister Crowley and Frieda Harris, is considered by many to be the "standard" tarot deck. However, it is less widely used on the European continent, and there are now hundreds of other tarot decks available in every religious, spiritual, and metaphysical tradition imaginable.

Religious and Mythological Themes

Modern readers might be surprised to learn that the original imagery of the tarot included strong religious elements, specifically Christian. Historians differ about whether the imagery is entirely orthodox or whether there are some heretical elements, but most agree that it is typical of other artwork of the Renaissance era, consisting largely of religious, philosophical, and mythological elements.

It is difficult to definitively identify a coherent theme (if there was one) that the artists of the early tarot decks intended to portray. For one thing, the early decks did not have numbers on the trumps, and all the decks that we have in museums are missing at least a few (if not many more) of their cards. We do know that the oldest decks differed from one another in the order of their cards, and in some cases, even the numbers of trumps and court cards. Not knowing the exact number and sequence of the trumps makes it more difficult to imagine what the ideas behind their design might have been. However, several interesting theories have emerged from tarot scholars over the years.[2]

One idea was that the *trionfi,* or trumps, were related to or designed after the triumphal processions that were relatively common at the time, as well as Petrarch's poem *I Trionfi.* These were allegorical depictions of life in which one group triumphed over another, and was later triumphed over itself. For example, the first group might represent ordinary mortals, and consist of the trumps 0–5. This group would be triumphed over by the virtues and the fates in the middle of the trumps, as well as Death and the

Devil. This middle group would in turn be triumphed over by the celestial bodies and the Angel (an alternate name for Judgment), trumps 17–21.

A similar concept is that the trumps represent the universe, at all levels of perfection from lowest to highest. This starts with the lowly Beggar or Fool at the bottom, the Mountebank or Magician next, followed by worldly kings and queens, and the Pope. The cards that come next in the series represent various ideas that were important in the culture at the time, and were considered either virtues to aspire to or forces beyond the control of humans. The virtues that are clearly depicted in the early decks include Fortitude (Strength), Justice, and Temperance. In addition, there were cards in the middle of the series of trumps such as Time (the Hermit, then known as Chronos), Fortune (Wheel of Fortune), and Death, all of which controlled the fate of mortals.

The Hermit
Visconti Tarots

Set above all these was the Devil, and the Tower (possibly representing the destruction and chaos perpetrated on earth by the Devil). Above the Devil are the heavenly bodies (the Stars, the Moon, and the Sun), the Angel, and the World. In Christian symbolism, these last two cards may have represented Judgment Day and God presiding over eternal life. The central figure of the World card has often been compared to paintings of Jesus, but may actually represent the *animus mundi*, or soul of the world.

These are just a few of the ideas that have been put forth to explain the sequence of trumps from a Renaissance worldview. One of the most important ideas that emerges from these studies for a modern tarot reader is that tarot cards are not and never have been antireligious or the Devil's work, as some still believe. Although currently considered by many today to be outside the mainstream of organized religion, they contain strong religious, spiritual, and philosophical elements that are reflective of the culture and the era in which they were developed.

EXERCISE 1: SPIRITUAL THEMES

As tarot readers, we will often be questioned about the place of tarot cards in our religion or those of our clients. One of the most personally rewarding ways that we can use tarot cards is to express our spiritual path and fundamental beliefs about religion, spirituality, and philosophy. Think about your own personal beliefs, those you grew up with and/or your current beliefs, if they have changed. Imagine how the tarot cards and trumps in particular can be used to portray central concepts and teachings within your belief systems, both past and present. How could this be useful in readings, either for yourself or others? ✪

Correspondences

An older system of astrological and mythical correspondences is based on Renaissance art and mythology, and more closely follows the mythological portrayals of the gods and goddesses, beasts, and other symbols that are associated with these signs and planets. At that time, only seven planets were known, so not every card has an astrological correspondence. No particular attention is paid to signs being in order or having one sign per card, since this was most likely not an issue in the original development and ordering of the cards.

In addition to astrological signs, many of the cards are associated with Greek or Roman gods and goddesses, or other familiar figures of the culture at that time. To better understand why these cards have the assignments they do, you may want to look at an early version of the trumps in one of the Renaissance decks, and check out some of the references listed at the end of this chapter.[3] One interesting note is that some of the cards that we think of as being largely allegorical today, like Death, the Devil, and Judgment, may have had more literal meanings to the people of the time.

0. The Fool: Fool or court jester, Dionysus.

1. The Magician: Mountebank or conjurer, Hermes, Mercury.

2. The Papess: Historians differ about whether this card could refer to the legendary Pope Joan or the historical Manfreda Visconti and thus represent a heretical take on the church, or whether she is simply a feminine counterpart to the Pope and the church, much as the Empress to the Emperor; other associations include Juno, Persephone, and Taurus.

3. The Empress: Demeter, Hera, Mary mother of Jesus, Cancer.

4. The Emperor: Zeus, Jupiter.

5. The Pope: Sagittarius.

6. The Lovers: Venus, Aphrodite, Eros. This card was originally called Love or the Lover, and featured Cupid rather than an angel overhead, and a man choosing between two women.

7. The Chariot: Mars, Aries.

8. Justice: Athena, Libra, the virtue justice.

9. The Hermit: Saturn, Chronos (Father Time), possibly associated with the virtue prudence, though this link is less clear than the card links with the other three virtues of justice, strength, and temperance.

10. The Wheel of Fortune: Fortuna, the Three Fates, Gemini.

11. Strength: Heracles, Leo, the virtue strength.

12. The Hanged Man: Prometheus, Odin, Capricorn.

13. Death: Hades.

14. Temperance: Iris, Aquarius, the virtue temperance.

15. The Devil: Satan, Pan, Scorpio.

16. The Tower: Tower of Babel.

17. The Star: Ganymede, Aphrodite, Virgo.

18. The Moon: Moon, aspects of the Triple Goddess, including Artemis, Demeter, and Hecate (maiden, mother, crone), as well as other goddesses associated with the moon, such as Athena and Persephone.

19. The Sun: Sun, Apollo, Helios, Castor and Pollux.

20. Judgment: The Resurrection, Judgment Day, Archangel Michael, Pisces.

21. The World: Gaea, Paradise, the four elements, *animus mundi.*

EXERCISE 2: MYTHOLOGICAL ASSOCIATIONS

Look up one of the references in the previous list that intrigues you, and find out why this mythical figure or concept might be associated with a Renaissance version of this card. Write an essay that explains how well you think this association works for you—what fits and what doesn't, and how you can use this idea in a reading. Could you use this association with a modern deck? Why or why not? ✪

EXERCISE 3: THE VIRTUES

In addition to the four virtues that were believed to be inherent in mankind (strength, temperance, justice, and prudence), there were three additional virtues—faith, hope, and charity—that were believed to come from God. This was a very important concept in Renaissance times, and the virtues appeared in other tarot-like card decks of the period. Three of the first four virtues are obvious in the tarot, while various authors have had to stretch a bit to assign prudence to a trump. Similarly, some of the additional virtues of faith, hope, and charity are easier to assign to trumps than others. Go through a deck of this period and see if you can assign the seven virtues to certain trumps, and write a short explanation of your choices. After doing this exercise, do you think either the four or the seven virtues were intentionally included in the tarot or not? ✪

Measuring Your Progress

Study Goal 1

Spend some time reviewing one or more of the references listed in the first endnote of this chapter. Once you have done this and absorbed the material in this chapter, write a series of tarot FAQs (Frequently Asked Questions) or a short essay from memory explaining the historical origin of tarot cards. Practice what you might say if a client asked you questions about it or presented you with one of the many widely held but inaccurate beliefs about this subject.

Study Goal 2

Take two tarot decks, one a modern deck and one a pre-twentieth-century deck, and place the two sets of trumps in rows for comparison. Explain how the mythological, astrological, or spiritual associations and meanings of the trumps may differ in the two decks, being as specific as you can. Give at least two examples of how the deck you are using might affect the way you would interpret an actual reading.

---

1. For further reading on the history of tarot, the following printed and on-line references are useful: R. Decker, T. Depaulis, and M. Dummett, *A Wicked Pack of Cards: The Origins of the Occult Tarot* (New York: St. Martin's Press, 1996); S. R. Kaplan, *The Encyclopedia of Tarot, Volumes I, II, and III* (Stamford, CT: U.S. Games, Inc., 1978–1990); T. T. Little, *The Hermitage: A Tarot History Site,* www.tarothermit.com; J. W. Revak, *Villa Revak: A Tarot Website,* www.villarevak.org; and *The TarotL Tarot History Information Sheet,* www.tarothermit.com/infosheet.htm.

2. See the following for further reading on the possible basis for the design of early tarot decks: Gertrude Moakley, *The Tarot Cards Painted by Bonifacio Bembo for the Visconti-Sforza Family: An Iconographic and Historical Study* (New York: The New York Public Library, 1966); Robert V. O'Neill, *Tarot Symbolism* (Lima, OH: Fairway Press, 1986); and T. T. Little, *The Hermitage: A Tarot History Site—Tarot as a Cosmograph,* www.tarothermit.com/cosmograph.htm.

3. For further reading on the mythological symbolism of early tarot decks, please see the following: Brian Williams, *A Renaissance Tarot,* deck and book set (Stamford, CT: U.S. Games, Inc., 1987); and Juliet Sharman-Burke, *Mastering the Tarot: An Advanced Personal Teaching Guide* (New York: St. Martin's Griffin, 2000).

ten

Using the Major Arcana in Readings

Study Goals

1. Gain an understanding of how to interpret the Major Arcana in readings.
2. Develop elemental and astrological associations for modern tarot trumps.

This chapter covers important things you need to know when working with trumps in a reading, including what it means to get a trump in a reading, and where they fall within the numerological and elemental cycles we have already learned. Astrological uses of the trumps are also covered for those with an interest in and knowledge of astrology.

What Does It Mean to Receive a Trump in a Reading?

Trumps are special and important cards, and they deserve a prominent place in our readings. One of the first things we should do when scanning a reading of any size is to notice whether there are any trumps, what reading positions they fall into, and what proportion of the cards received are trumps. The following are some ideas about what it means to receive one or more trumps in a reading.

Majority of Trumps

If all or most of the cards in your reading are trumps, this is usually an indication that the question itself is a very important one to the client, the situation contains spiritual or psychological overtones, or that this decision or question represents a major turning point in her life. On the other hand, if there are few or no trumps in the reading, the question is a more mundane and everyday question for this person. In large readings, half or more trumps is enough to be considered unusual, since trumps make up about one-quarter of the deck.

Control

Some older tarot books state that the trumps represent powerful influences that are not in the client's control. This is an idea that was very prevalent in the belief systems of past centuries, in which people generally felt that they were subject to the whims of the gods, nature, the church, and nobility, and only the smaller things in life were in their personal control. However, as we saw in chapter 8, a more modern view of the Major Arcana is that they are about our own spirituality and our psychological health and well-being. While it may be more difficult and time-consuming to alter our spiritual path or psychological nature than to take action in a more routine part of our lives, it is even more critical that we recognize that we are in control and are responsible for our own spiritual and mental health.

Positions

Whenever you receive trumps in a reading, look at what positions they are in, as this may tell you a lot about the situation. If the trumps are in the past, then the most difficult decisions, issues, or turning points may already be over. If they are in the present or future, this also gives valuable information. If they are in one position of a Mind-Body-Spirit or elemental reading, then that area may be the most important one to focus on. If a positive or upright card, it may be an area that the client can draw a lot of strength from, and if a negative or reversed card, it may be the biggest obstacle they have to overcome, and one that could take a long time to work through.

Occasionally, a trump may be no more significant than the other cards. This may happen when you have built an association with that trump that is not represented by any of the Minor cards. Then, if you need that particular message, the tarot will give you that card because no other card fits. Here is one example of this effect, using a Mind-Body-Spirit reading about the health of a woman in her middle 40s.

The Moon
The Gilded Tarot

In this case, she received a reversed Queen of Swords in the Mind position, a reversed Moon in the Body position, and the Nine of Swords in the Spirit position. The "health" associations she built with these cards over the years led her to read this as migraines, hormonal imbalances, and insomnia/anxiety, respectively. The hormonal imbalances may or may not be any more important than the other two, in terms of her overall health, but since there is no Minor card that she associates with hormonal cycles, she received the Moon. She read this as a physical issue because it was present in the Body position, so it may be a relatively straightforward symptom of menopause rather than a major spiritual or psychological crisis. However, because this physical change can cause mood swings and other related symptoms, it would still be worth considering these Moon-related meanings.

A trump may also be weakened by other cards around it, as in elemental dignities (see chapter 16), and Minor cards may be strengthened. Cards may also be stronger or weaker based on how the spread positions are defined (for example, an "overall influences" or "most likely outcome" position may be given the most weight). So, while trumps are often considered the most important cards in a reading, use your judgment based on other factors.

EXERCISE 1: TRUMPS IN READINGS

A client asks: "I have been offered a new job in an architectural design firm. How will this work out for me?" The spread chosen here is Intellectual-Emotional-Financial, and the cards received are as follows:

Intellectual: Hanged Man

Emotional: Four of Cups

Financial: Nine of Pentacles

Do an interpretation of this spread that gives the appropriate weight to the Major Arcana card (Hanged Man), and also uses any additional active/passive, elemental, suit, or numerological meanings you feel are useful. ✪

EXERCISE 2: INTERPRETING THE MAJOR ARCANA

Using a three- to five-card spread of your choice, design a reading for the following question: "I am in serious relationships with two different men, and I love them both in different ways. How can I make the right decision for my future?" Place special emphasis on any Major Arcana cards that appear, and use all the tools we have learned so far in interpreting this reading. ✪

Numerological and Elemental Associations

In previous chapters, we learned about the numerological cycle and elemental associations with the Minor Arcana. The next step in learning to use the trumps is to figure out how they fit into these cycles. Trumps also have numerological and elemental attributes that can be used in many ways.

The numerological associations between the first ten Major Arcana (Magician through Wheel) and the Minor cards of the same number are very strong. One way to think of this is as the Minor cards being reflections or refractions of the archetypal energy of the Major Arcana, filtered down into four different aspects of our daily lives—the expression of the divine in the mundane world. If you receive one of these ten trumps along with Minor cards of the same number, these cards strengthen that numerological energy in the reading; for example, Threes along with the Empress, or Sevens along with the Chariot. Higher-numbered trumps are less related to the material world and to the Minor cards, but may also have a weaker association with the number that they reduce to—for example, Justice (11 = 1 + 1 = 2) with the High Priestess and the Twos.

If you are using elemental or active/passive associations in order to read elemental dignities, it is helpful to know the elemental associations of the trumps. These are listed in appendix D, and are primarily derived from the astrological sign or planet associated with that trump. As with all such attributions, it is fine to change them or work out attributions of your own, according to how you view and understand each card. Note that the elemental associations of the trumps may lead them to have closer associations with the number of the suit that has the same elemental energy. For example, the Empress may be more strongly linked to the Three of Pentacles than the other Threes, and the Emperor with the Four of Wands. They will still resonate with the other Minor cards of the same number, but perhaps less strongly so.

EXERCISE 3: CONNECTIONS WITH THE MINOR ARCANA

Lay out the Major Arcana cards 1–10 (Magician through Wheel of Fortune) in a row. Place the 1–10 Minor Arcana cards of the four suits below the Major Arcana card of the same number. Look at each group of cards of the same number, and see if you can identify how the energy of the Major Arcana card works through the Minor cards of the same number. Do you see a common theme or pattern? Are there any cards that don't seem to fit? How can you expand your concept of either the Major or Minor cards so that they do fit? ✪

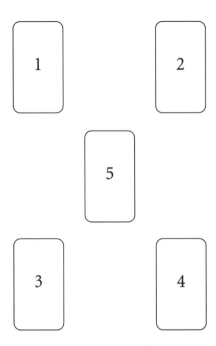

Elemental Square

EXERCISE 4: ELEMENTAL SQUARE

Do a five-card "whole person" reading for yourself, as follows:

Card 1: My emotions (Cups).

Card 2: My thoughts (Swords).

Card 3: My health (Pentacles).

Card 4: My actions (Wands).

Card 5: My spirit (trumps).

Notice how the elementally opposite positions are placed opposite one another, and the central spirit card binds and balances all the cards. Write out an interpretation of this reading, looking at the following issues:

1. How well does each card fit the natural suit for that position (strengthened or weakened)?

2. Which suits predominate in the reading, and is there a balance of energies?

3. Are there any numerical patterns or repeated numbers?

4. Which positions do the trumps fall into?

5. Are the trumps related to any of the other cards numerically or elementally?

6. How does each card relate to those that it connects with in the diagram, numerically and elementally?

Not all of these numbered elements may be important for every reading, but it is a good idea to keep these possible relationships in mind as you look over any reading you have just laid out. ✪

Astrological Associations

Using astrological (or mythological) associations along with the trumps can add a new dimension to your readings, but should generally only be attempted if you are quite familiar with astrology or the mythology represented by the trumps in your deck. If you have studied these areas, these associations will suggest additional meanings that may be relevant in some readings, and you should feel free to make these associations if they seem appropriate. For example, if a question is about the type of man that would be the best partner for the client, and you receive the Emperor, you may comment that the Emperor is often associated with the astrological sign of Aries, and then describe the personality traits of an Aries along with those of the Emperor. Or if you receive the Hermit (Virgo) as a possible approach to a problem, and you know something about how a typical Virgo would work through an issue, this may allow you to suggest that the client go on a retreat and remove outside distractions in order to hear her inner voice clearly (Hermit), and then approach the problem logically through a detailed analysis of all the factors involved (Virgo).

I often use these astrological associations in larger readings, particularly one called the Astrological spread,[1] where one card is placed in each of the twelve astrological houses. In this case, if you receive the Tower in the tenth position, this is similar to having Mars in the tenth house in an astrological chart. To an astrologer, this would bring up immediate associations and could add depth to the reading. Lastly, because I find most of the astrological associations to be fairly intuitive, I use them simply as a memory aid to remember the elemental associations of the trumps. These are just a few examples of how the astrological associations may be used, and there are many other possibilities. The main point here is that the more associations you develop, the more you can draw on them during readings to add depth and meaning to the interpretation. However, they should be built slowly through experience—it is possible to be overwhelmed at the beginning by trying to learn too many associations and not being sure when or how to use them.

EXERCISE 5: HOROSCOPE READING

Conduct an astrological/tarot reading as follows: First, have a basic astrology book available that gives the meanings of the planets and signs in the twelve houses.[2] On your birthday or that of someone you know, do a tarot reading where you place one card in each of the twelve houses. (You can also do this reading when it is not your birthday, but think of it as covering the period from your last birthday to your next birthday). If you'd like, you could also place one card in the center to show overall influences for the year. This is similar to a "solar return" chart in astrology, and shows the energies at work in various areas of your life for the coming year.

Read about the meanings of each of the twelve houses, and then interpret the tarot cards in each house as you normally would. Think of the houses with trump cards as the ones where the most significant events will take place, and the houses with Minor cards as areas of lesser importance, but still having a message. Look for any numerological or elemental patterns (remember that each of the twelve houses has its own elemental energy). When you are finished with this part of the reading, focus on the trumps again from an astrological perspective. Each one represents a sign or a planet, as shown in appendix C. In your astrology book, look up the meaning of that sign or planet in the house in which that trump appears, and see if provides you with any additional insight into your reading and the coming year. ☉

Evaluating Your Progress

Study Goal 1

Explain how you might interpret any trumps that appear in a tarot reading differently from the Minor Arcana cards you receive. If their significance would vary according to the type of reading you are doing, imagine several different topics for a tarot reading, and explain how they might be used in each.

Study Goal 2

From memory, list the Major Arcana in order and write down the elemental and astrological associations you have chosen for each card. Give one example of how you personally might use an elemental association with a trump card in a reading, and one example of how you might use an astrological association with a trump card.

---

1. For more information on the Astrological spread, see chapter 1 of my book *Designing Your Own Tarot Spreads* (Saint Paul, MN: Llewellyn Publications, 2003).

2. One good beginning astrology book is *Parkers' Astrology: The Essential Guide to Using Astrology in Your Daily Life* by Julia and Derek Parker (London, New York: DK Publishing, 2003).

part four

Reading for Yourself and Others

———— eleven ————

Working with the Question

Study Goals

1. Develop a positive, informative, and effective introduction to your readings.

2. Learn techniques for working with vague, complex, or poorly worded questions.

3. Develop personal guidelines for whether, when, and how to rephrase questions.

Before we begin a reading for another person, there are things we do to set the stage for the reading, such as introducing ourselves and our reading philosophy to the client and working with the question that is asked. Many readers are unaware of just how important this first impression is to the client. How you deal with the question and introduce yourself and the reading are critical to how receptive the client will be to your reading and whether he feels you understand his question and problem. However, it is often the case that you will be presented with a question that is difficult to work with as it is—it may be too complicated, too vague, not phrased in a way that you feel will produce helpful answers, or simply outside your ethical boundaries. This chapter will give you some tools for introducing your reading and working with the question that is asked, and the next chapter will help you develop a code of ethics and practice setting boundaries for your readings.

Developing an Effective Introduction

Our opening statements, whether verbal or written, are the first impression we make on the client, and set the tone for the entire reading. I have seen wonderful readings that were ruined by a negative comment at the beginning, and other readings in which the introduction was so informative and inspiring that it was worth the price of the whole reading. Here are some tips and general guidelines for developing verbal introductions or written opening paragraphs:

- Introduce yourself.
- Thank the client for the opportunity to do a reading for him.
- Acknowledge or repeat his question (preferably in its original form).
- If you plan to rephrase the question, explain why, and restate the question in its new form.
- Make any ethical or philosophical statements that seem appropriate, which will guide how you approach the reading in this particular case.
- Describe the deck and spread that you plan to use.
- Practice your opening statement and make sure that every part of it is positive and respectful. Any appearance of negativity in the opening paragraph will set the tone for the whole reading and put off the client. Here are some examples of phrases to avoid:
  - "I am not a psychic, fortuneteller, etc." Tell the client what you are, not what you are not.
  - "The tarot cannot do (whatever it is) . . ." Tell the client what the tarot can do. Don't assume limitations that may not really be in the tarot, but in the reader's choice of how she uses tarot.
  - "It is very important that you understand . . ." This is overly instructive.

- "You need to . . ." or "You should . . ." These phrases tend to make people feel defensive.

- Try not to point out problems with the client's question. Instead, try some of the suggestions discussed below, and use positive rather than negative statements about the best way to phrase a question. One good rule of thumb is to avoid the word "you" in this context—use the word "I" instead. This way it is portrayed as your choice of how to handle the question he has asked, and it is less likely to make him feel defensive about his question. For example, instead of saying, "James, you have asked six questions, and the tarot can only answer one question at a time," you can say, "Since we only have fifteen minutes to work with, I believe it will be helpful if we focus the reading on one or two of these questions." Then give him the choice of which question is the most important to him to have answered now.

- Avoid absolutes in your philosophical statements. Remember, no one really knows how tarot works, what it can do, or what it means. Present your beliefs as simply your beliefs rather than statements of fact. This way the client will not be as confused when the next reader he encounters has different views. You are not required to explain or defend your views on how tarot works, so keep in mind that you only need enter into such discussions if you want to.

Techniques for Working with Vague Questions

Sometimes a person may not be sure what she wants to know, and may ask a very general question like, "What does my future hold?" or "What advice do you have for me?" She may say something like, "Oh, I don't really have a specific question in mind." In some cases, she may not want to tell you her question—there may be a lot of reasons for this, and it is better not to assume that she is just trying to test or trick you. The setting may be too public for her to express her concern out loud (at a tarot fair, for example), or she may be too embarrassed to do so. There are also many readers, as well as clients, who actually prefer not to have clients state their questions because they believe this will help minimize any possible bias in the reading (a reading without a question is sometimes called a "cold" reading).

First and foremost, don't be concerned or upset by a lack of information. Your reading will be just as good as ever, even if you do not fully know the situation. Trust the tarot to give you the cards the person needs for her situation, and place yourself in the hands of the universe or your guides. If you have some tools and techniques ready to handle this ahead of time, then it will not seem difficult when the time comes. Here are some ideas for dealing with these situations:

- *Use an all-purpose, general spread.* Especially if you are reading at a tarot fair or other public event where these situations are likely to arise, have some general tarot spreads handy for answering these types of "nonquestions." For example, one that I like is a three-card Health-Wealth-Happiness spread that looks at the near future. Or you could do a spread like Work-Family-Personal Life. Another option would be to use a Situation-Challenge-Path Forward spread and simply ask a question like, "What is the most important thing that John needs to know about in the next month?" Readings of this type will be more general and vague, but don't let this worry you. Remember, it is the client's choice whether to ask a specific or a general question, and he will get an answer that is commensurate with what he asks.

- *Ask questions.* If the client doesn't know what to ask, perhaps because she's nervous or new to tarot readings, gently guide her with some questions you have prepared in advance for this kind of situation. For example, you could say, "I can do a reading about some area of your life over the next few months. Would you like it to focus on work, love, family, friends, or something else?" Sometimes providing suggestions will encourage her to narrow the focus a bit. You could also have two or three general reading options listed on a card or poster, and ask her to choose one of them.

- *Make up your own question.* In a situation like this, I will often ask a question like, "What is the most important thing that Eileen needs to know right now?" That's pretty general, but it still provides a framework for the reading, and allows the reading to be guided to areas that the client might not even have thought of asking about. This approach also works when the client tries to ask too many questions at once.

- *Do a "textbook" reading.* When the client knows the question but doesn't want to tell you, the first thing to do is to tell yourself that this is okay, and that your reading will be just as good even if you do not know the context for the reading. Simply describe each card along with the position it represents as if you were teaching someone about the card and the symbols on it (that's why I call this a textbook reading). In this case, you must simply trust that the client will be able to discern how your description relates to his situation. When you're done, you can ask whether he has any questions about specific cards, which often brings out more information, especially if he is now convinced that your reading is accurate and relevant.

- *Incorporate a "question" card into the spread.* Spreads such as the traditional Celtic Cross are very good for cold readings, because they incorporate card positions that describe the question or situation being asked about. In the case of the Celtic Cross, the first three positions describe the client, the situation, and the challenge she is facing.[1] For smaller readings, or e-mail readings, you may wish to choose one or more cards that tell you what the area is that she is asking about, and simply define these as "question" cards. Then choose an appropriate spread to answer the question and do the reading as usual. For reasons already discussed, you may not want to do this in a public reading situation where the client does not have adequate privacy.

EXERCISE 1: CHOOSING ALL-PURPOSE LAYOUTS

Imagine that you are preparing to do a tarot fair, and you will have twenty minutes to do each reading. Prepare in advance two general, all-purpose readings that you can use for people who don't have a specific question in mind. ✪

EXERCISE 2: COLD READINGS

Do a "cold" reading for someone you know well, using any reading format you are comfortable with. Ask your friend to hold his question in his mind while you prepare to conduct the reading and shuffle the cards. After the reading, discuss what his question was and how he felt your reading answered the question. This will give you confidence that this approach works, and some practice so you will be more comfortable using it. ✪

Techniques for Focusing Complicated Questions

Some clients will have the opposite problem—they will have a dozen different questions about a situation that they want answered, or several questions that are clearly unrelated. Sometimes the number of issues they want to cover would be difficult or impossible to address with the number of cards or the amount of time you have available. Here are some techniques for focusing a reading when the question is complex:

- *Generalize the question.* Think about all the questions the client is asking and whether they all really pertain to one overall situation. If the questions really address a single issue, then you may be able to generalize her question in such a way that it covers her issues; for example, "How can Jane solve her problems at work and create a more productive environment for getting things done?" or "How can John turn his life around in a more positive direction?" Don't worry too much about the exact wording of the question. The important thing is to keep in mind everything the client has told you or asked about the situation, and form a kind of mental image or picture of the situation—then ask the tarot what this person needs to do in this situation. Don't worry that the issue is too complex. Remember that the more information you have about her situation, the more specific and helpful your reading can be.

- *Eliminate dependent aspects of the question.* Sometimes a client will ask a question, and then add on a follow-up question that is dependent on the first question coming out a certain way; for example, "Will I be fired from my job, and if so, will I be happy in the next job I find?" or "Will Susan marry me, and how many kids will we have?" The second half of these questions is contingent on the first half coming true. In these cases, you can simply explain to the client that to answer the second half isn't possible until you know what will happen with the first half. Go ahead and do a reading on the first part and see how it comes up. Then if there is time and it seems appropriate, you can follow up with another reading. Usually the second half is so far in the future that it may be inappropriate for a reading, at least until the first part is settled. Let him know that he has some control over his future, and that he can affect the outcome of the first part. Once he has gotten through that part, it would then be appropriate to seek a reading on the second part.

- *Ask the client to tell you which issue is the most important.* If the client's questions are truly unrelated to one another, and you can't generalize them into an overall situation, then explain to your client that a reading generally works out best if it focuses on one main question, and ask her to choose which one is the most important to her right now. If possible, give her some resources for later, such as your business card or the addresses of some free tarot reading sites on the internet.[2] This way she will not feel as if she has no way to get her other questions answered afterward.

- *Ask the tarot to tell you which issue is the most important.* If it is not convenient to consult with the client, or if he is not sure what to answer, then let him know that you will ask the tarot what is the most important thing he needs to know right now, and then conduct the reading as usual. Choose one extra card at the beginning, and treat it just like the "question" card described above, except that you will limit your choices to the various questions he has asked about. Whichever question that card seems to relate to the most is the one that the tarot or the universe feels is the most important for him to have answered at this time. I have often found that this approach works well—clients seem satisfied that a higher power has chosen which question should be answered.

• *Define your layout using the client's questions.* Another approach is to define the positions of your layout using the client's questions—if she asks three very specific questions and you have three cards to work with, you can use one of the cards to answer each question. This only works if the number of questions is small enough to accommodate in the time you have available. There is nothing wrong with doing a spread this way; it is just like doing three mini-readings instead of one larger reading. The trade-off is she will get a more limited answer to each question rather than a detailed answer to one question. This approach works best if the questions are all related in some way, for example if they all have to do with her marriage, or work environment, or family. This helps because then sometimes the cards do build on each other, and you can see an overall pattern to the situation.

EXERCISE 3: SIMPLIFYING A QUESTION

You are assigned a reading by a free tarot reading site on the internet. The question reads as follows: "I would like to know whether I will get the job I applied for on Tuesday. Also, if I will meet someone nice soon and what they will be like. And whether my sister and I will be able to agree on whether to sell some family property." The client was only supposed to ask one question, and you only have one card to work with. Choose an extra question card to help you decide which of her questions is the most important to answer right now, and explain how the extra card helped you make this decision. Then do the one-card reading. ☉

EXERCISE 4: BREAKING UP QUESTIONS INTO PIECES

Now imagine you received the same reading request, but you have three cards to work with. Try conducting this reading using one card for each question. Do you think this worked out well or not? Would you use this approach again in the future? ☉

Rephrasing Questions

Rephrasing questions is a technique that is commonly used and taught to tarot students. It has a great deal of value as a learning tool, because it requires readers to struggle with and set their own personal reading boundaries around ethics, personal empowerment, and reading style. There are indeed times when a question cannot or should not be answered as asked, but these are relatively few and generally deal with ethics violations (we will cover those in the next chapter). The remaining situations are those where the reader feels that the question would be more effective, empowering, or appropriate if worded differently.

However, there are a number of issues involved with rephrasing that have led me to become less comfortable with it over time:

Issues with Rephrasing

1. Rephrasing a question can come across as somewhat patronizing, and clients may perceive a lack of respect or understanding of their concerns. I do not believe that clients are incapable of asking the questions they really want to ask. The fact that we, the readers, may feel there are better or more empowering questions they could ask does not diminish the client's interest in their original question. They often do not understand that we have their best interests at heart, and may feel that we are simply not hearing them.

2. It is a well-respected counseling technique to repeat back the client's questions or concerns in her own words. This lets her know that you are really hearing her. When you rephrase her question, this sends the message that her question was somehow inappropriate or inadequate, and that you know better than she does what she really should have asked. Even if you are right, this will not make her feel good and will distance her from the reading, just when you want her to be the most receptive.

3. Even after rephrasing, the answer to the original question often pops back up in the tarot reading, either in the cards themselves or in the reader's interpretation. The energy of the question is there and does not go away because we try to ask a different question. Rephrasing can be ineffective—it just may not work. Remember that your conscious mind, your subconscious, and your higher self are all involved in the tarot reading, and the overall mental construct you have of the ques-

tion may well be more important than the specific wording your conscious mind gives it. Other parts of your self may think in images or more abstract concepts, and may not "get" the rephrasing.

4. On occasions when clients have been asked, many have reported that they don't like rephrasing and feel offended by it (if you are not sure whether this is the case, I encourage you to try it). They may dismiss the reading if they don't feel their questions are being answered.

5. Unless it is handled very carefully, rephrasing can be a somewhat clumsy way of dealing with a poorly worded question, and may get the reading off to a negative start. There are other ways of dealing with a poorly worded question that are more subtle, friendly, and helpful than dismissing the client's question right off the bat and substituting one of your own, no matter how nicely you try to do it. And without a lot of practice, many readers don't do it that well.

Alternatives to Rephrasing

This alternative approach works well for me, most of the time:

- Let the client know that you have concerns about the way the question was phrased *without* substituting one of your own.
- Define the card positions and meanings carefully so that the client is empowered to make choices and take action even if he has not asked the question that way.
- Read the cards in such a way that the client gets the help and information he needs without handing him the answers.

This approach preserves the client's original question while still providing, by example, the empowerment and tools he needs. I believe this is a much more respectful approach than rephrasing the question yourself, and is equally effective.

For example, a woman asks, "Will I leave my husband?" Here is an opening paragraph that avoids rephrasing this question, even though it is clearly not one we would want to answer directly:

"Dear Susan,

Thank you for stopping by our website for a reading! Your question is, will you leave your husband? Susan, only you can answer a question as important as this one. Your future is not predetermined, and you can affect your fate through your own actions and free will. However, the tarot can assist you in looking at this situation and can give you helpful information with which to make this decision. For this question, we will use a three-card reading in which the first card represents strengths of your marriage, the second card represents issues or problems in your marriage, and the third card represents what consideration will be the most helpful to you in making a decision about whether to stay or leave your marriage."

This opening paragraph is respectful of the client, avoids rephrasing her question, and yet puts the burden of the decision squarely back in her hands while still providing valuable information to help her make her decision. An alternative spread could have looked at the likely outcomes of staying and leaving, with the same third card as a decision tool—not telling her whether to stay or leave, but just giving her information about what each choice may lead to. Notice that the issue of empowerment and choice that underlies rephrasing is handled by informing the client directly of her power of free will and through the reading itself—it is not necessary to actually change the question that is asked. The layout that the reader chooses and the way the cards are interpreted are much more important steps in giving the client a valuable reading. This also ensures that the reader will stay on track with the central issue of concern (the decision she has to make about leaving her husband), and doesn't head off in another direction by rephrasing this to a more general question, such as, "What does Susan need to know about her marriage?"

Other Alternatives to Rephrasing

It's a good idea to consider why you want to rephrase the question. If the reason is because it is a reading that is not unethical but is one you are just not comfortable with, you can always decline the reading and refer the client to another reader. For example, for a while I was not comfortable with pregnancy readings no matter how they were worded, but many readers are happy to do them, and I always knew someone I could refer those readings to. Timing readings are another category that some readers do and some don't. If you are not in a situation where you can pass along the reading, you have the right to set boundaries about the types of readings you will do. Let the client know in a respectful way that this is not a question you feel comfortable with, and why. Give him some options for rephrasing or asking different questions so that the choice is put in his hands.

If the question is one that is outside your ethical boundaries, then you can explain the ethical issues to the client and ask her to rephrase the question to fall within the scope of your personal ethics. This is much better than you doing it for her—because then it's her question again and she has learned how to ask a good and ethical question. Clients are often grateful and interested to learn that tarot readers have a code of ethics, and this gives them a sense that we are responsible professionals, not just fortunetellers and entertainers.

Suggestions for Rephrasing a Question

If you feel it is appropriate or necessary to rephrase a question, here are some suggestions:

1. Acknowledge to yourself and to the client that you, the reader, are making this choice to rephrase the question because of your personal views on how readings should be done. It is not because of limitations of the tarot or because there was anything actually wrong with the question (assuming it was ethical). I have seen rephrasings that start like this: "Because the tarot can only answer one question at a time . . ." or other openings that make it sound like the client asked the wrong question. The tarot itself does not have these limitations For example, there are many tarot spreads that handle multiple aspects of a client's life and the interactions between them. It is the reader's choice (and usually a good choice for a small reading) to focus on one question. A better phrasing might be this: "I find that my readings are clearer if I focus on one question at a time. Since you seem the most concerned about X, I have chosen this question for our reading today."

2. Make sure you know why you feel it is necessary to rephrase the question, and explain this to the client. Some readers seem to get into the habit of rephrasing every question, with little or no explanation. Clients cannot learn to ask better questions unless we explain to them what the issues are.

3. It might be best to avoid the word *rephrase*. Even though we know that is what we are doing, the word itself may offend some clients. Try something like this instead: "I would like to ask the question this way . . ." or "Based on what you have told me, I would like to focus the reading on . . ."

4. Remember that each client and each question are individual and unique, and try to keep your reworded question as close as possible to the original question. Many readers use the rather generic rewording "What does *X* need to know about *Y*?" This is an easy way out that is often much less specific than the original question, and has some semantic problems as well. What the client most needs to know about the situation may in fact be the inappropriate question he originally asked—like exactly when he will get his money, or whether his wife is cheating on him. And you, the reader, will find yourself with a reading that you are not comfortable with.

Try making the reworded question more specific. For example, a client asks: "My husband seems really distant lately. Is he having an affair? I am worried I will lose him." Many readers prefer not to do third-party readings—readings that involve someone who has not given permission for the reading—because it is thought of as an invasion of their privacy. Instead of asking the question "What do I need to know about my marriage?" which may tell you that yes, he may very well be having an affair, try this instead: "Is there any reason for me to be concerned about our marriage, and if so, what can I do to improve the situation?" This way you are sure to get a reading that is helpful and avoids straying into unethical areas.

EXERCISE 5: OPENING PARAGRAPHS

Write an opening paragraph for a three-card reading for the question "Should I quit my job and look for a new one? How will it work out if I do?" Handle this opening paragraph without rephrasing the question, and design a three-card reading that will give your client the information he needs without making his decisions for him. ❂

Evaluating Your Progress

Study Goal 1

List the elements you expect to include in your introduction to any reading, and explain why you have included them. Also list any elements you might add under special circumstances, which would not necessarily always be included (for example, special ethical considerations or rephrasing issues). Write an example opening paragraph for a written reading. Practice your opening statement in face-to-face readings until you are comfortable with how it sounds and it is easy to remember.

Study Goal 2

Imagine that you are reading at a tarot fair, and you have twenty minutes allotted for each reading. Explain how you would handle each of the following situations:

- A woman has signed up for a reading but does not seem to know what to ask and appears reluctant to state what is on her mind.

- A man arrives at your table with four or five questions that cannot possibly all be addressed in the time available (and there are other people signed up after him).

Study Goal 3

Write down a description of the circumstances under which you would rephrase a question. If you prefer not to rephrase questions, explain how you would address a poorly worded question in a different way. If there are situations in which you would rephrase a question, give an example of the original question and how you would rephrase it. Then take your example to a friend or one of your querents and discuss with them how they would respond to the approach you have taken. See if they would feel satisfied that their question had been answered (to the extent you think it is responsible or ethical to do so), and whether they feel comfortable with the approach.

---

1. For more information on the Celtic Cross spread, see chapter 9 of my book *Designing Your Own Tarot Spreads* (Saint Paul, MN: Llewellyn Publications, 2003).

2. One free reading site is the American Tarot Association's Free Reading Network, www.freetarot.us/.

————— twelve —————

Boundaries and Ethics

Study Goals

1. Explore your beliefs about tarot and how it works.

2. Establish clear-cut ethical boundaries for your readings.

3. Develop a written code of ethics.

This chapter continues the discussion of setting personal boundaries for your readings, both ethical and practical. One very valuable tool for professional readers is developing and using a code of ethics. A code of ethics sets standards of behavior for your readings, both in terms of positive statements about what you want to offer your clients in your readings, and in terms of the types of activities or behaviors you do not consider appropriate for readings. It may also include "client's bill of rights" elements—things that the client should expect from you when receiving a reading. Another issue that readers grapple with is that of predictive readings. Many clients will ask us to predict the future in one way or another, and we need to know what our own personal boundaries are in conducting this type of reading.

Predictive Readings

Because dealing with free will, deterministic questions, and predictive readings are all part of developing a good code of ethics, we will deal with this issue first. In chapter 17, we will discuss approaches to timing questions, most of which involve predictive aspects. There are many other kinds of "predictive" questions that deal primarily with questions such as what will happen, whether something will happen, who will be involved, and how something will happen. There are two main issues surrounding these types of questions:

1. Free will versus predetermined fate.
2. How the future is formed, and how accurate a prediction can be.

It is very helpful when receiving a question like this to have a clear sense of your own beliefs surrounding the future. That way you can communicate your ideas to your clients, set appropriate boundaries for your readings, and most importantly, stick to what you are comfortable with and not agree to do readings that may get you in over your head or may even be uninterpretable or inaccurate.

Clients often ask for definite and specific answers. Many readers are uncomfortable with such predictive readings, while other readers feel perfectly at home doing them. Each of us has to decide whether we want to do predictive readings, and if so, to what extent we believe predictions can be done with tarot. These issues are a matter of personal philosophy and belief, as well as overall reading style. Let's look at each of these factors separately.

Discomfort with doing predictive readings relates to the idea that we should have at least some control over our future. Some people even believe that we can affect anything about our future, that we create our own reality. This is a relatively modern idea, and is one reason that older spreads often tend to appear overly definite to readers today. In earlier times, the belief that one's destiny or fate was preordained was much more prevalent, and still prevails today in some religions and cultures. Many people felt truly powerless in comparison to the Church, nobility, powerful land owners, disease, nature, and other forces that seemed to determine the course of their lives, apparently at whim.

Today the concept of empowerment and tarot as a tool for spiritual enlightenment has gained credence. In addition, Jungian psychological concepts have made their way into tarot work, and have moved many readers in the direction of using tarot as a tool for self-awareness and personal development. These approaches have given rise to a different reading style—one in which the client is not given all the answers and the reader is not an all-knowing authority. Instead, the reader uses the tarot to help provide a deeper understanding of the situation, the client's motivations, goals, and feelings, alternatives open to the client, and possible plans of action to obtain a desired result.

However, because our clients often demand predictive readings, most readers will find themselves doing them to some extent, even if they prefer a more facilitative style. On the other hand, even tarot readers who are comfortable with predictive readings will occasionally be asked questions that go beyond the bounds of what they feel is reasonably predictable. The question then remains, to what extent can the future be predicted? This is a philosophical question that readers must ask and answer for themselves, and it depends a great deal on your concept of how the universe works and how tarot readings work. Being able to explain your views to your clients may be helpful when you are asked a question that you believe is not possible to predict with any likelihood of accuracy.

There are also limitations associated with the medium. For example, most tarot readers feel that the visual nature and the limited number of tarot cards in a deck preclude highly specific predictions involving names or places. But there is at least one deck on the market that includes letters you can use to spell out names, so there really is no general consensus on the issue.

In thinking about this question, it is helpful to remember that many people's jobs involve predicting the future: weathermen, investment brokers, sports writers, and insurance analysts, to name just a few. In the physical world, the future can be predicted to some extent based on the present situation, known trends extending into the future, and past patterns of behavior—and things may be just the same in the metaphysical world. Some similar rules may apply—for example, the sooner the event being predicted, the more likely an accurate prediction can be made. Or the more ordered and less chaotic the system, the more likely the future can be predicted. If a future event is strongly based on events that have already taken place, it can probably be predicted by tarot cards as easily as a current situation can be explored. On the other hand, if the future is highly dependent on actions or decision that have yet to be made, a prediction is less likely to be correct.

This is how I see it, anyway. Certainly, other people may have different views of the future and how it works. So to me, the question is one of reasonableness. Is it reasonably likely that the question being asked can be predicted based on what is happening today and patterns of events that are likely to occur? If a client asks me whether he will live to an old age, and he is only eighteen years old, I would say that is not a reasonable question, as it depends on too many unknown factors. If someone asks whether she is likely to get a job she interviewed for last month, and the committee has already met but not yet announced their decision, I would say that this future can be predicted with reasonable likelihood, as it is based on events that have already happened. In practice then, a decision on whether or not to do a predictive-type reading is best made on a case-by-case basis, based on your evaluation of whether the question is a reasonable extrapolation from events and forces already in motion.

EXERCISE 1: DEVELOPING A TAROT PHILOSOPHY

Think about the following questions and answer them for yourself. They will form the basis of your beliefs about predicting the future.

1. When I answer a question about the future, what am I really seeing in the reading?

2. Do we always have control over every aspect of our future? Why or why not? Give some examples.

3. How far into the future can we look and still be accurate in our predictions?

4. Does the act of looking into the future change it?

5. What is the most important thing to emphasize when doing a predictive reading for a client?

6. What would be the value of doing a reading about the future? What are some possible pitfalls or traps to be aware of? ✪

Keep in mind that your answers to these questions may change and evolve over time, as you become more experienced and as you have more time to think about them. It is okay to change your mind, and also to change your code of ethics and reading boundaries as you think through this and gain experience.

Developing a Code of Ethics

A code of ethics is required to belong to some reading organizations, such as the American Tarot Association, and also gives your clients confidence that you are an ethical person who takes tarot reading seriously. While not necessarily required at a beginning stage of your practice, it is never too early to develop a code of ethics. For one thing, it will make you feel more confident and assertive about the approach you choose to take when reading for others, and will most likely prevent you from getting into reading situations that make you feel uncomfortable later on.

The following steps will help you develop a code of ethics:

Step 1. Think about the positive affirmations you want to make. What positive behaviors or services do you want to offer your clients? If you were to visit a tarot reader, what would you expect from him or her? Try formulating these positive attributes into several clear statements.

Step 2. Read some examples of other readers' codes of ethics. You can find my code of ethics at www.tarotmoon.com/aboutme/aboutme.html, and many other professional readers also have their code of ethics posted on their websites. The American Tarot Association provides a minimum set of ethical standards for tarot readers at their site.[1]

Step 3. Think about the more difficult ethical areas that can be encountered in readings. These might include doing predictive readings, doing third-party readings (readings about someone other than the client, which may invade that person's privacy), readings that could have harmful consequences, readings in which the client is trying to force or influence someone else to do something, health or legal questions, readings about pregnancy, readings on death and dying, finding soul mates, reincarnation, etc. All of these are tough issues that a reader will face sooner or later. Formulate some statements that will help you define your boundaries with respect to these kinds of questions, and explain them to clients who may ask questions you prefer not to answer.

EXERCISE 2: SETTING BOUNDARIES

The following is a list of real questions that I have received over the years, which may help you grapple with these issues and define your boundaries. Some are perfectly reasonable questions, while others are borderline, and still others are clearly beyond the pale. In your opinion, which of the following questions can be answered as is (Group A), which are borderline and should be refocused somewhat (Group B), and which are outside the boundaries of your personal reading ethics (Group C)? For those questions that need to be refocused, write a sentence or two to the client explaining why this is necessary and how you would suggest doing so. For the purposes of this exercise, assume that you can use three cards for the reading. For those questions that are outside the boundaries of your ethics, what related questions could you suggest to the client as alternatives?

- When will I finally meet my soul mate?
- How can I get along better with my mother-in-law?
- I really need to know if my husband is having an affair!
- I have a lawsuit going on right now. Will I win, and when will I know for sure?
- I am considering a new career as a writer. I am wondering whether this has any chance of success and whether I will be happy.
- How can I make my teenage son stop getting in so much trouble?
- Am I pregnant? If so, who is the father?
- What is the name of my future husband?
- I don't know what the question is, but I really need to know the answer! (This is not a joke—I'm serious.)
- Will I be able to sell my house before June 7?
- Does Bobby love Heather, or does he love me?
- What can I do to improve my chances of getting a raise and promotion at work?
- Will I be healthy and rich when I die? ✪

And, just a reminder that ethical boundaries are a touchy and very personal area for many readers. It is not important or necessary for us all to share a code of ethics or a single approach to reading—it is only important that each reader works with these issues and remains true to her own choices.

Step 4. Now take your positive affirmations, any statements about how you intend to conduct business and treat your clients, and statements that define your personal reading boundaries, and organize them into a personal code of ethics. This can and should be revised over the years as you gain experience and your philosophy evolves, and will continue to provide a good touchstone to keep you on track and feeling comfortable with your readings. It is also immensely helpful in working positively with clients who ask inappropriate questions or ones you are not comfortable responding to. You can then direct the client to your code of ethics, explain the issues around his question, and suggest or request alternative questions—without making either of you feel defensive or uncomfortable.

Evaluating Your Progress

Study Goal 1

Write down what you would say if a client asked you how you believe tarot works and whether it can really predict the future. Keep in mind that you need only say as much as you are comfortable with about your own personal spirituality and philosophy. Now ask someone you know to ask you these questions and see whether you are able to answer them to their and your satisfaction.

Study Goal 2

List any types of readings that you would not do, which you consider outside your personal ethical boundaries. Choose two of these and explain what you would say to a client who requested a reading of this nature.

Study Goal 3

Create a written code of ethics, and describe how you will incorporate it into your tarot practice.

---

1. See www.ata-tarot.com/ethics.htm.

thirteen

Reading for Yourself

Study Goals

1. Begin reading for yourself in an everyday setting.
2. Learn techniques for overcoming difficulties in your personal readings.

Learning to read for yourself is a key part of using tarot and can be a valuable tool for personal growth. Many people do not use the tarot at all for divinatory purposes, and choose instead to study tarot as a spiritual tool, learning about the cycles of life and our personal journey through the physical, mental, and spiritual planes. Reading for yourself is also a very good way to become familiar with a new deck and learn how the symbols and visual images manifest themselves in your personal life and the world around you. If you follow this practice consistently, eventually you will build up a series of associations between the cards and everyday events, problems, and issues that will serve you well in reading for others. For example, science and technology and problems associated with it are not represented pictorially in most tarot decks or in their associated books. However, if you consistently do small daily readings, you will eventually come to associate a suit and/or certain cards with this important part of modern life.

By reading for yourself, not only will you learn what the cards represent, you will gain added perspective into your own life, since the patterns and cycles in the cards are just reflections of patterns and cycles that actually exist. When something truly terrible and earth-shattering happens in your life, you will now have a tool to say, "This is a Tower experience—and I know that this has a purpose." Not only will you have a way of understanding what that purpose is, you will know that the Star follows next, and then you can have hope for the future. It is immensely comforting to be able to see the tarot archetypes in action in your life, and be able to recognize what they mean for your future and your spiritual growth. Learning the lessons of each card will help you deal with these events in your own life. Doing personal readings and gaining practice linking the tarot to your daily life will bring the tarot alive for you in ways that reading a book never will.

17 The Star

The Star
The Shining Tribe Tarot

Some tarot books you may have read actually state that you cannot or should not read for yourself. This is an old superstition that has no basis in reality. Many readers do have trouble reading for themselves, for lots of very good reasons discussed later in this chapter. However, this creates a block in their ability to really live and learn the tarot, and it is something that is important to work on and overcome. At the beginning, it helps to start small, with one-card daily or weekly readings, which is usually easier for most people to learn than doing large personal readings. If you find that you ever have difficulty reading for yourself, check out the last section in this chapter, "Common Problems and Helpful Solutions," or the following chapter on overcoming reader's block.

Getting Started with Daily or Weekly Readings

The quickest way to learn to read for yourself is to do one-card daily or weekly readings. You could do one reading each week, a reading each day, a few daily readings whenever you feel like it during the week, or any combination that works for you. This is also a great way to learn a new tarot deck before using it in readings for others. Start small— try to avoid the temptation to use too many cards or do too many readings in a short space of time. This can result in information overload, which is not really useful in helping you work through the deeper meanings and messages of the individual cards, especially the more difficult ones.

Pick a time when things are relatively quiet and you have a moment of peace. If possible, make it a routine to do a daily or weekly reading. It doesn't take much time, because all you have to do is choose one card—you can think about what it means all day long, rather than doing a reading then and there. Take out your journal and write down the deck and the card, leaving some space to write in later. If you are going to be around the house, keep the card out in a prominent place where you can see it. If not, take a minute to fix as much of the card image in your mind as you can.

There are many different ways you can work with a daily or weekly reading, and it's a good idea to choose a particular type of question each time you do it. Also decide whether you want to use reversed cards (it might be better not to at first, unless you already have practice with this). Here are some ideas for questions you can ask:

Predictive: "What kind of a day/week will I have?" This is great for learning how the cards manifest in everyday activities.

Helpful: "What energy or approach should I take to successfully accomplish my goal today?" or "What mental attitude will help me talk to my teenage son about his late nights out without getting into a fight?" This type of question is good when you have certain things you need to get done, or if you are expecting an unpleasant or difficult event and want help or advice for getting through it.

Healing: "What healing energy will help me feel better today?" or "What can I do to cheer the kids up?" This type of question is great when you need a pick-me-up, and is especially good when people are feeling sick or down. It works great with healing decks like the Herbal Tarot, but any deck will do.

Living the Tarot: "Which card do I need to experience more thoroughly?" When you choose your card, think about how you can use the energy of that card during the day, and consciously try to act in a way that matches what you understand about that card. See if it helps you with anything you are doing.

Setting Priorities: "What is the most important thing I should be focusing on right now?" This is helpful when there are too many things going on and you need to set priorities. It is especially good as a weekly reading.

Lessons: "What can I learn from what is going on right now?" This can be either general or with regard to specific things you are dealing with.

Specific: Ask any specific question you want about the coming day or week. For example: "What do I need to know about the meeting tomorrow?" or "How can I make up with my sister after the fight we had last night?" or "What is the best way to approach my supervisor about a raise?"

As you go through the day or week, notice how aspects of the card come into play. At the end of this time, take a few minutes to think about the card and how it manifested, and write down any observations that come to mind. If you have learned something new about the card, or how it may relate to typical situations, add these meanings on the page for that card in your tarot journal. Notice especially if you get the same card over and over, or if you get a series of the same number or the same suit. This is most likely a message to you about something important going on in your life. Above all, have fun and enjoy the new insights you will gain!

Common Problems and Helpful Solutions

Reading for yourself is not only something you can do, but something that is an integral part of using tarot for your own spiritual and personal development. When you can lay a spread for yourself, and recognize how all the cards relate to you—positively and negatively—then you really know yourself; and knowing yourself is a big step toward loving yourself, making the best use of your strengths, and being able to reach your goals.

Yet, many tarot readers have difficulty reading for themselves. In this section we will look at some of the reasons why this happens, and also some solutions to these problems. Knowing why it is happening will help you figure out what to do about it.

Size of the Spread

First of all, the spread may be too large. The larger and more complex it is, the harder it can be to make sense out of things, particularly when you are first learning and when you are emotionally close to the subject. Information overload can make the other problems listed below even worse. Practice reading for yourself by starting small—pull one card for a week, and then when the week is over, spend some time thinking about how that card came into play in your life. Don't worry if you don't have any idea what the card means when you pull it—you'll know by the end of the week! If you do this continually and faithfully, eventually you will come to know which cards show up for you most often and what they are connected with in your own life.

If you see an interesting spread that you really want to try, but it is bigger than those you are accustomed to using, try simplifying it—break it down into three- to five-card sections and work with one part at a time. This may be more manageable at first than jumping in and trying to do the whole reading. Similarly, if you're having trouble reading for yourself, use a deck you really know, one that feels comfortable and familiar. Save experimenting with new decks for easier situations.

Rushing Through a Reading

A different problem is not giving ourselves the gift of a thorough and complete reading. Many experienced readers have a tendency to skim their own readings, click off the cards in succession—"Yep, I know what that means!"—and then sweep the cards up and put them away. It may seem hard to justify the time in our busy lives, but by doing this, we miss the subtle messages in the cards that are meant just for us—the special symbol that may stand out, and the patterns that we would see if we spent as much time on our own readings as we do for our clients. Some readers overcome this problem by pretending the reading is for a client, and then recording or writing it as if it were a paid reading. After all, we deserve the benefit of our own insight, don't we?

Objectivity

It is hard to be objective when reading for ourselves. This causes several problems, one of which is something like going into shock. When you lay out a spread for yourself, and see a lot of reversed, difficult, or scary cards, there's a kind of self-protective distancing that sets in, and it becomes hard to make yourself work through it—you have to fight off the desire to shuffle all those cards right back into the deck and start over! This happens, in spite of the "tough love" and words of wisdom that we are more than capable of giving to others in the same situation. This self-protective mechanism may be extreme enough that we convince ourselves that the cards make no sense or the reading is somehow confused or wrong.

We all have things that we hide from ourselves, some more so than others. One of the "problems" with reading for ourselves is that these things have a pesky way of surfacing. If you are having trouble reading for yourself, it could be because there is something your subconscious is trying to tell you that your conscious mind really doesn't want to know; like, you're really not happy in your marriage, or you feel like the last six years of graduate school were a total waste of time and you really want to quit without getting your degree. These are very scary and difficult things to face in any context, and if you are a tarot reader, they will come out in your personal readings. This can be very tough to deal with, and causes some people to avoid ever reading for themselves. One hard and fast rule I have for myself and my clients is "Never ask a question if you are not prepared for any possible answer that may come up." Don't ask a question solely in the hope of finding reassurance, because you may not get it.

Lack of Self-Confidence

A very common problem among beginning readers is a lack of self-confidence or trust in their reading abilities. Just because you are not objective when reading for yourself does *not* mean that you will lay the wrong cards, or that the cards will somehow be biased or skewed. Trust me, the cards themselves will be fine. It's our interpretation of them that can be confused. So as you're doing the reading, trust that the universe, or your guides, or your subconscious will choose the right cards even if your conscious mind has no idea what they mean. Then give yourself some time and space to interpret them. This will keep you from worrying that there is something wrong with the reading itself—knowing that the cards are right is a liberating feeling and cuts through a lot of possible confusion.

Pessimism and Fatalism

One last problem that often surfaces when reading for ourselves is pessimism and negativity. I don't know how many times I've seen good and supportive readers suddenly turn doom and gloom when it comes to their own cards. We all know that cards are neither inherently bad nor good, yet when reading for themselves, some readers take a very negative slant—they choose the worst possible interpretation for the cards that appear, and don't see the positive messages these same cards can hold for them. This is a self-perpetuating problem, because people who perceive that they always get bad cards will eventually become reluctant to do a reading at all, and become frightened and worried by the readings they do attempt. We try our best to be honest yet positive for our clients, and it is important to give ourselves the same pep talks, and avoid unnecessary negativity. We counsel our clients to take their future in their own hands, yet sometimes become fatalistic or overly deterministic about our own readings. This is not to say that we should sugarcoat our readings; just that being overly negative is also a form of untruth, and is equally harmful and unfair to ourselves.

Five of Cups
The World Spirit Tarot

The first thing to do if you are having trouble doing a reading for yourself is to think about the various problems that we just discussed, along with more typical problems, like not really making a quiet place or time to do your readings (these are listed in the next chapter). See if you recognize any of these as possible contributors to the problem, and then you will at least know where to start.

Solutions

Here are some ideas to help overcome any difficulties you may encounter when reading for yourself:

1. Start with small personal readings—one to three cards that cover a short period of time. This is both easier to process and less scary, because it's okay to have a bad week, but a bad year is a lot harder to handle.

2. If you have a large spread to interpret, or if the issue is unusually emotional, try some of the techniques listed in chapter 18 for analyzing large readings. These will help get you started on interpreting the reading objectively by giving you a standard set of questions to ask about the reading, and will help break the reading down into manageable pieces.

3. Trust that the cards you choose will be right, and don't worry if you don't figure out what they mean right away. Struggling with difficult readings is one of the best ways to learn. Write down the cards you received, and any meanings for cards that are clear. Note which cards are confusing or unclear, and commit them to memory. Then give the reading some time. It may be months before you understand what those cards were telling you, but when you finally know what it is, it will be an illuminating experience and much more powerful than having someone else tell you what they think.

4. Before you start, commit yourself to following through on the reading, regardless of the outcome. Be sure you are really mentally prepared to receive an answer to the question you are asking—no matter which way it goes. If you have a very strong stake in one particular outcome, it will be much more difficult to handle if you don't receive a reading compatible with your wish. In this case, it may be better to reword your question. Rather than asking whether it will happen, ask how you can make it happen.

5. Consider the positive and negative of every card, and realize that more than one aspect of the card may apply to your situation. Don't assume the worst, or the best, but try to take a middle ground. Imagine what you would say to a good friend or client if they received those cards, and realize that you are deserving of the very same interpretation.

6. Pay attention to each card individually—try hard not to skip over any cards, as the ones you most want to skip over may be the ones with the important message from your subconscious. Spend an equal amount of time celebrating the good cards as you do worrying about the bad. Think of reversed and difficult cards as opportunities to improve your future or change something about your life that isn't working.

7. If you think you know what a negative card represents, try a follow-up empowerment reading that focuses on what you can do to solve that problem. This can be especially helpful if there is one card that comes up over and over, as you will keep getting it until that problem is solved. The follow-up reading will give you a plan of action and a feeling of control.

Evaluating Your Progress

Study Goal 1

Do a series of frequent readings (daily or biweekly) using one to three cards consistently, for at least a month. Record the readings in your journal. Write down your initial thoughts when you first do the reading, and write down any experiences during that day or week that seem to relate to the reading. At the end of the month, evaluate whether you are more comfortable now with small everyday readings for yourself, and whether this practice has given you any new insights into the cards and how they apply in your personal life.

Study Goal 2

Choose a topic of great importance to you in your personal life, and do a larger reading about it (for example, a ten-card reading using any spread of your choice). Consciously note the areas that are easy to interpret, and those that are harder or that provoke strong emotional reactions. Review some of the techniques listed at the end of this chapter for getting over the rough spots, and try applying them to your reading. Describe whether and how they helped you with the interpretation.

fourteen

Overcoming Reader's Block

Study Goals

1. Identify the situations that can lead to reader's block.
2. Learn some techniques for solving this problem when it arises.

Most of us are probably familiar with the feeling of laying out a tarot reading, only to find that one of the cards sits there stubbornly refusing to speak or reveal its meaning. I call this situation "reader's block." Although it is most common when you are first learning the cards, it can happen even to the best and most experienced readers. This can be very confusing and frustrating, particularly when a client is sitting in front of you waiting for her reading. This chapter presents some tips for overcoming reader's block, including both logical and intuitive approaches.

Eight of Swords
The Fey Tarot

Relax and Slow Down

When doing live readings, it is hard not to be nervous, especially at first. Anxiety and nervousness contribute to reader's block by not allowing our intuitive subconscious mind to flow and bring the images and ideas we need into our conscious mind. It may help to simply take a deep breath, center yourself, and tell your client that you are going to take a moment to meditate on the cards. When I am doing large readings with my friends at the corner coffee shop, I sometimes send them off to get a latté, to give myself time to sift through all the cards and allow them to fall into place.

Create a Receptive Reading Environment

When doing readings at home, or even on the road, many readers create a special environment for tarot readings that helps them trigger a receptive state of mind. This may include setting aside a certain place to do readings, or using a particular cloth, candles, incense, music, or other environmental cues. Centering and meditation rituals can also be helpful. Positive visualization techniques can be used to imagine yourself giving the perfect reading and having your interpretation flow easily. All these techniques work best if they are used regularly, and if they are set aside especially for tarot readings. With regular use, you will come to associate these environmental cues with a receptive state of mind, which they will help trigger automatically, releasing the tensions of everyday life that can intrude and block your flow of intuition and awareness.

Try Alternative Approaches

We get used to reading cards a certain way, and forget that there are many different levels on which each card can be read. One of the main causes of reader's block is relying too much on a particular idea or keyword that you have assigned to the card, which may not fit every situation. Sometimes it helps to quickly run through all these levels again, and remind yourself of alternative meanings and approaches to reading that card. There are at least five levels on which a card can be read, one of which may provide the key you need for the reading:

Pictorial: Look carefully at the picture on the card. Forget about your normal interpretation of that card, and read it very literally. Imagine the client is in the card, preoccupied with her question. What is she thinking or doing? What is happening to her? Is there anything about the scene depicted in the card that could shed light on her question?

Symbolic: Review the colors and symbols you see; for example, red usually means passion and action, green may mean growth and fertility, water stands for the subconscious mind, twin towers are gateways, etc. How do these recognizable features interact with what is happening to the client in the card? For example, a boat traveling over water may mean a relatively safe journey across the subconscious mind. Pay attention to any details that stand out, like whether the water is calm or choppy, and what this might say about the client's state of mind.

Keywords: If you have a tarot journal in which you wrote keywords for each card, go back and look at all the different keywords you wrote. Often we write down as many as we can think of at first, and then we tend to narrow it down to a few that we use most often in our readings. If you look, you may find some you had forgotten about that are appropriate to the situation. You may also want to try looking up the cards or symbols in tarot books or on-line, to get other perspectives and ideas.

Suit: Think about the suit of the card all by itself. Ask yourself whether it is appropriate to the question, or what it might say about how the client is approaching the question. For example, if the client asks about love and receives only Pentacles in her reading, this alone gives you information you can use in the reading—she may actually be preoccupied with work or not feeling a strong emotional attachment in her relationships.

Number: Think about the number of the card, and reflect on its numerological meaning with respect to the question. What stage of the cycle does this number represent, and how does that influence the interpretation? Sometimes there is a message in the reading that has more to do with the repetition of a certain number (or suit) than with the individual cards. A group of reversed Fours, for example, might indicate an unwillingness to leave a safe and stable situation, leading to stagnation and lack of opportunities for personal growth.

Let It Rest

If you have the luxury of time, such as when you are doing an e-mail reading, lay the cards out and fix them in your mind. Run through all the cards once, noting those whose meanings seem clear right away, and those whose meanings you are unsure of. Then go do something else—housework, chores, business, whatever—even sleep on it if you want. As you are doing other things, your subconscious mind will be working on the meanings, and often they will pop into your head at random times. As you go through the day, you will find that the cards "click," one by one, and soon you will be able to sit down and write out the full reading. I often use this technique when I have a reading order and can't start on it right away. I will still take just a moment to meditate on the person's question, lay out the cards, and look at them carefully. Then I know that by the time I am free to write up the reading, I will be much further along mentally in having the interpretation finalized.

Start Somewhere Else

If you need to start your reading and are still not sure what all the cards mean, remember that it is usually not necessary to conduct a reading in a strict order. Normally, when you lay out a reading, the meanings of some of the cards will be very clear right away, while others may take longer to reveal their meanings. It often helps to begin with those you know, and allow the others more time. First, take a moment to look carefully at all the cards. This fixes them in your memory and allows your subconscious mind to begin working on those that are still unclear. Then proceed directly to the cards you are sure of, and either begin explaining them to the client, or begin writing them up (depending on what form of reading you are doing). This gives your mind time to work on the problem, and often by the time you finish the cards you started with, the others will fall into place.

Ask the Client

If the client is sitting there with you and you are really stuck, try this approach. You can tell the client, if you choose, that one of the cards is unclear to you, and because she knows her question and situation the best, she may be able to help you with what it represents. Or, simply state that you would like to hear what she sees in the card. Remind her of her question, and the specific meaning that that position in the reading corresponds to, and then ask her to look carefully at the card, imagine herself in the card, and have her describe her impressions. How does the card strike her? What does she think of when she looks at it? What is happening to her when she enters the card? What the client tells you about the card may give you a great deal of information about what this card is intended to represent in her reading. The card may mean something special to her that you would have never imagined on your own. This approach can be used more generally as an interactive technique for exploratory readings or counseling.

Use On-Line Resources

If you belong to an internet reading organization or discussion group, you can put your card and the question it pertains to on the discussion list. Don't be embarrassed—this happens to everyone, and other readers will be more than happy to help out. Usually you will get such a wide variety of possible interpretations that one or more of them will provide the key you need. If you have a teacher or mentor, you can also ask them for help. Finally, there are lots of resources on the web now where you can look up card interpretations and read through alternative ideas.

Let It Go

After all is said and done, there may still be a card that refuses to speak. It may even appear blank or unusually featureless. In some cases, this may represent an area where the client does not want you to see what is happening, or does not want to know what is happening (this can happen in readings for ourselves, too), or where the future combination of events is so unlikely that the card just does not seem to make sense. In these cases, it is okay to say: "At this time, the meaning of this card is not apparent to me. It normally means such and such, but it's not clear how that relates to your question. It is likely that its meaning will become clear over time." Then wait to see what happens. More often than not, at some point in the future you will find out what that card meant.

The main thing to remember is that there isn't only one right way to interpret the cards, so be open to new ideas that fit your reading. It is these experiences that help us learn and grow as tarot readers, and that open the door to a deeper understanding of the patterns and associations of tarot.

Evaluating Your Progress

Study Goal 1

List as many reasons as you can why you might have trouble interpreting the cards in a reading for others (or for yourself). Which of these can be overcome with time and practice, and which are likely to occur even as an experienced reader?

Study Goal 2

For each of the reasons you just listed, identify techniques to use in each situation that will help you avoid and/or overcome reader's block. These can be things you could implement over time and practice with each reading, or they can be things that you could try on the spur of the moment, depending on the situation. Give these a try, and come back after a few months to read over your list. See if you feel more confident and comfortable with the approaches you are using, or if you need more work in any areas.

— part five —

Intermediate
Reading Techniques

fifteen

Methods for Reading Reversals

Study Goals

1. Become familiar with a wide variety of different ways to read reversed cards.

2. Develop your own personal approach to using reversals in readings.

3. Learn ways to handle readings that are all or almost entirely reversed.

Reading reversals can be a challenge for beginning and experienced readers alike. However, there are many misconceptions about reversed cards that may contribute to the problem. Most tarot books you will read have assigned some fairly unpleasant meanings to reversed cards, which may seem superficial and overly negative. Many of these meanings are "left over" from when tarot cards were used in a fortunetelling sense, and it is not recommended that you use this approach if it makes you uncomfortable. Tarot students may be daunted by the idea of learning an additional seventy-eight meanings for the cards to read them in reverse, but this is really not necessary. If you have learned the primary meaning of the card, you can read it in reverse, and will learn how in this chapter.

The Hanging Man
The Gilded Tarot

Every card has positive, neutral, and negative aspects contained within it, a full spectrum of meanings centering around a core concept represented by that card. In a sense, you can think of the basic card as "neutral"—neither positive nor negative, but representing a group of ideas, lessons, or concepts (see chapter 2 for exercises in developing a range of meanings for each card). This basic energy can act helpfully or unhelpfully in any given situation. When reading without reversals, all of these aspects of the card need to be considered, and it is sometimes difficult to tell exactly how the card should be read in any specific situation.

When you add reversals to your reading tools, remember that you are also adding uprights—the positive balances the negative. Now it is possible to determine whether the forces represented by that card are acting in a positive or negative, helpful or un-helpful, obvious or hidden manner in the situation. And in the next chapter, when we add elemental dignities, we will be able to recognize even more shades and nuances to the card meanings. This helps us use the limited number of cards in a tarot deck to re-flect the myriad situations and possibilities that occur in real life.

Using reversals helps you identify whether the overall situation is positive or nega-tive, pinpoint areas of blockage or difficulty, and aid clients in devising strategies to sur-mount obstacles they are facing. Reversals can uncover hidden issues or problems that the client was unaware of or is hiding from herself. In many cases, these are the very is-sues with which a client most needs help, and may be the reason she turned to you for a reading to begin with. Using only uprights often leads to each card being labeled "good" or "bad," and requires the reader to make a value judgment about which category each card is placed in. With a full spectrum of cards that can act in a variety of different ways, a whole new world of meanings is available to the reader.

While it is not strictly necessary to use reversals, they are one of many tools that should be evaluated and learned as part of your tarot studies. Each reader can then make an informed decision after trying them out and after serious practice and reflec-tion. Elemental dignities and other approaches can be used instead of, or in addition to, reversals, and we will cover this in the next chapter. The goal of this chapter is to present you with a variety of tools relating to reversals, so that by the end you will have tried them all and can choose one or more that work for you, comfortably, consistently, and reliably.

Approaches to Reading Reversals

As with all things in tarot, there are many different ways to read reversals, and each reader develops her own individual style with practice. As long as you understand how you are using reversals in your readings, that is how your cards will fall for you. As you learn more techniques for using reversals, you may find yourself using different ap-proaches depending on the question, situation, layout, or position in the layout in which the card falls. This is entirely appropriate, and if you ever feel that a reversed card just isn't making sense, it is worth reviewing the list of possibilities to see if another ap-proach to reversals might help explain its meaning. Here are some of the approaches to reversals that you can use:

- An area in which the client is having difficulty or problems.
- Obstacles or issues that affect the question.
- Something that is not likely to happen.
- An energy, resource, or path forward that is available but temporarily blocked.
- Something that has been repressed, or needs to be released.
- A negative or unhelpful influence.
- Negative or unhelpful aspects of a personality (court cards).
- Something that is hidden, deceptive, or not what it appears to be.
- An internal influence or process, as opposed to external.
- An approach or course of action to avoid; something you are being warned against.
- The normal energy of the card, but out of balance or taken to an extreme.
- New moon energy (as opposed to waxing, waning, or full moon energy).
- Any other meaning you assign the reversed card to have.

With each of these approaches, the upright cards should be considered to have complementary meanings; for example, an area that will go well for the client, resources he can draw on, something that is likely to happen, something that is externally focused or obvious, a positive influence or helpful personality, etc. It is a good practice to decide not only what the reversed cards will mean, but what the upright cards will mean, and it may even be appropriate to communicate this to the client before the reading begins.

All of these suggested approaches are explored in this chapter and illustrated with exercises. Some approaches to reading reversals with round decks are also provided. In addition, there are times when an entire reading will come up all or nearly all reversed, and this special situation will also be discussed. Finally, there is a section on how to decide which approaches work best for you and are appropriate for any given reading.

You may notice that there are a few approaches to reading reversals that are not included on the previous list, and which I do not advocate. These are described below, along with my reasons for excluding them. However, I support each reader's right to choose which approach she would like to use, and if you prefer one of these approaches, you are welcome to use it. If you would like to try out or practice any of these methods, please feel free to use the questions suggested in the exercises that follow, and compare your results to other methods described.

Opposite of the Upright Meaning

I believe that each card has a core set of ideas and concepts that it represents, and that any way you modify the card—reversals or dignities—should be a variation on the theme of these basic meanings. Sometimes the opposite of a card is too much like another card, and I would expect the tarot to provide that other card if that is the meaning that is needed. Using the opposite of an upright meaning tends to result in cards being initially classified as positive or negative, and the opposite of that is used in the reversal.

Little White Book (LWB) Meanings

Most of the LWB meanings for reversed cards are highly superficial and should not be relied upon. Many of them use the "opposite" approach just described, or draw from highly negative fortunetelling-type meanings prevalent during the early days of tarot divination. Many are not recognizable as modern meanings, and may cause confusion as well as unnecessary negativity. It is much better to develop your own system, and use it consistently.

Diminishment or Weakening of the Upright Card

In this approach, a reversed card's effect is considered to be diminished or weakened compared to the upright card. This method may have developed because readers perceived some cards as already too negative to make worse (for example, the Tower or the Devil), and because some cards seemed too positive to ever have a negative meaning (for example, the Sun or the Ten of Cups). However, this approach relies on the idea that cards are mainly either positive or negative, while I believe that all cards have a full spectrum of meanings. A weakening or diminishment of meaning does not seem to me to have much value in a tarot reading compared to other approaches.

For each of the following methods and exercises, keep a journal in which you record how you feel about each reversal approach. Try each one, even if you think you won't like it, and keep your interpretation as close as possible to the method description as you can. When you are done, write down any thoughts you have about the approach. Did it help you answer the question? Did it make it easier to understand what to do with the reversed cards? Did it feel comfortable or uncomfortable? You may need to try some of them more than once, so feel free to use and practice these methods as you are doing your other readings for yourself, friends, or clients. These notes will help you choose one or more approaches that fit your own style of reading.

Obstacles and Problem Areas

One of the most straightforward ways to read reversals is as obstacles or problem areas for the client in the situation asked about. This is a very helpful approach because it gives the client information needed to remove obstacles and clear up problem areas. Any time you read a reversed card this way, it is useful not only to tell the client what the problem is, but what he can do about it. This turns a negative into a positive, and it is these readings that can prove to be the most life-changing and empowering. Sometimes knowing about a potential problem in advance makes all the difference in preparing for and/or avoiding it.

For example, if a client asks about her marriage, and receives a reversed Empress, she may be feeling that she is unable to develop her creative side and pursue her own interests in the marriage. Perhaps she has been too busy taking care of her kids and husband to do anything for herself, or anything to express herself. She may feel much more satisfied in this marriage if she sets aside some time for herself each week to take classes, work on a creative project, garden, or just do things for and by herself. This may require her to set boundaries and communicate her needs to her family. Another possible interpretation is that she really wants kids, but has been repressing the desire because she is afraid her husband does not want them. This is a serious issue that should not be left unresolved, and may require counseling to address.

EXERCISE 1: REVERSALS AS PROBLEM AREAS

Do a three-card reading using any spread of your choice on the question "What can you tell me about the new job I am about to start?" Select specific meanings for each of the three card positions, related to the new job (for example, the work itself, the coworkers, and opportunities for advancement). Read any reversals as possible problem areas, and give the client specific advice about how he can resolve these issues. Also, develop a specific approach to interpreting any upright cards you receive in this reading—what will these cards be telling you? ✪

EXERCISE 2: REVERSALS AS OBSTACLES

Do a three-card reading on the question "What would it take for me to get a raise at work?" Read uprights as suggested approaches that may work, and reversals as obstacles that will need to be overcome. In this reading, use a more freeform style without specifically defined positions. ✪

Reversed cards can be used in Yes/No spreads to identify the likelihood of things working out the way the client wants, and specific issues that, if addressed, will improve the chances of this happening. For any yes/no question, you can lay three or more cards. Any upright card shows areas that are likely to work out, and strengths or resources the client can draw on. Any reversed cards show problem areas or obstacles that need to be addressed if the situation is going to work out. Using this method, the number of reversed cards gives an indication of the likelihood of the event, but your client also learns why it is or is not likely to work out, and what specific obstacles need to be overcome to improve her chances. If all three cards are upright, the situation is probably clear sailing, and she has little to worry about. If some cards are reversed, the answer is "Possibly, if these specific issues can be addressed." If all cards are reversed, the chances are very slim; but it is still worth going through the specific issues, and then she can decide for herself whether she wants to do the hard work to overcome all these obstacles.

EXERCISE 3: YES/NO QUESTIONS

Do a three- or five-card reading on this question: "I just had a huge argument with my best friend. Are we going to be able to patch this up, or is this the end of our friendship?" Discuss the overall number of reversals in answering the yes/no part of the question: read the upright cards as strengths they can draw on in their friendship, and the reversals as specific problem areas they are going to have to resolve. Provide some guidance on resolving each problem area, as suggested by the card. ❂

Moving Forward in Life

People often come to us with questions about reaching a future goal or getting themselves out of a bad situation. In these readings, reversals can be helpful in pinpointing the specific things that need to be done to move forward. When clients have a future goal they are trying to reach, any reversals in the reading will show paths forward that are currently blocked and what areas they need to pay special attention to in order to get where they are going. One frequent reading request is wondering whether it is possible to start a new business, and whether it will actually work out. You can design a spread that takes into account a wide variety of different factors, and then look for any reversals as areas the client needs to pay special attention to, or wait to resolve, before starting their business. For example, if a client receives a reversed Seven of Wands in a position relating to the marketplace, it could mean he is going to have so much competition that it will be hard for this business to stay afloat. In this case, he needs to rethink the product he is offering, and make sure that it has unique features that are marketable and distinguishable from those of his competitors.

Seven of Wands, reversed
Lo Scarabeo's *Universal Tarot*

EXERCISE 4: MOVING FORWARD

Do a three-card reading on this question: "I want to go back to school and get a master's degree, but I am worried about our finances and who will take care of the kids. Is this possible right now?" Define the three cards as major issues of potential concern (you choose the issues), and then look for reversed cards to see which areas may actually be a problem and which ones will work out fine. For upright cards, identify the resource represented by that card that can help in that area. For reversed cards, offer any suggestions you can on how to overcome these obstacles. Look at the overall picture to see how feasible this idea is right now. If two or three cards are reversed, try reading the reversed cards as what has to happen before she can go back to school. This will give her hope that it can be done in the future, if not now. ✪

Another typical situation is a person who feels completely stuck in his life, but doesn't really know what the problem is, or how to solve it. Reversals are very helpful in "diagnosing" the problem and offering suggestions on how to fix it, especially when the client is hiding something from himself or avoiding the real issue. Often there is something or someone in the past that needs to be released in order to move on, and reversals will identify this. For example, if a client feels that he has trouble forming positive relationships, and receives a reversed Five of Swords, he may have experienced abuse in the past that he needs to reconcile in order to build trust, perhaps through counseling. Until he resolves and releases this old situation, he may be unconsciously trying to resolve it by choosing unsuitable and abusive partners. This approach is especially helpful for relationship and marriage "counseling"—and we do a lot of informal counseling as tarot readers.

EXERCISE 5: IDENTIFYING THE PROBLEM

Do a Mind-Body-Spirit reading on this question: "I feel so depressed and sick all the time. I just have no motivation to get out of bed in the morning. I can't figure out what is wrong with me. Can you help me?" Look for reversals to get an idea where the problem lies, then offer appropriate advice. Do a follow-up reading to get more specific details on the area(s) suggested by this reading. ✪

Negative Influences or Personalities

Generally speaking, the basic meaning of a tarot card is always the most important, and the reversal is simply a modification of that meaning. Each card has positive and negative aspects to it, although some seem more inherently positive and some more negative. Whether a card is positive or negative may depend entirely on the situation. A Two of Swords may be a very good card if it represents calming an emotional situation and finding a compromise or truce. It may be a problem if it represents a person stuck in indecision, unable to make a difficult choice. A reversal helps you identify whether a given influence represented by the card is acting for better or worse in a particular situation. This is particularly true of court cards, as every personality type represented in the tarot has both good and bad aspects to it, just as each of us has our good days and our bad days, things we have done that we are proud of, and things we did that we wish we could undo. Never fall into the trap of thinking that a particular card or personality represented by a court card is always good or always bad, or you will have difficulties with reversals. In one interpretation, a reversal simply indicates that a thing or person is having a negative influence on the situation, whether intended or not.

EXERCISE 6: POSITIVE AND NEGATIVE INFLUENCES

Do a four-card reading as follows. Ask the question "What two things or people are having the most positive influence on my life right now?" Pull two cards from the deck, and place them upright. Now ask the question "What two things or people are having the most negative influence on my life right now?" Pull two cards from the deck, and place these reversed (or imagine that they are reversed). Explain to yourself how each of these factors is affecting your life at the moment. Now imagine that you are doing this same reading for a friend, and you receive the same cards in the opposite positions. How does this change how you would interpret each card? ✪

EXERCISE 7: LOOKING FOR ANSWERS

Do a five-card reading on the following question: "I am having great difficulty dealing with my teenage daughter. I don't know whether it is me, her, or outside influences that are the biggest problem, or whether this is just normal mother/daughter teenage "stuff." What's going on, and is there anything I can do about it?" Use three cards to identify the factors having the strongest influence on the situation (good or bad), and after you have looked at the first three cards, draw two more cards to suggest possible strategies for resolving any problem areas identified in the first three cards. Pay special attention to any court cards that come up, and how they may be influencing the situation. ✪

Hidden, Deceptive, and Unrealized Factors

Reversed cards can identify hidden wishes, problems, or influences, and they can identify unresolved wishes or issues. For example, in a relationship reading, a reversed Ace of Cups could represent a relationship that is not actually real—wishful thinking, a crush on someone from afar, or an internet romance that has no chance of going anywhere. If someone asks when his Mrs. Right is going to show up, and he gets a reversed Queen of Wands, it could very well be that she is already here, but for some reason he hasn't noticed her yet. She may not look the way he expects, or he may be looking in the wrong places, or overlooking an old friend. He may not realize the type of woman that would actually make him happiest.

Reversed cards can also be helpful in providing warnings about things that appear to be something they're not. For example, if a woman asks about someone she just started dating, a reversed King of Cups could represent a man who appears romantic and loving, but actually has a hidden drinking habit, or who may form an unhealthy emotional attachment and eventually become a problem. Reversed cards definitely act as warnings from time to time, and often they warn about hidden situations or personality problems. This is most likely to occur when a person is asking about a new situation or the future consequences of a course of action, but reversed cards can also uncover things that are seriously wrong that the client has no idea about (to give one actual example, an employee embezzling funds from a small business). If all the cards in your reading are reversed, it is worthwhile to consider whether this may be a strong signal from the tarot, depending on the question, and take advantage of this opportunity to provide the client with information she can use to protect herself.

EXERCISE 8: HIDDEN FACTORS

A client is planning to meet a woman whom she has been corresponding with on the internet. She believes they have a chance at a meaningful relationship, but is trying to be cautious. She would like to know if there is anything she should know about this person that hasn't come up in their conversations on-line, or if she should go ahead with a meeting. Do a reading that is focused on whether anything in this relationship has been hidden, or whether all is as it seems. You may also add cards, if you wish to evaluate the likelihood of their in-person relationship being successful. ✪

EXERCISE 9: BREAKING THE BAD NEWS

You conduct a three-card reading on a new relationship that a client has just entered into, and receive the Queen of Wands, the Four of Pentacles, and the Devil, all reversed. Your client is a doctor, recently divorced and lonely, and the woman he is involved with is quite a bit younger than he is. Complete this interpretation, and decide what you will tell your client about this new relationship. Learning to give bad news gently and constructively is one of the most important skills you can learn in tarot reading, and is worth practicing. ✪

It is important to remember that reversed court cards, especially, may represent hidden issues or insecurities within the client's own mind or personality. Often these are things the client actually knows, but hasn't faced up to as a problem affecting her current situation. A reversed court card may actually represent both the client and the people she attracts into her life, since like energy often attracts like.

In a reading about the future, especially readings that try to look far into the future, a reversed card may simply mean something that will not happen for a long time, or something that cannot happen until something else is resolved first. In this sense, these cards are telling you that they are only potentials that are still somewhat conjectural, or energies that are not yet in play.

Extreme or Unbalanced Energies

Another way to read uprights and reversals is to view the upright card as the natural, balanced energy of that life lesson or activity, and the reversal as the same energy or activity, but unbalanced or taken to an unhealthy extreme. An example is the Ten of Pentacles, which upright might represent a healthy and financially well-off multigenerational family, and the passing down of traditions and family possessions in a loving and positive way. Reversed, this card could suggest a family obsession with inheritance and progeny, and an unwillingness to part with family lands or possessions regardless of the cost, perhaps entangling the family in feuds or lawsuits.

This approach could be used in any tarot reading, but might be especially useful in identifying the source of a problem and specific areas that need to be brought back into balance to improve a situation. Occasionally, it may be hard to interpret the reversal, as there are potentially two ways in which the natural energy of a card may become unbalanced—too much of the energy or too little. Normally, the nature of the tarot suggests that the energy of the card would become intensified and unbalanced in the same manner as the normal energy of the card—strengthened for active cards, and weakened for passive cards.

EXERCISE 10: BALANCE OF ENERGIES

Use this approach to conduct a three- to five-card reading about the current status of your life. Assign each position to an area of your life that is important to you. Read upright cards as positive, balanced energies that are active in that area of your life, and reversed cards as areas where something is out of balance or extreme, and then imagine what you could do to improve these areas. Develop affirmations to help yourself make the necessary adjustments. ✪

Unhelpful Aspects or Approaches

At the beginning of this chapter, we touched on positive, neutral, and negative facets of the cards. Here is where that really comes into play. For example, a positive statement about the Four of Pentacles might be "a person creating a responsible financial foundation for her family's future." A negative statement might be "a greedy, materialistic, or stingy person." A neutral statement could be "a person who tends to be conservative with her money." This last one could be good or bad, depending on the situation. Rather than making value judgments, it attempts simply to describe a person or an approach to a situation. I say "attempts" because sometimes one person's value judgment is another's neutral description.

Using the positive/negative approach for uprights and reversals is more like making value judgments, and we should be aware of how it might come across to a client, and also of the possibility of our own values and biases creeping into the reading. However, in some cases, making value judgments may be appropriate. For example, in exercise 8 in this chapter, you were asked to complete the reading for the doctor and the new person he was seeing. Your reading of the cards may have contained some fairly strong negative statements about the woman in question, which could also reflect on the doctor. This could easily make some readers uncomfortable. Yet, in this hypothetical situation, the doctor came to us essentially asking for a value judgment (by the universe, not by us) on this new person he was seeing. In these cases, and especially when the cards speak out strongly and tell a coherent story (good or bad), it is okay to make strong positive or negative statements, which may inevitably contain some value judgments.

An alternative approach, which may feel a lot more comfortable in some cases, is to stick to the neutral meaning of the card, and imagine that this neutral meaning is acting helpfully or unhelpfully in this specific situation. The neutral meaning may describe an aspect of our personality, or an approach to a situation we have been considering. This works best when doing a reading for ourselves or other people we know well, when we will instantly recognize a card as representing some familiar aspect of our personality. For example, I have a tendency to vigorously defend my ideas, even if strongly challenged by others. I might represent this tendency with the Seven of Wands. This tendency can be good in some situations, and bad in others. If I receive this card in a reading, I can use whether it is upright or reversed to let myself know whether this is an appropriate time for me to exercise this particular trait. One good exercise to prepare for this method of reading is to think about your own personality, and come up with as many descriptive sentences about it as you can. Try your best to make them nonjudgmental—neither positive nor negative, just descriptive. If you assign a tarot card or cards to each statement, then you will recognize another possible meaning of that card when it comes up for you in a personal reading.

Here's an example of how this approach differs from the traditional positive/negative one. A woman asks for a reading about an important decision she needs to make, and her birth date shows that she is a Libra. You're doing a one-card reading, and you pull the Justice card. If you were using the traditional upright/reversed approach, a reversed card might suggest that she is about to make the wrong decision or is not seeing the bigger picture. She's getting lost in the details and on the wrong track, or making a choice that is not fair to others and will create negative karma—or whatever you think of when you think of the dark side of the Justice card.

Using the neutral approach instead, you might say:

Intro description: "Being a Libra, you have a tendency to want to weigh all the details of both alternatives and examine the pros and cons very carefully before making a decision. You want to know the big picture and the karmic implications of your actions and decisions. You want your decisions to be logical and fair to all concerned."

If upright: "This approach is appropriate in this situation because there are facets to this decision that may only become evident after careful consideration. The details are important, and your decision may affect others, whose needs should be carefully weighed. Take your time, and don't make this decision until you feel you have examined all the issues. If it would help, make a list of the pros and cons, for both yourself and others."

If reversed: "This approach may not work well in this situation. There may be a need to make a decision quickly in order to take advantage of an opportunity that could disappear if you wait too long. Or, this may be one of those times when you have to make a decision without knowing all the things you would like to know. This could be a time when emotions and gut feelings are more important than logical weighing and balancing, and it might be time to let your conscious mind rest and try to access your intuition and feelings about this situation."

Using this method, we have said less about whether her decision is likely to be right or wrong, and more about what might be a good approach to making this decision. She goes away with some valuable guidance, and still has ultimate ownership over the decision. It's more about process than outcome. Whether this is appropriate will depend on what the person wants, what type of question it is, and what you as a reader are comfortable doing.

EXERCISE 11: VIEWING YOURSELF OBJECTIVELY

Choose a goal you would like to reach, or a problem you would like to solve. Draw three cards, and before interpreting them, develop a value-neutral statement for each one that describes you or a possible approach you might take to your question. Then use the fact that each card is upright or reversed to determine whether that aspect of your personality or possible approach is likely to be helpful or unhelpful in this situation, and why. Work hard when doing this to be nonjudgmental about yourself, recognizing that nearly every aspect of your personality has its pluses and minuses at various times. ✪

Reading Reversed Court Cards

Every one of the sixteen personality types represented by court cards has both positive and negative attributes or potentials. Depending on whether the court card in question represents an aspect of self or another person, the reversal may be read in a variety of different ways. Here are some of the most useful ones:

- A person who is having a negative influence on the situation, whether intentionally or unintentionally.
- A person whose negative personality traits have become dominant.
- A person who is thwarting your goals or actively opposing you.
- A negative or difficult aspect of the client's personality, or a character trait that, while normally positive, is contributing to a problem in the current situation.
- An undeveloped area of the client's personality.
- A hidden or subconscious influence in the client's mind.

- An area in which the client feels uncertain, afraid, or blocked.
- An impulse or desire that will lead to problems if acted upon.

EXERCISE 12: STRENGTHS AND WEAKNESSES

Using only the court cards, do a three-card reading for a thirty-six-year-old female client as follows:

Card 1: My approach to parenting.

Card 2: My approach to work.

Card 3: My approach to marriage.

Read any upright cards as strengths and any reversed cards as areas that need work and could be improved. Be sure to give specific suggestions for improvement based on the card, or draw a second card from the rest of the deck to suggest actions that could be taken in these areas. ✪

EXERCISE 13: THE SHADOW SIDE

Think about common personal and relationship problems, such as anger, violence, physical or verbal abuse, insecurity, low self-esteem, alcoholism or drug use, manipulative behavior, affairs, dishonesty, and any other character or personality problems that you have experienced in yourself or others. While it may be unpleasant to think about, realize that many of the people who seek our advice are experiencing difficult situations in their lives, in which one or more of these problems may be a factor. Imagine which court cards (probably reversed) might represent these situations in your readings. ✪

Assigning Special Meanings to Reversals

Reversed cards can actually mean anything you want them to, as long as you specifically define their meaning before you conduct the reading. This provides an added versatility that can be helpful in some situations. For example, you receive a reading request on a one-card free tarot internet reading network that asks, "Would it be better to leave before December 6 or after?" No additional context or explanation has been provided. You could assign the upright position to mean "before," and the reversed position to mean "after," and use the card itself to explain why to the client. In this case, since you are only allowed to use one card, you can use reversals to help deal with questions that ask about two different alternatives. The reversed card is not actually read as reversed, but is simply assigned to the second alternative. You can also assign uprights and reversals to the pros and cons of a situation, or any other meaning that is helpful to the reading. Reversals are just a reading tool, and you should feel free to use your imagination in working with them.

EXERCISE 14: ADVANTAGES AND DISADVANTAGES

Do a five-card reading on the question "What are the advantages and disadvantages of starting my own business in the next six months?" Interpret uprights as advantages, and reversals as disadvantages (notice that the disadvantages are not read as obstacles, but more like pros and cons). One of the benefits of using this method is that the number of advantages and disadvantages is not fixed, but is decided by the cards themselves. ✪

EXERCISE 15: EVALUATING ALTERNATIVES

A client asks whether moving to New York City or Los Angeles would be better for her acting career. Conduct a three-card reading as follows:

Card 1: Ease of getting established.

Card 2: Getting rewarding acting roles.

Card 3: Making enough money to live on.

Use upright cards to suggest that New York City would be better in that area, and reversed cards for Los Angeles. The card itself provides additional commentary on why that city would be better in that area. ✪

Reading Reversals with Round Decks

There are at least three methods for reading reversals using round cards that may be helpful with decks like *Motherpeace, Tarot of the Cloisters, Songs for the Journey Home,* or *Daughters of the Moon.* First, and simplest, you can use any of the methods described in this chapter with round cards by simply assigning them to the upright position if they are closer to upright, and to the reversed position if they are closer to reversed. This may be easiest if you are used to traditional decks and not looking for added complexity.

Shakti, the Life Dancer
from Ffiona Morgan's *Daughters of the Moon Tarot*
www.daughtersofthemoon.com

A second way of reading round cards is to use upright and reversed for cards that are clearly in that orientation, and add shades of meaning for those cards that "tilt" either to the left or right. The farther they tilt, or the closer to lying on their side they are, the stronger the modifier becomes. Here are some possible meanings for left/right tilts:

- Associated with the past/forward-looking.
- Associated with or influencing the card to the left/right.
- Feminine/masculine.
- Passive/active.
- Held-back energies/forceful or aggressive energies.

EXERCISE 16: READING TILTS IN ROUND DECKS
Choose one of the left/right approaches just listed, and do a three-card reading with a round deck on the question "How can I change my approach to be more effective at my job?" ✪

A third way of reading orientation with round cards is to assign different positions to phases of the moon. A fully upright card represents a full moon, or influences that are fully active, apparent, and realized. A reversed card represents a new moon, or influences that are only potentials or are hidden. A card tilting to the right represents influences that are waning, and a card tilted to the left represents influences that are waxing (or the opposite, however you choose). Any number of shades of these orientations can be used. For example, a card at 1:00 could indicate an influence that is just beginning to wane, while a card at 5:00 indicates one that has almost fully passed out of your life.

EXERCISE 17: PHASES OF THE MOON

Use the phases of the moon approach described in the previous paragraph with a round deck to do a three-card reading on the question "What influences do you see affecting my love life?" ❂

Completely Reversed Readings

Occasionally, we may lay out a reading and find that it is completely or nearly all reversed. These situations almost always have a larger meaning that goes beyond that of the individual reversed cards. The overall reversal gives the big picture, and the details are provided by the individual cards. In general, the tarot is usually trying to state in the most unequivocal way possible that something in the situation is either backwards or seriously wrong. Here are some possible meanings for a reversed reading—which one will apply depends on the type of question being asked, the spread being used, and the cards that appear:

- The approach being asked about is the exact opposite of the approach that should be taken.

- The tarot is trying to warn the client of something very important that may go wrong.

- The whole situation that the client is asking about is a problem, and should be avoided.

- The answer lies in the past rather than the future—time flowing backward.

- The situation contains a very strong hidden or suppressed component that must be examined.

- The question being asked is misguided, inappropriate, or unethical.
- The client or reader should examine their assumptions, questions, or reading, and try a different approach.

These meanings are really just generalizations of a variety of possible meanings for card reversals, applied on a higher level. Once you have the overall message, you can determine whether it is necessary to read each individual card as reversed. For example, if the message is that the answer lies in the past, you may want to read the individual cards as if they were upright, but possibly in the reverse order that you normally would—moving from the future back to the past. If the overall message appears to be a warning of something that may go wrong, it may be appropriate to then read each individual reversed card, to get a sense of the specific details the client needs to know. Finally, in the last two cases just listed, it might be better not to complete the reading, and instead take a day or two to think about a more appropriate approach.

Choosing Your Method of Reading Reversals

Once you have conducted all the exercises and readings in this chapter, and have experimented with all the different approaches, go back through your reading journal and decide which ones you like the best—which ones seemed to work best in your readings, and which ones helped you interpret the cards, and made sense with the questions. Choose at least one and no more than four of these methods to practice with intensively for a month or two. You can change your mind later, and you can make exceptions to the rule, but it will help in becoming comfortable with reversals to always have some basic approaches in mind as you do your readings. Too many choices can sometimes lead to overload and indecision, so start simply and add complexity or additional choices as you get comfortable with each approach.

No matter what approaches you choose, make a conscious choice of approach *before* starting each reading. This is not a hard and fast rule that you have to follow once you become very experienced with readings, but it is a good way to start. As you shuffle your cards, review in your mind what you know about the question and situation, the card positions and spread you plan to use, and the method you will use to read uprights and reversals. Then stick to the method you have chosen—don't change it after laying the cards. Sometimes it is tempting to change it if it doesn't seem to make sense, but whatever you had in mind when you shuffled and dealt is how the tarot will provide you with cards, so it is important to stay consistent with that.

Once you become "fluent" in reversals, you can relax and vary your approach to whatever seems to suit the question, reading, spread, and deck the best. I consider this step to be part of the spontaneous spread design that I do as part of a custom reading. To give you an example of how this could work, here are some reading requests and the choices that a reader could make about how to use reversals in each case:

Q: "What do I need to do to reach my goal?" The spread is designed to show the steps along the way and the things the client needs to do. The reader decides that reversed cards indicate the steps that will be most difficult for the client.

Q: "Why am I having so much trouble getting a job in the field I have trained for?" The reader decides that upright cards will indicate external factors (job market, etc.), and reversed cards will indicate internal factors (attitude, expectations, etc.).

Q: "How will my move to Los Angeles work out for me?" The reader assigns card positions to different areas of the client's life, and decides that upright cards indicate areas that are likely to work out well, and reversed cards indicate areas in which the client may encounter challenges.

Q: The client asks a yes/no question. The reader plans to draw three cards, and decides that upright cards will indicate factors in favor, and reversed cards factors against. The number of upright and reversed cards will indicate the overall likelihood of a yes answer, and the cards themselves will explain why.

Q: The client asks a timing question (see chapter 17). In addition to whatever method the reader may choose to do timing readings, the reader decides that reversed cards may indicate a delay while the particular issue represented by the card is worked out.

Q: The client asks whether she should take a job that is being offered to her. The reader decides that upright cards will indicate pros or benefits to the position, and reversed cards will indicate cons or problems with the position. The client is still left to make the ultimate choice.

Q: The client asks about a new person she has just met, and whether a relationship with this person would be a good idea. The reader assigns upright cards to strengths and positive factors in the combined relationship, and reversed cards to problem areas or hidden issues to watch out for.

These are all just examples of the myriad ways in which reversals can be used. An experienced reader may or may not be this explicit about choosing her approach to reversals before every reading, and may be able to do it more intuitively. But I find that this approach is very helpful when first learning to read reversals. When I read, I sometimes explicitly assign the upright/reversed positions, and sometimes I read it more freeform. While I think it is best to know what your card positions and reversals will mean ahead of time, it is also important to remain open to other messages the cards may bring you. Just like with the meanings of the cards themselves, doing many readings over time will teach you new ways of using reversals.

Evaluating Your Progress

Study Goal 1

Write down as many different ways of reading reversals as you can think of, without looking at your notes. Next to each one, indicate the type of situation in which this approach could be used, unless it is one that you are not likely to ever use or feel comfortable with. Mark several that you found yourself most comfortable with as you worked through this chapter, a few more that you might use on rare occasions, and those that you didn't really like.

Study Goal 2

Write a few paragraphs about the overall approach you have developed for reading reversals, or explain it to someone with whom you read. If you use more than one approach depending on the spread and/or the card, include a description of how you will decide what method you will use in each situation. Decide whether you will explain this to your clients as part of your introduction to your readings.

Study Goal 3

Imagine that you have laid out a ten-card reading, such as a Celtic Cross or other spread of your choice, on a current situation that a client is asking about, perhaps a romantic involvement with another person. Nine of the ten cards come up reversed. Describe how you would interpret this spread and what you would tell your client.

sixteen

Elemental Dignities

Study Goals

1. Develop elemental associations with all the cards in the deck.

2. Choose and remember a system of elemental interactions.

3. Learn to use these dignities or interactions in tarot readings.

4. Explore advanced methods of using dignities in association with spread positions and/or reversals.

As we discussed in previous chapters, each tarot card has an elemental association with earth, water, fire, or air. As these cards sit next to each other in a tarot spread, their elemental qualities interact to strengthen or weaken each other, as well as having other effects. This is what is known as "elemental dignities." A card is said to be "well dignified" if the other cards around it are elementally compatible with that card, and a card is said to be "poorly dignified" or "ill dignified" if the other cards around it are elementally incompatible with that card. Elemental dignities can be used instead of, or along with, reversals to provide added insights and nuances to readings.

The World
The Robin Wood Tarot

Like reversals, not everyone approaches elemental dignities the same way. The following is one way to do it, and common variations on this approach are also described. As you become experienced working with the elemental qualities of the cards, you should feel free to develop and use an approach that is intuitive and makes sense to you, whether it is one of the systems described here or one of your own design.

Developing a System of Elemental Dignities

In chapter 3, we began to get familiar with elemental interactions, starting with the table of elemental compatibilities shown again here. This table can be used as the basis for a system of elemental dignities.

Compatible	*Neutral*	*Incompatible*
Fire and air	Fire and earth	Fire and water
Earth and water	Water and air	Earth and air

In an alternative traditional system used by the Golden Dawn, there is no neutrality: elements are either compatible (called "friendly") or incompatible ("unfriendly") with each other. To use this system, place all of the Neutral interactions listed in the table into the Compatible column, with the result that the majority of interactions become Compatible. In addition to the element combinations in the table, all interactions between cards of the same element strengthen each other (fire with fire, water with water, etc.). This degree of strengthening is not always beneficial—too much of any one element can lead to an imbalance of energies.

To use any system of elemental dignities, you first need to decide which cards you want to associate with which element. Many people use the Golden Dawn associations, which are based on their astrological associations for the tarot cards. However, some decks interchange the suit associations for air and fire, and if you use an older (pre-Golden Dawn) deck, planetary or mythological associations with the trump cards may be very different, which could lead to different elemental associations. None of these is more valid than another, but one may be more appropriate to the deck you are using or to your personal philosophy and associations. Appendix D provides a table of elemental associations based on the Golden Dawn system, but feel free to substitute your own.

EXERCISE 1: ELEMENTAL ASSOCIATIONS

To get started using elemental dignities, choose which elemental associations you prefer for your cards, and which system of interactions you plan to use. Practice these choices by drawing two random cards from your deck, and deciding whether they are compatible, neutral, or incompatible toward each other. Do this until you can easily remember the elemental associations of all your cards, and the quality of the interactions between them. ☉

Assigning Meanings to Elemental Dignities

The next step in developing a system of elemental dignities is to figure out what you want the interactions to mean in your readings. There are a couple of different ways that elemental dignities can be used. To use elemental dignities, look at the cards that surround a card to see if it is weakened or strengthened by them. Traditionally, compatible elements or cards of the same element strengthen each other, neutral elements are neutral, and incompatible elements weaken each other. For example, if a Wands (fire) card is surrounded on all sides by Cups (water) cards, the energy of the Wands card will be considerably weakened (you can think of it as all that water putting out the fire). This can add another dimension to your reading, by noting which cards are in the strongest positions, or which cards are strengthened or weakened by other cards. Of course, this approach is only applicable if you are using more than one card—a difference from using reversals.

It is entirely up to you what meanings you assign to compatible (well-dignified), neutral, and incompatible (ill-dignified) interactions. Here are three possible ways of using elemental dignities (and there are probably others), including the traditional Golden Dawn approach (#2 below):

1. Positive/Negative

Compatible: A more positive interpretation of the card combination.

Neutral: A basic or neutral interpretation of the cards.

Incompatible: A more negative interpretation of the card combination.

2. Strong/Weak

Compatible: Energies of the cards are strengthened, and are more powerful and dominant in the situation.

Neutral: Energies of the cards are unaffected, and are read normally.

Incompatible: Energies of the cards are weakened, and have less influence on the situation.

Note that in the system above, trumps are often considered to be naturally stronger than Minor cards, and can be adjusted accordingly.

3. Supportive/Unsupportive

Compatible: Whatever the cards represent support each other and work together.

Neutral: Whatever the cards represent don't interact with each other.

Incompatible: Whatever the cards represent interfere with each other.

The first method is like a replacement for reversals, with the added nuance of neutral meanings. With this method, it is not recommended that you also use reversals. The other two approaches can be used on their own, or in conjunction with reversals. In the second method, a strong or powerful card may be positive or negative, depending on whether it is reversed and other factors in the spread, and the same is true of weakened cards.

For example, suppose we are using the second method for elemental dignities, and we are also reading upright cards as positive and reversed cards as negative. In this system, two ill-dignified upright cards would be read as a positive influence, weakened by the unfriendly elemental interaction; for example, good intentions not followed through on, or someone who means to be helpful but is prevented by circumstances from helping very much. Two reversed but well-dignified cards could indicate negative influences that are made all the stronger by the elemental affinity of the two reversed cards.

EXERCISE 2: TRYING OUT DIGNITIES

Lay out a three-card reading on a question of your choice. Choose one of the three methods just listed to interpret the elemental dignities of your cards. Look at the interactions between the first and second cards, and the second and third cards and decide whether they are well dignified, ill dignified, or neutral. For the first and last cards, you need only compare them to the middle card. The middle card will have two interactions that need to be taken into account. Interpret your cards, using the method you have chosen. Now, choose one of the other methods, and apply it to the same cards. How does your reading change? Which method do you prefer? ✪

Using Elemental Dignities in Readings

The next step is to decide which cards interact with which in your readings, and whether you also want them to interact with elemental energies of the card positions and/or the question. This may vary by spread—some spreads are designed with the card positions having elemental qualities, and others are not.

Working with the Card Interactions

I prefer to design spreads of any size so that cards that influence each other are adjacent in the spread. This geometric arrangement of cards assists in many aspects of reading besides elemental dignities. For example, consider a three-card spread. If your spread is Mind-Body-Spirit, and you believe that all three aspects influence each other equally, you might wish to place these cards in a triangle. If, on the other hand, your spread is Past-Present-Future, then placing the cards in a linear manner makes more sense, as the first and last cards do not influence each other as much as they influence the middle card.

Once the cards have been arranged in this manner, each card can be read separately for elemental dignities by looking at what cards are adjacent to and touching it in the spread, and adding up their influences to see how positive/negative or strong/weak that card is. In addition, you can see groupings of cards from an elemental perspective that may support or hinder each other.

_____

EXERCISE 3: ANALYZING ELEMENTAL INTERACTIONS

Conduct a reading using any spread and question that you wish—do not use reversals. Select one of the three methods listed in the previous section to use with elemental dignities in your interpretation. For each card, make a list of all its interactions with adjacent cards, and summarize it into one overall conclusion, weighting each of its neighbors equally in terms of their influence. Now use these results in interpreting your reading. First, list the neutral meaning of that card in that position, with respect to the question. Then determine how the use of elemental dignities changes the interpretation of each card, modifying it from its original meaning. ✪

Another approach derives from an older Golden Dawn tradition. In this approach, the spread consists of a large number of cards in a line, usually an odd number. The central card becomes the primary focus or resolution of the spread (alternatively, a significator may be chosen and placed in the center of the line). The cards are read from the outside in, pairing up each card with its opposite in the spread. Card pairs that are unfriendly cancel each other out and are not considered to influence the central card. Using this method, the card positions are not specifically defined, but are read more as a story line, in a freeform manner.

There is a great deal more to this approach and related spreads, including dividing the deck initially into four piles representing the four elements, looking in the piles for where the significator lies, using a counting technique in which each type of card is assigned a particular value to determine the order of the cards in that pile in the spread, along with a variety of other complex manipulations. For readers who would like to pursue this approach, I recommend Aleister Crowley's *The Book of Thoth, Appendix A,* for a complete description of the shuffling, counting, and laying of this spread, known as the Opening of the Key.

Working with Spread Positions

Certain spreads are designed to make use of elemental energies, such as the Elemental Pentacle or Elemental Square. One very effective version of this spread is to place positions representing the four elements in the four directions (N, S, E, W) and a position for spirit in the middle. Opposite elements may be placed opposite one another in this spread, or you may place them according to how you normally call the elements in ritual, or the directions you associate with the elements. The four surrounding elemental positions represent various aspects of your life, corresponding to the natural suit associations, and the central spiritual position corresponds to the trumps.

In this type of spread, the cards not only interact with each other, but they are also affected by the definition of the card position. For example, a natural card in the Water position would be any Cups card or any trump that is associated with the element of water. A card that has an unfriendly interaction with the position it is in will be poorly dignified, in addition to any effects from neighboring cards. When you have two types of elemental dignities operating in a spread like this, it can get really complicated. One way to handle this is to consider the card position as just another card interaction, and weight it equally with all the rest. Another way is to use one method for the position interaction (e.g., strengthening/weakening) and another approach for the card interactions (e.g., positive/negative).

For spreads in which the card positions are not defined in terms of suits or elements, consider the card positions to be elementally neutral.

EXERCISE 4: USING ELEMENTAL POSITIONS IN SPREADS

Use the five-card spread just described to look at influences on different areas of your life over the coming month, using only upright cards. Work through each card in turn, identifying the elemental influences from both the card position and adjacent cards. Choose a method to use for both types of influences, and then apply it to determine how the combined influences affect each card. ✪

Working with the Question

It is also possible to assign the overall reading an elemental "backdrop," based on the type of question that is being asked (for example, water for a relationship reading). This would be read as yet another elemental interaction with the cards. This approach would work well with the Opening of the Key spread described earlier in this chapter, since in this approach the significator for the linear reading is found in one of four elemental piles to begin with, and the other cards in the reading come from that pile.

Example Reading Using Elemental Dignities and Reversals

The following is an example reading using both elemental dignities and reversals.

Question: "How can I become a better tarot reader?"

Position 1: What I already do well—Temperance, reversed.

Position 2: What I need to work on—Queen of Cups.

Position 3: External resources for improving—Knight of Swords.

Position 4: Internal approaches for improving—Four of Wands.

Position 5: Overall advice—Seven of Cups.

Rather than doing a full interpretation, we will just look at the reversals and dignities. Overall, there is only one reversal in the spread, which suggests a generally positive outlook for becoming a better tarot reader, and that the resources and approaches suggested by the spread are likely to be accessible and learned without undue difficulty (energies flowing freely). The one reversal is in the position of areas in which this person is already doing well. Since this is by definition a positive spread position, the reversal might be read less negatively than usual—perhaps something the reader actually does well but thinks she does poorly, and is therefore not allowing her full potential to shine through. (This is an example of "positional dignities"—defining card positions as positive or negative, and then modifying the meaning of the card accordingly).

As an example of upright meanings for the other cards, the Knight of Swords could be read as an intelligent mentor or acquaintance who could bring a burst of new ideas or enlightenment to the reader and rapidly cut away old and unproductive ways of thinking—as opposed to his more negative and destructive character traits that would appear if he were reversed.

Now, let's look at the dignities and add them to the reading. Temperance (fire) has a Cups card next to it (water), weakening it significantly. This would suggest that even though it is a trump, it should be given no more importance than the Minor Arcana cards in the reading, and we have already seen that the reversal is somewhat weakened by the card position. These two cards are antagonistic, suggesting that what she already does well is in opposition to what she needs to learn to do better. Perhaps the fire ener-gies are more her natural strengths, and the water energies are harder for her. She may be having difficulty learning to deal with the emotional aspects of tarot reading because she relies instead on her natural strengths in other areas. This is also suggested by the last two cards in the reading. However, Temperance requires a blending of fire and water, and that is probably the most important message for her from that card—she needs to learn to use these energies in more equal proportions and blend them together.

The Queen of Cups (water) has a weakening card to the left and a neutral card to the right. That weakens it a little. The Knight of Swords has a strengthening card to the right and a neutral card to the left, and is somewhat strengthened in the reading. The Four of Wands has a strengthening card to the left and a weakening card to the right, and is neu-tral overall. Finally, the Seven of Cups is strongly weakened by the Four of Wands. The strongest card in this reading (relatively speaking) is therefore the Knight of Swords, and this is where the reader should look first in becoming a better tarot reader. This is the area where the reader is likely to get the most help. The Knight also supports the cards on either side—what she needs to improve and her own internal processes.

She should be aware of the fact that her natural abilities and intuitive approach to tarot revolve around fire energies, and it appears that this is making it harder for her to develop her emotional or nurturing side, which is needed to bring elemental balance to her tarot readings. She can use Swords (air or intellect) to help bridge these elemental opposites, and should look for a mentor or discussion partner to help stimulate new ideas and ways of doing this.

There are a couple things to notice about interpreting elemental dignities that are brought out by this reading. First, if a central card has a strengthening card on the left and a weakening card on the right, it will be neutral overall. Yet, it will be drawn to and supported by the card on the left, and will draw away from and be interfered with by the card on the right. This type of analysis can provide great insights into the interactions in the situation being asked about. Second, the overall elemental balance in the reading is important. In this reading, there is no earth energy at all, so she may not be grounding herself adequately or paying enough attention to practical matters.

Also, there is a pattern of antagonism between water and fire, held together by the central strong air card. The bridging function of elements is important in suggesting ap-proaches and solutions. As already discussed, this reading suggests that a person repre-sented by the "air of air" Knight of Swords could assist in bridging her current fire abil-ities with her needed water abilities, perhaps finding ways to blend them and turning the Temperance card upright. Whenever two incompatible elements interact in a reading, it is helpful to imagine what third element could help reconcile them and bring the warring elements into harmony by interposing itself in the middle.

EXERCISE 5: COMBINING REVERSALS AND DIGNITIES

Do your own reading using both reversals and dignities using the question and spread just discussed. Analyze the reversals and dignities that appear, as well as the other ways in which the elements interact in the reading. ✪

Evaluating Your Progress

Study Goal 1

From memory, list all the cards in your deck and the elemental qualities you have assigned to them. Include multiple associations for any cards for which you feel it is appropriate (for example, court cards or certain Major Arcana).

Study Goal 2

From memory, make a table of elemental interactions according to the system you have chosen.

Study Goal 3

Explain the system you have chosen for reading elemental dignities (do not include reversals or other complications for this goal). Conduct a reading of at least six cards to illustrate how you use this system in your interpretation. Explain how the elemental interactions modify the meaning of each card and/or the reading as a whole.

Study Goal 4

Decide whether you plan to use elemental dignities in combination with reversals or other aspects of the spread (such as card positions with inherent elemental associations). If so, describe the system you will use to combine elemental dignities with reversals or other aspects of the spread. Illustrate this approach with a reading as described for study goal 3.

seventeen

Timing Readings

Study Goals

1. Become familiar with a variety of ways to conduct timing readings.

2. Choose one or more approaches to handle "When" questions in your readings.

Timing questions are some of the most difficult that tarot readers face, and this chapter will provide you with a wide variety of tools for handling them. These tools range from qualitative and general approaches to highly specific timing methods. Many readers feel uncomfortable doing something as specific as timing readings with tarot, since it is primarily a visual and conceptual tool—in which case the narrative method described in the next section may work for you. While it is true that astrology, being a more mathematical and time-oriented system, may be more useful for working with timing issues, the tarot can also be used as long as you develop a system and stick to it. The goal of this set of exercises is to give you an opportunity to try all of these methods, and find one that works for you.

Since these are only practice readings, I encourage you to try each method, even those that you are initially uncomfortable with. You may find that your views about an approach change after trying it, and that your comfort level with timing questions may increase as you have more practice with them. If after trying these methods you still don't like them, you need never use them again—but at least you will know what methods are available, and you can return to them later if you need them.

Narrative

The first approach is the most straightforward and also very useful for readers who do not wish to use numeric or deterministic approaches to timing. This approach is great with one-card readings, and simply answers the question "When?" with a narrative answer also starting with "When." For example, if the client asks, "When will I get a raise and promotion?" the answer might be, "When you are able to develop a better relationship with your boss" or "When you improve your communication skills" or "When you move to a different department." None of these answers predicts a specific time when the event will occur, but they tell the client what he needs to do to bring about the wished-for event, or what needs to happen first. In fact, if you wish, you can think of the original question with the "When" being replaced by "What do I need to do to..." or "What needs to happen before..." depending on whether or not the things that have to happen first are under his control or depend on outside factors.

One inherent problem with "When" questions is that they contain an assumption that the event will someday happen. For example, the question "When will John ask me to marry him?" assumes that John *will* ask her to marry him—which may or may not be a safe assumption. Although clients may often ask their questions this way, don't fall into these assumptions yourself. Reword the question, or be on the lookout for cards that imply that the event may not happen at all, or is very unlikely, or is too up in the air to predict whether it will or will not occur. These questions can still be handled as originally worded, as long as the reader is aware of this issue. For example, if you are doing a three-card reading and all three cards are reversed, you could say something like: "This and this and this would need to happen in order for you to get a raise in your current job, but the chances of all these things happening are remote due to problems in each of these three areas. You either need to prepare yourself for the possibility that you may never get a raise if you stay in this job, or work very hard to overcome all these obstacles."

EXERCISE 1: NARRATIVE APPROACH

Do a one-card reading on the question "When will our family finally be able to afford a house of our own?" Use the narrative approach in answering the question. ☼

Active/Passive

Active and passive cards can also be used in timing spreads to get an idea of how quickly an issue may be resolved. This is an especially good method to use when the timing element is just part of a larger question or reading. You can do the main reading first, and then look at the cards as described in the example below to get a sense of how quickly the issue will be resolved. Active suits are Wands and Swords, and passive suits are Cups and Pentacles. Note that court cards can have elements of both: active courts are Knights and Kings, and passive courts are Queens and Pages/Princesses, modified by their suit. Trumps are assigned to active or passive depending on the element or astrological sign with which they are associated, and some may be considered to be neutral. Here is an example of how to use this method with a three-card spread:

Three active cards: Happening now or being resolved within a matter of days.

Two active cards: Time frame of weeks.

One active card: Time frame of months.

No active cards: Time frame of years.

The specific numbers on the cards can be further used to provide a numeric range, if you wish. For example, a three-card reading with the cards the Two of Pentacles, the Four of Cups, and the Three of Swords would equate to a time span of two to four months (one active card, numbers on cards ranging from Two to Four).

EXERCISE 2: ACTIVE/PASSIVE APPROACH

Do a three-card reading on this question: "We need to sell our house, but the market isn't very good right now. Is there anything we can do to improve our chances, and how long might this take?" Use any spread of your choice or design, and use the active/passive approach just described to answer the "When" part of the question (with or without the numeric range). ☼

Suits/Elements

This approach is similar to that described above, but uses the energy of the suits and associated elements to provide a time frame estimate. This approach is especially good when you have only one "timing card" in a spread. This approach uses only the Ace-10 cards of the four suits as timing cards; the courts and trumps are dealt with differently, as described below. First the suits are ordered in terms of their volatility or permanence—you can choose any order that makes sense to you, for example switching Swords and Wands if you like. I chose this order intuitively, and by looking at the movement and speed of the horses in the Knights cards.

Swords: Days.

Wands: Weeks.

Cups: Months.

Pentacles: Years.

Court cards: The time frame depends entirely on the decisions or actions of the querent or another person, which have not yet been finalized.

Trumps: Will happen once the issue presented by the trump is dealt with—no time frame specified. These cards represent major life issues that may take anywhere from days to decades to resolve.

If you want to be specific, the numbers on the cards can be used to give an indication of the number of days, weeks, months, or years. As with any of the methods discussed in this chapter, reversals should also be examined, because these can represent obstacles to resolution of the issue. The timing only provides a potential for when things could happen, if any obstacles are removed. A spread that is mostly or entirely reversed may represent a situation in which the event being asked about may never happen, or in which there are many obstacles to overcome. A card such as the Wheel of Fortune may indicate that random factors are influencing the outcome in unpredictable ways.

EXERCISE 3: SUIT APPROACH

Do a three-card reading on this question: "I've been alone for three years after a difficult divorce and am ready to meet someone new. When will I find someone, and what kind of person should I look for?" Use the following spread along with the timing approach just described to answer this question:

Knight of Swords, Wands, Cups, Pentacles
Lo Scarabeo's *Universal Tarot*

Card 1: What kind of person will make her happiest?

Card 2: What she needs to do to find this person.

Card 3: How long this might take. ✿

Seasonal

The seasonal approach is another way of using the associations between suits and seasons. To use this method, you must first decide which season you associate with each suit—this may vary from deck to deck or you may choose to use the same associations with all decks. Here are the associations I most often use for readings:

Cups: Spring (water—spring rains, new growth, creativity).

Wands: Summer (fire—fullness of life, sunny, hot).

Swords: Autumn (air—cutting back, harvesting, planning for the winter).

Pentacles: Winter (earth—dormancy, putting down roots, quiet).

Using this method, the suit gives the season, and the number on the card gives the week of the season, all the way through the courts. Each season has thirteen weeks, Ace through Queen. The Kings are traditionally considered transition cards, and indicate the cusp between seasons. In this method, only the Minors are used. The trumps represent major issues or events that cannot be easily timed, and are read narratively. Reversed cards may indicate a delay in the normal time frame, and are sometimes read as one year of delay while the issue indicated by the card is worked out. It is important to recognize that this method is only capable of predicting timing for events that are likely to take place within the coming year. Any event that may take more than one year to occur (and relationship questions usually fall in that category) should be explored using another method.

EXERCISE 4: SEASONAL APPROACH

Use the seasonal method above to answer the question "When would be the best time to ask Joanna to marry me?" Use the spread below or one of your choice:

Card 1: When would be the best time.

Card 2: Why this would be a good time.

Card 3: What he can do to have the best chance of success. ✿

Astrological

There are various approaches to timing that incorporate astrology, based on astrological associations with the cards. In some systems, the Minor cards represent specific planetary transits (for example, Mars in Libra). Each card can therefore be associated with a certain time frame when that transit will take place, of various durations depending on the planet and its transit time. Similarly, certain trumps and court cards traditionally are associated with certain signs of the zodiac. Some trumps are associated with planets, and if these planets are near other cards that indicate signs, a transit may be indicated by the combination of the planet and the sign. Or, if a card associated with a planet is reversed, it could be that a retrograde period is indicated. The Golden Dawn assigned all 360 degrees of the zodiac to the two through ten cards of the Minor Arcana. Court cards, Aces, and trumps are overlaid on these, and rule larger parts of the year. This system could also be used to determine the time of year when something is likely to happen.

Because there are so many ways to associate tarot and astrology, it is helpful to have some basic knowledge of astrology before attempting one of these methods. You may choose at that time to develop your own astrological associations with the cards, and your own system of combining them, or use one of the methods just described.

Deck-Specific

Certain deck designers have developed their own timing systems in which they assign their cards to certain days of the year (for example, *Ancestral Path*), or to certain periods of the year aligned with solstices and other natural cycles, such as the Celtic Wheel of the Year (for example, *Greenwood*). Whenever you acquire a new deck, it is worth checking to see what underlying systems, including timing or seasonal systems, the author may have attributed to the cards, as you may find this energy present in the cards even if it is not a system you are familiar with.

Evaluating Your Progress

Study Goal 1
List several different approaches that you tried for conducting timing readings, and describe your experiences with each one. Would you use different approaches with different questions or decks, and if so, why? Can you think of any approaches not described in this chapter?

Study Goal 2

Describe which approach(es) you are most likely to use for timing readings. What approach would you take to a more general question versus a more specific one? What would you tell a client who pressed you for a definite time frame?

eighteen

Interpreting Tarot Readings

Study Goals

1. Integrate everything you have learned so far to feel confident conducting small tarot readings on a routine basis.

2. Learn some systematic tools to aid in interpreting larger readings.

Small Tarot Spreads

In the preceding chapters, we covered almost everything you need to know to interpret smaller spreads. The main thing to do now is practice, practice, practice! So this list is really just a summary of the things we have learned so far, which can serve as a kind of mental checklist as you prepare for a reading session, or just as a reminder from time to time:

1. Create a positive space for your readings—a centered frame of mind, and enough space to lay out your cards and sufficient time to read them. Use whatever small rituals you may have developed to prepare the space and the energy around the reading.

Queen of Cups
Avalon Tarot

2. Make sure the question is well worded, as it will be harder to interpret a question that is not clear to you. Ensure that the question falls within your ethical boundaries, or you may find yourself with an interpretation you would prefer not to give.

3. Create a layout appropriate to the question, being as specific as possible with the card positions, given how the question is worded. Know in advance what each card position means, and how each relates to the others.

4. If you have followed the preparatory steps thus far, then you can always trust that you have received the appropriate cards for the question. Don't worry that the reading hasn't come out right or think that you have to do it over. Use the cards you are given, even if it takes many months before the meaning becomes clear. Trust the tarot.

5. When you are conducting the reading, make sure your interpretation adheres to the question that was asked and the positions you have defined for the cards, since this is what you had in mind when you laid the cards and this is what the

tarot has answered, even if something else seems to make more sense to you now. Don't shy away from difficult or negative interpretations; this is often what the client most needs to hear.

6. Unless you are just practicing, wait to use reversals or dignities until you have a clear concept of how they work and how they will be used in the interpretation. In practicing these concepts, start with smaller readings (such as reversals in one- or three-card readings), and work your way up. Simpler is better, at first.

7. When beginning the interpretation, start by looking at each card separately. Remind yourself what the card means to you, and then match up the possible meanings with the spread position you have defined for that card. Finally, relate that card and that position back to the question that was asked. You may do this either mentally or out loud—when you choose to actually start the reading is up to you. Some people talk as they go along, while others figure the whole thing out before speaking (or writing).

8. Once you have looked at each card separately, find the overall story that the cards are telling, and make the interpretation into a coherent whole.

9. Look for any patterns that appear in the reading. These could include:
   - Mostly trumps or no trumps.
   - Mostly one suit or element represented.
   - Repeating numbers (Minors and trumps) that may have numerological significance.
   - Sequences up or down within a suit or trump series.
   - Most or all cards reversed or upright.
   - Elemental dignities.

These patterns should only be used if they stand out and seem to be clearly related to the question. Don't make things more complicated than they need to be or spend too much time on "mechanical" interpretations—trust your intuition to tell you when a pattern is important. The main thing is to remember to take a moment to look for these things, but don't assume that you have to find something. For example, in a three-card reading, it is not unusual or necessarily significant to find one or two suits missing from the reading, since it is not possible for all four suits to be represented by only three cards.

10. Involve the client in the reading if it is possible to do so. As you go along, get his impressions, answer any questions, and receive feedback on the possible meanings of the cards. Adjust your interpretation as you receive new information and insights. Try to strike a balance between being too invested in your own interpretation (the "reader is always right" attitude) versus being firm about the message of the reading when the client may be engaging in wishful thinking or deluding himself about the likelihood of an outcome. This requires being both confident and open-minded. Be aware of possible sources of bias in your own interpretation, as well as in the client's view of the situation and their hopes and fears about it.

11. Once the reading has been conducted, you may draw additional cards to expand on areas that are still vague, but don't use clarification cards to replace cards that aren't clear or to answer the original question—define a new question for any clarification or expansion cards based on the areas that need to be further addressed.

12. Wrap things up with a summary of the main messages of the reading, in a few sentences.

Large Tarot Spreads

Reading larger spreads can be difficult and confusing, as sometimes it seems that there is an overwhelming amount of information. The natural tendency is to give each card less attention, but then you may lose much of the depth and insight that the reading has to offer. When interpreting a large spread, I find it helpful use some objective analysis techniques to start off (this is especially important when reading for yourself, because it provides some emotional distance). Here are some questions you can ask to guide your interpretation:

1. Trumps

How many trumps are there: lots, a typical amount, or none at all? What does this say about the significance of the question being asked in the big picture? Are there more trumps in any particular part of the reading? Which Minor cards reinforce or strengthen the energy of the trumps that appear, and which seem to work against them?

2. Suits

Which elements/suits are most strongly represented? Does this change from one part of the reading to another? Are any missing entirely? What does this say about the types of elemental energies or issues in the reading and how they are changing? Think of each suit as a different area of life, and focus on them one suit at a time to see what they are doing throughout the reading.

3. Reversals and Dignities

Where are the reversals, and how many are there? Are most of the reversals in any particular suit, time frame, or area of the reading? How do the elemental dignities look— are neighboring cards reinforcing or weakening each other? Do they support or work against the card positions they are in?

4. Court Cards

Which of these court cards feel like part of yourself and your own personality (or your client), and which ones do you think might represent other people and why? Is it possible that some of the court cards don't represent people at all?

5. Numbers

Are there any numbers that stand out or are repeated in the spread (don't forget to look at numbers of trumps)? If so, what do these numbers usually represent? A repetition of numbers may indicate the overall energy or theme of the reading.

6. Progressions

Do there seem to be any progressions in the numbers in different parts of the reading, especially within a single suit or trump? Progressions could indicate a learning process, working successfully through an issue, or regressing to an earlier stage.

7. Repeaters

Are there any cards that you or the client has received repeatedly in other readings? If so, they may be especially significant messages about important transitions or issues that need to be resolved.

8. Stories

Look only at the pictures on the cards, and think of the whole reading as a picture or storybook. Is there a story being told that you can see visually in the cards?

9. Record

After running through all the overall patterns, make a list of each card, and write down meanings for the ones that seem to make sense—and just put question marks next to those that don't. It's okay to have an incomplete reading at first, as the gaps will get filled in eventually. If you really have a block on one or two cards, see chapter 14, "Overcoming Reader's Block," for further ideas.

Once you have finished this entire analysis, you will have a pretty good handle on what's going on in your reading, and you will also know which cards you are still having trouble with. Notice that most of the questions in this analysis are not about individual cards, but about patterns in the reading. When you do larger readings, the interpretation has at least as much to do with the overall pattern as with the individual cards. At first, it may seem like a lot of work to run through each of the steps, but with time, this will become a kind of mental checklist that will run through your mind automatically as you look over a large reading.

Another technique is to take a really big reading and focus on individual aspects of it one at a time. Break it down into two- to four-card parts, and on the first day, choose one part to focus on. On the second day (or whenever you feel you understand the first part), work only with the second part, and so on. Breaking it down into manageable parts, and giving yourself lots of time, can be really helpful. Big, significant readings are really worth spending some time on, and should only be done occasionally. A very good time is at year-end, birthday, solstice or other significant festival or holiday, or at a time of major change, because of the value large readings have in processing the past and setting direction for the future.

Evaluating Your Progress

Study Goal 1

Get involved with an activity that gives you an opportunity to do frequent small readings, such as three-card readings. This could be an on-line reading group, such as the

American Tarot Association's Free Reading Network, or a tarot discussion list that swaps readings, your own website, reading in a local bookstore or community center, or signing up for a New Age fair. You can decide whether to charge for your readings—the main purpose is to give yourself some practice. Practice using the tips in this chapter and what you have learned so far until you feel confident and comfortable doing small readings on a frequent basis.

Study Goal 2

Do a large reading of eight to twelve cards on a topic of importance to you or another person, and follow the steps in the last section in analyzing it. Below is a spread you can use, or choose one of your own. Record your answers to the questions in each step. Don't be concerned if you don't find anything significant for some questions—it is usually the case that only some of these patterns appear in each reading. Once you have analyzed the overall reading, work through the individual cards, and see if the patterns you noted helped you gain an understanding of any of the cards or helped complete your understanding of the reading. Try this again using different spreads and different questions (no more than once a week at first) until you can easily run through the patterns to look for in your mind and feel comfortable with your interpretations.

The Wheel of Fortune Spread—Coping with Change

This spread is designed to make use of the unique energy and symbolism of the eight-spoked Wheel of Fortune card in the *Rider-Waite-Smith* deck, to help the querent cope successfully with changes in her life. The first four cards work with the alchemical symbols on the Wheel to provide an understanding of the changes, and help effect the transformation that needs to occur. The middle card sits at the hub of the wheel, the place that turns but does not move. This card helps us find our center and provides some stability through the change. The last four cards work with the astrological and elemental energies in the corners of the Wheel of Fortune card to provide additional information and to give the querent a plan of action for working with the changes.

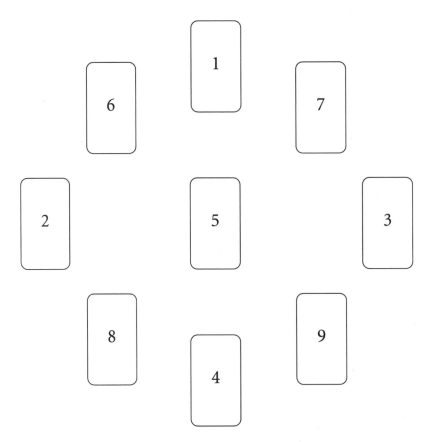

The Wheel of Fortune Spread

Card 1: Mercury/integration—The energies I need to balance and integrate at this moment.

Card 2: Sulfur/expansion—The energies that are coming into my life.

Card 3: Salt/contraction—The energies that are leaving my life.

Card 4: Water/dissolution—That which I need to let go of.

Card 5: Center—The part of myself or my life that remains unchanged.

Card 6: Aquarius/air—What I need to know about these changes.

Card 7: Scorpio/water—My emotional response to these changes.

Card 8: Taurus/earth—Where I can find stability and practical support.

Card 9: Leo/fire—What actions I can take to make the most of these changes.

Keyword Self-Test

This self-test is designed to give you an idea of which cards you know really well already, which cards you are starting to learn, and which cards need more work. Don't be discouraged if many of your cards end up in that last category right now; you will improve rapidly as you continue learning. The idea is to give you a baseline with which to judge your progress.

This self-test will help you see what you have learned from your studies and practice so far, and which cards still need special attention. If you are a very new reader, you may want to wait to take this test until after you have looked at chapters 1 through 10, and have had a chance to try out the book that comes with your deck. If you have already been working with the tarot for a while, it might be a good idea to try it now. Most readers have certain cards that give them trouble (court cards is a common group), and this will help you identify your problem areas. Then, later you can do the test again to see how much you have learned. When all your cards fall into categories A and B, you are ready to begin reading for others, although you may not feel fluent or comfortable right away—practice is the best way to learn more at that point.

Eight of Pentacles
The Gilded Tarot

Because there are 78 cards to go through, this test may take two to three hours to complete. You can do it all at once, or break it up into sections. But no peeking in between!

Step 1. Put away your journal and all your notes and books, and shuffle your deck thoroughly. Use the cards only in their upright positions. Have a blank piece of paper handy, or use your computer. Also have a timer, or some other way of noting the time.

Step 2. Turn over the cards, one by one. For each card, allow yourself two minutes, and write down or say out loud a variety of keywords, phrases, or concepts for that card. If possible, include some positive, neutral, and negative ideas for each card.

Step 3. Review the keywords or phrases you wrote down or spoke out loud. Place each card into one of three piles, as follows:

   A: You were able to come up with at least three keywords or phrases for the card within two minutes, which are not all negative or all positive, but show how the card may function in a variety of different situations. These are the cards you know quite well and can use fluently.

B: You were able to come up with one or two keywords or phrases, *or* your keywords were all positive or all negative. You know these cards well enough to begin using them, but may want to work on them more until you are comfortable with them in a wider variety of situations.

C: You were not able to think of any keywords or phrases, or for whatever reason you are not satisfied with the ones you have learned so far. These are the cards you should focus on the most as you work through the rest of the book. Don't be surprised if entire categories of cards end up here at first, like all the Aces or all the court cards—this is not unusual at all.

Numerology and the Tarot

This appendix provides some ideas on the numbers as they relate to the tarot, to the Minor cards in particular. These should be considered personal thoughts rather than hard and fast rules. Each reader, through her own tarot practice, will build up her own personal meanings for the numbers based on how they manifest in her readings. The thoughts shared here may serve as a starting point for your own study of the numbers.

Aces

Aces seem to me to require consciousness. In other words, especially in the context of a reading, they are not just raw powers, unfertilized seeds, or hidden gifts, although they may be these things as well. The Aces represent the point of conception and conceptualization. Their number is one, which represents consciousness of self—"I am"—and is related to the conscious mind of the Magician. They represent the point at which an idea, thought, feeling, gift, or energy first becomes known in our lives. It is not yet acted upon, manifested, or maybe even thought about, but it identifies itself and its potential.

Here are some examples from life that I associate with Aces:

Cups

A rush of unexpected emotion that wakes you up to something you're subconsciously feeling, the moment you realize who your life partner may be, a gift of something beautiful or aesthetic that brings peace or calm, a spiritual vision, a creative inspiration, the moment of conception (for a woman).

Wands

The moment of conception (for a man), the moment you realize what direction you want your career to take, the flash of inspiration that eventually gives rise to a creative work of art or writing, a moment of personal revelation about yourself and your life, the moment when you realize that you need to a take a life-altering course of action.

Swords

The first idea or emergent concept that gives rise to a line of philosophical inquiry or research, a flash of insight into how to solve a problem, any "first thought" that leads you in a new direction, the moment when the pieces of the puzzle suddenly click together.

Pentacles

Conceptualization in the mind's eye of a thing or creation—a visualization of a new garden, woodworking project, craft, or anything you create with your own hands. The moment when you realize you can build or create something tangible, such as your own business, or writing a novel. The day you decide you want to own a home or have a family. A sudden gift of funds that changes your life—a grant, scholarship, inheritance—or even the idea to seek such funds and what you want to do with them. The moment when you first realize you want to change something about your body, health, or physical surroundings.

What these all have in common is consciousness of an emergent idea—a seed, yes, but visible, germinated, and ready to put down roots (the Twos) and then flower (the Threes). Almost by definition, the minute you turn over an Ace in a tarot reading, the client will become conscious (if they are not already) of the potential of that energy to manifest in his life. This is the moment when some elemental power in the universe manifests itself in a particular form in your life and says, "I am" or perhaps "I can be if you will it so."

Twos

In the Twos, we find the next step in manifestation of this new idea. The Twos are associated with the High Priestess, and represent a reflective, thoughtful, feminine energy stage. Here we take our new idea and we ponder it, plan for it, start the preparations, and begin weighing the possibilities. A choice between two alternatives is a key aspect of the Twos—to keep what we have or try for something new—to evaluate our new idea, and decide whether to actually do it. Here we must look at our new idea, lover, emotion, etc., and make a choice about committing to it, or setting it aside and waiting for the next possibility to arise. In the Twos, there is interaction with others—the self versus the not-self—and decisions to be made that have long-term implications.

Here are some real-life examples of the Twos:

Cups

Our rush of feeling for someone else has turned into a real relationship. This is the stage where we get to know each other closely, and decide whether or not to commit to this relationship over the long term. We learn each other's good points and bad points, compatibilities and incompatibilities, but as yet have not made any decisions. In the meantime, we begin to think about what a future with this person might be like, even if we have not yet spoken of it.

Wands

We are considering starting a new life. We have something stable already built, but are considering leaving it and heading out into a new direction, to become a new person. We are weighing the risks against the potential expansion of our horizons, but have not yet left the security of our homes. This could be an adolescent considering moving out of his parent's home, a person deciding whether or not to leave his marriage, or a businesswoman considering moving to a new country to take a new job. At this time, all the considerations are weighed, and any planning or preparation is done that is needed.

Swords

The first time we take our new idea and tell it to someone else. We perceive their reaction (good or bad). We try to decide if it really is a good idea and should be acted upon, or just a wild imagining. We do some research to see whether others have already had this idea, and what they thought about it, and whether it is something we can realistically do. We hold actual activity in abeyance until we have thought our idea through some more, and then decide whether to pursue it.

Pentacles

Here we are faced with a physical or material decision that has emotional undertones. We are keeping our options open by juggling more things than we can really handle over the long term. Meanwhile, we struggle with the internal process of deciding which of these things to keep and which to let go. A new opportunity (Ace) has entered our life, but to take advantage of it, other things must be dropped. An example might be working long hours to build a consulting business while still holding a full-time job, knowing that eventually either the consulting business will take off and you can quit your job, or it will fail and you will go back to your first job without the extra hours of work. Here we try to determine if this new financial or material opportunity is really viable and worthy of our full attention and investment.

Threes

The Threes can be associated with the Empress, and are the productive and fertile union of the pure male principle (embodied in the Magician) and the pure female principle (embodied in the High Priestess), and are considered balanced and harmonious for this reason (all the multiples of three are). The Threes therefore represent the traditional as-sociations of fertility and abundance, but also the first earthly manifestation of the new gift or potential that came with the Aces, which has been pondered, planned for, evalu-ated, and decided upon in the Twos.

Even at this point, the journey is by no means finished. In fact, it is just getting started—but the first actual steps toward making it a reality have been taken. Another aspect of the Threes is the intervention or involvement of three people. The Twos deal with duality, which often involves another person, but the Threes take this one step fur-ther—leading to even greater productivity or greater difficulty, joy or pain.

Here are some card associations corresponding to these aspects of the Threes:

Cups

Friends or family celebrate a commitment to a relationship, such as a betrothal—this is the stage where the relationship has been publicly announced and celebrated, but the mar-riage has not yet taken place. A pregnancy or adoption. The first harvest of the season, cel-ebrating, and sharing these fruits with others.

Wands

After long planning, a person starts a new business and gets his first contract. A person makes a decision to change her lifestyle and begins to take the actions required to achieve this change. A person takes his first independent steps out into the world and goes exploring. A new job offer is accepted that reflects a change of career. The expan-sion of a business to include employees or a new partner.

Swords

The moment that a new direction of thought is manifested; for example, a person writes the first chapter of a new book. A grant is received and a scientific research program begun. A person presents his ideas at a conference, and gets public or professional feed-back and criticism. The intervention of a third party into a previously stable relation-ship, resulting in jealousy or heartbreak.

Pentacles

The first actual use of a newly learned skill to make something. A project moves from blueprints to construction. A family moves into their new home after deciding to move across the country and start a new life. A financial investment pays off with dividends. Working in teams to accomplish something practical.

All of these situations lead to growth, sometimes painful, sometimes joyful.

Fours

Fours are identified with consolidation, security, stability, building foundations for the future, resting, and regenerating. Just as the Threes are expansive and creative, the Fours represent consolidation, contraction, and conservation of energy. They are the natural counterbalancing force to the Threes, and a restful stop before continuing on to the unstable energy of the Fives.

We can liken the first four numbers to the seasons of the year. Aces are springtime—the germination of the seed, the first shoots of the plants, the thawing and beginning of a new cycle. The Twos are summer—putting down roots, and sending up stems and leaves—the potential of the plant beginning to be realized. The Threes are autumn—the fruiting, ripening, and harvest of the plant, and celebration of the harvest. And the Fours are winter—resting, conserving energy, established plants putting down deeper roots during dormancy, preparing for the next cycle.

Here are some real-life examples of Fours:

Cups

Here we begin to see that all is not love and perfection in our relationships with others. We have gotten past the breathless excitement, romance, and passion of our early relationships, and reality and familiarity are setting in. This is a test of our ability to see things as they really are, to establish a deeper relationship with someone that is not based on transient pleasures. Or, we may discover that there is nothing really solid there, and we are bored. This could be likened to a midlife or midmarriage crisis. If a couple gets through this stage together, then their marriage nearly always comes out the better or stronger for it. Or, they may do something they bitterly regret later (Five of Cups).

Wands

In this card there is celebration, but also a formalization of a business or romantic relationship into a partnership that lays the foundations for the future. Here we are making a final commitment, and agreeing to live by certain promises, rules, or ethical standards freely given to one another that will set some limits on future activities, but also provide a solid and stable foundation for growth together with our chosen partner.

Swords

Restful contemplation after a painful experience that has expanded our understanding of ourselves, others, or the world. Time is needed to heal our mental wounds and to integrate what we have learned in a positive manner. During this time, we try to fit what we have experienced into a mental framework, and make sense of it. This could be a solitary vacation or retreat to try to sort out your direction in life; rehabilitation after surgery, a mental illness, or drug addiction; or simply taking some time off after the completion of a particularly demanding or difficult project at work.

Pentacles

This card represents consolidation of our finances or material possessions. In a positive light, after the expansion and risk taking of the Threes, we pull back a bit and make sure that we are providing for our future. We may focus on building our assets carefully, rather than investing in dot.coms. We establish bank accounts for our kids' future college expenses and for retirement. We protect our investments through insurance and careful money management, and put a hold on any risky activities. We pay attention to our diet and exercise, trying to hold on to our youth and good health.

Fives

Fives are an interesting dichotomy in tarot—in traditional decks they are painful, negative cards, and yet in some more modern and feminist decks they are cards of spirituality, magick, and womanhood. The same duality can be seen in their associated trump, the Hierophant. On one hand, he represents in some decks and to some readers all that is wrong with organized religion: corruption, hypocrisy, greed, and intolerance. On the other hand, he represents the link between the divine and the mundane, the Word of Spirit brought to earth. Some decks assign the Hierophant to the element of earth, in his association with Taurus. To other minds, he is best represented by spirit rather than one of the four earthly elements.

In traditional numerology, Fives represent instability and change. After the highly stable (and some might say rigid) Fours, a fair amount of destabilizing energy is needed to push oneself out of this stable or stagnant situation to allow further growth. One characteristic of the Fives is that the change is generally not voluntary or expected; therefore, it can be frightening, and there may be a real or perceived lack of control over the situation and one's reactions to it. Hence the traditional associations of the Fives in tarot with the most negative situations in life. The movement from the Fives to the more harmonious Sixes can also be brought about through a personal or spiritual transformation, or through the grace of God/dess—and this is where the other side of the Fives can be seen, even in the traditional decks.

The number five is also associated with women, and with magick. These associations may have been frightening to some originally, and added to the negative associations with the Fives (as in the fifth sephira of the qabala). However, some newer decks, such as *Wheel of Change,* have begun to celebrate these as positive associations. The symbol of the upward-pointing pentagram is one that often appears, as well as four elements or directions integrated into central white energy in a ritual circle.

I have developed a Tree of Life that encompasses the scientific aspects of creation, as well as spirituality, and some of the ideas that are forming relate to the trumps numbered 0–5—they can be likened to the natural creation of the earth, as follows:

0. The Fool: Spirit, nothingness, the origin of the universe.

1. The Magician: Air, coalescing of swirling gases and elements into matter and molecules.

2. The High Priestess: Water, the formation of the earth's oceans and atmospheres, the creation of the necessary conditions for life.

3. The Empress: Earth, the abundance of plant and animal life that arose next.

4. The Emperor: Fire, the spark of consciousness and self-awareness that arises in humans, organization of humans into civilization, the arts of agriculture, trade, law, and government.

5. The Hierophant: Spirit, the reaching out of human civilization for something greater than itself, a return to our connection with the origin, but filtered through our perception of the material world.

Notice that the trumps 0–5 comprise the four elements, bracketed on either side by spirit.

Here are some real-life examples of the Fives:

Cups

Loss of a relationship, coping with the death or illness of a family member or friend, grieving and making peace with losses, emotional instability (positive or negative), self-doubt, fluctuating self-esteem, creative change.

Wands

Intense competition at work or in the marketplace, a clash of wills while the argument is still going on and no one is sure who will come out on top, internal conflict caused by uncertainty about one's identity or a challenge to deeply held ideals, instability that threatens a marriage or business partnership, a scattering of energies due to a lack of focus.

Swords

Being confronted with new ideas that feel threatening to the established order of things, rampant idealism overriding calm reason, facing a harsh reality, mental instability resulting in cruelty or victimization, verbal battles or contests, a period of revolutionary change.

Pentacles

Financial instability, loss or sudden change of job or living situation, being physically out of balance or ill, facing a period of hardship, rejection or isolation, physical violence or accidents, stress.

Sixes

After the instability and stress of the Fives, the Sixes bring a welcome feeling of success after having overcome difficulties and obstacles. After sorrows and travails, joys taste even sweeter, especially since we have worked hard to reach this point. Now we enter a time of relative stability, but unlike the rigid stability of the Fours, this is a stability in which there is flow and interaction. I think of the Sixes as being in harmony with the world around us, letting energy flow through, into, and out of us. Here we understand the rewards of giving and are open to the blessings as they return to us in equal measure.

We are no longer rigidly afraid of change, nor so unstable that we are out of control, but somewhere in the middle, and the light shines on us in this happy state.

This centered existence is the pivot around which our soul turns, and having once experienced this, we can climb to even greater achievements. The Fives and the Sevens both have their challenges, but the difference is that the Fives are often thrust on us when we are not prepared and are not willing to let go of the Fours. Sevens, on the other hand, are challenges we choose freely that will lead us to greater maturity and mastery in the end. Without our successful and centered time in the Sixes, we would not be ready to take up the challenge of the Sevens. Indeed, the Sixes are so wonderful that there may be many times when we wish to just stop at this point in the cycle and not move on. We cannot really do this, but we can stop and rest for a while, and use this time to recharge, energize, and enjoy life.

Here are some real-life examples of the Sixes:

Cups

Being in harmony with a friend, sibling, or lover, finding or creating a safe and relaxing place, enjoying simple everyday pleasures like gardening or walking, feeling protected, spending quality time with your children, being on vacation, feeling at peace, simplifying your life.

Wands

Getting that job you always wanted and finding that it's a perfect match for your abilities, getting a promotion, receiving recognition for something you deserve and can feel good about, winning through skill or ability, achieving a goal, being a good role model.

Swords

Overcoming fears and looking ahead, seeing the light at the end of the tunnel, moving steadily toward a destination of your choice, having your plans and ideas in order and the means to carry them out, making good progress after a period of intense difficulty, enjoying the journey.

Pentacles

Feeling relaxed about your money, believing and experiencing that the universe will provide for you, feeling the pleasure of sharing your wealth with others, enjoying your possessions without being overly attached to them, being in good health.

Sevens

One concept of the Sevens centers around the idea of challenges, chosen by and for ourselves as part of our path toward personal mastery (the Eights). After the harmonious existence of the Sixes, if we are completely satisfied there, we might never choose to move above that level. Indeed, for many people who achieve success in life, however they choose to define it, they may try to stay happily in the Sixes and never think of looking beyond their good fortune and where their hard work has brought them. Others feel an urge, a tug to go beyond anything they have achieved so far and meet a personal challenge. In life from the Aces through the Sixes, we have been learning to live successfully in the world, and reach a harmonious balance with it. From this point on, any further we go is a more personal journey. In the Sevens, we choose our next challenge to focus on.

The concept of personal choice here is critical. In the Fives, we are faced with difficulties and challenges that were not of our own choosing, and which we are forced to deal with in order to reach the Sixes. We are often unprepared for the Fives, clinging to the stability of the Fours and refusing to look ahead. In the Sixes, we are prepared and we can see. We have reached a point of maturity and capability that allows us to look ahead without fear to new horizons and challenges. If we think of the primary Seven card in the Major Arcana, we can clearly see this concept. Here the driver of the Chariot carries with him all the forces he learned to balance in the Sixes: positive/negative, the four elements, the twelve astrological signs, etc. He starts out with the tools he needs for success, and he chooses to leave his familiar city and go forth on a journey of self-adventure (one can think of the great heroes of Greek mythology and their quests). This is what the Sevens are about for me. If he succeeds, he will reach new levels of self-knowledge and mastery in the Eights (Strength) and Nines (Hermit).

Here are some real-life examples of the Sevens:

Cups

A challenge of values, emotions, dreams, or desires. Reaching a point in your life where you feel you can set your own goals, and trying to work out what those should be. Questioning the values you were raised with, and deciding for yourself what you believe in. Beginning to understand what drives your response to other people and your relationships, and learning how to choose positive life partners. Working through a childhood issue that has been blocking your progress in life. Giving up unproductive fantasies or dreams, and replacing them with dreams and hopes that are realistic and achievable.

Wands

A challenge of personal identity or beliefs. Coming out of the closet. Deciding to live according to a personal philosophy that runs against the mainstream. Defending a doctoral thesis. Taking on a career that does not pay well, but is important to your belief structure. Working for change when outnumbered by the system. Quietly explaining to your Catholic family that you are a pagan and you plan to read tarot cards for a living.

Swords

A challenge of ingenuity or ethics. Taking a calculated risk with a possible significant gain or loss. Coming up with a creative and unorthodox solution to a difficult problem. Taking a stand on ethical issues in the company or institution that you work for. Knowing when to walk away, even if it means taking a loss, and calmly and maturely making the best of what remains. Learning to make do with less in order to reach a longer-term goal.

Pentacles

A challenge of long-term planning and practicality. Setting long-term goals for your life, and working steadily to achieve them. Learning to value incremental progress over instant gratification. Learning to have patience with yourself and others. Saving money for retirement, a college fund, or other important purchases. Buying a home, and remodeling it little by little. Planting a garden that will take twenty years to reach maturity, and taking enjoyment in each small change. Making a five-year plan to get an important promotion at work.

Eights

The tarot is grouped numerologically into three groups of three, plus the Ten, which is a transitional number. Each group culminates with a multiple of three—3, 6, 9. The Eight is midway through the third group, starting with the Sevens and culminating with the Nines.

The Eights represent the mastery and accomplishments for which we are aiming in the Sevens. Once we have defended our ideas, made mature choices about our values and relationships, evaluated our ethical boundaries and willingness to take risks, and established a long-term plan (all Sevens), we begin to see these steps create results. In the Eights, we have reached a position of strength and maturity. Eights are a doubling of the Fours, almost like building another story on top of a firm foundation—very stable and solid (hopefully not too much like a Tower!). At this point, we do not only live in the world, we begin to shape our environment and our reality to resemble our personal vision. The Eights can be associated with the Strength card in the Major Arcana. After passing the tests, breaking free, and moving forward on sheer will alone (Chariot), we come to exist with a deep personal strength that arises from setting and meeting our own challenges, facing our fears and darker side, and mastering ourselves.

In the Eights, we are not resting on our laurels or enjoying the fruits of our accomplishments (that would be the Nines), but we are still actively engaged in the exciting project that we began in the Sevens. Right now our world revolves around what we are doing, and we are reaching new heights and depths. We may be acknowledged as an expert or master by the outside world, or it may be entirely internal, but in the Eights, we know who we are and what we are doing.

Here are some examples of the Eights:

Cups

A person, having decided what he truly values in the Sevens, begins to actually live his values, and takes steps to change his life. Many things may have to be left behind and few taken along, even friends and family on occasion, but the journey into self under the Moon of the subconscious is paramount. This is the person who walks the walk and talks the talk, and leaves behind hypocrisy or half-formed, equivocal values systems. Perhaps he gives up his automobile and heats his home solely on renewable energy sources. Perhaps she leaves behind a husband she no longer loves or shares values with, and looks for new companions in life. Perhaps after many long years of soul-searching, a person changes his religion to one he truly believes in. After the change, this person lives much more comfortably in the world, without the constant pressure of a lifestyle that doesn't match his beliefs.

Wands

Here we have successfully promoted our idea or concept, and it is all coming together for us. The resources are flying in to do what we need to do, communication is building, and activity is bustling to make happen what we believe in and have envisioned. Any minute now, these ideas will come down to earth and be materialized into something substantial. Imagine a businessman putting together a deal that will create a new company or launch a new product, or perhaps an architect who sees her revolutionary design for a bridge or building rise into the skyline. An artist gathers musicians from all over the world, and launches a successful album that crosses over into new markets. A woman joins the Peace Corps, and finds a way to bring together resources that provide water to an impoverished village.

Swords

This is probably the hardest card to fit into the Eight concept, based on the picture alone. If the Sevens present an ethical or risk-based challenge to our ideas or attitudes, in the Eights we are struggling to throw off the last bit of doubt, hesitation, or obstacles. All of these are in our minds, and here at least all Eight Swords are within easy reach—not falling out of our hands, as they were in the Sevens. The mastery in this card is in realizing that we can—it is mastery over our minds and self-doubts. We do have the mental tools to accomplish our objectives; they are gathered all around and are even relatively well organized. We just need to believe in ourselves enough to see it. The minute we do this, we will be able to use our minds as we wish to, make the connections we have been searching for, solve problems, and generate new ideas. The Eight of Swords, once the obstacles have been passed, represents the man who never learned to read but goes back to school, and not only learns but gets a college degree, the author who now has several books published and can feel secure that she really has a career in writing, or a person who overcomes abuse or trauma and goes on to live a successful and happy life.

Pentacles

A person reaches a deep level of mastery in a particular talent or area. In this card, I see the master craftsman, the woodworker, the musician. A talent honed by long practice, a deep love of the tools and materials with which he works, and a level of earned ability that goes beyond what he has been taught by others. Whether a bricklayer, a tailor, or a surgeon, this person is rock-solid in her ability and sense of self-worth, and her identity strongly resonates with her hands or work. She may teach, but more often serves as a quiet role model for others who learn by doing and apprenticing.

Nines

After setting a new challenge for ourselves in the Sevens, and rising to meet it with maturity and skill in the Eights, the Nines represent completion of this three-card triad, as well as the entire 1–9 numerological cycle (tens don't count in numerology—they are considered ones). As such, the Nines are associated with culmination, completion, finalization, wrapping up, winding down, enjoying the fruits of our labors, and reflection on our accomplishments. Being 3 x 3, the third cycle of three, they also represent the abundance and contentment that results from successfully reaching the end of a complete cycle. Alternatively, the cycle may have been a negative one, if things haven't worked out as we planned. Always, these cards represent an abundance and the final culmination of whatever we have reaped or created during the cycle—good or bad, loving or angry, joyful or sad.

Here are some ideas on how these concepts relate to the Nines:

Cups

Enjoyment of pleasures after a long day's work, taking a well-deserved vacation or retirement, basking in the enjoyment of having completed all tasks and having no more responsibilities at the moment, a sense of contentment and fulfillment from finishing a creative project, celebration of an accomplishment, a return to childlike enjoyment of life in old age.

Wands

Protection of accumulated resources, defending one's position at the top but being a little past one's prime, receiving recognition for lifelong career achievements, having a well-developed sense of self-identity and ego, being president of a company or having nowhere higher to go in one's chosen field.

Swords

Completion of an important thought process, publication of a major work, conscious realization of an issue that had been hidden or buried in the subconscious, the point at which a final decision is made and action must be taken, overwhelming thoughts that effect a transformation in the psyche, the culmination of a long and gradual shift in attitudes or beliefs.

Pentacles

Retirement, enjoyment of one's hard-earned possessions, living in the surroundings one has chosen for oneself, being a self-made person, a mature and beautiful garden but with no room to plant new things, the completion of a major project, financial reward for one's efforts.

Tens

Tens are the transitional number, the end of one cycle and the beginning of the next. Numerologically, tens are not stand-alone numbers, but reduce to 1 ($1 + 0 = 1$). In association with the Trumps, ten corresponds to the Wheel of Fortune, which is also all about cycles, endings, and new beginnings. However, the number ten can be looked at in many other ways. Associated with Capricorn, it could be considered a number of great responsibility and solidity—like $4 + 4 + 2$—a two-storied tower with a peaked roof (now our Tower is complete—ready to be struck down and rebuilt). Associated with Malkuth on the Tree of Life, it is the number of manifestation, the only number that corresponds to the material world in which we experience our lifetimes—in this association, it is thought of as $3 + 3 + 3 + 1$—the one sphere in the realm of Earth. Ten is a magickal number, produced by the addition of the first four numbers, $1 + 2 + 3 + 4$, important in Pythagorean and alchemical philosophy.

   With all this, what does the number ten really mean? We can see in it elements of solidity and stability, as well as transition and change. These apparent contradictions are key to the Tens—in the Wheel of Fortune, we have the stable hub and the unchanging elements, as well as a continuous cycle of change around the rim. In the material world, we also have a central core that remains as we cycle through many lifetimes or cycles within a lifetime. The material world we build remains, even as we ourselves are transitory through it. The Tens are about how we experience these transitions, what we take with us as well as what we leave behind, what we have built and what we allow to dissolve into the sands of time. It is interesting that the passive suits depict more positive transitions, while the active suits show more difficult transitions—this may have to do with issues of control and resistance to the turning of the Wheel.

Here are some examples of the Tens:

Cups

This is the card of happy endings, yet in real life we don't live happily ever after, unchanging. A moment of supreme happiness, when all that we have wished for is manifested. We cannot remain here long, because emotions and the water element are fluid and ever changing. In order to keep this relationship alive, we must look for new sources of inspiration and emotion. This card may also represent the completion of an artistic endeavor—the moment when we frame the canvas and put it on the wall unchanging, only to be gazed at from now on. We ourselves must move on to the next project, or risk stagnation and living in suspension.

Wands

Wands are integrally associated with our self, our ego, our ideas, and our career. Because we initiate Wands cycles, it is that much harder to let go of them when the time comes—so we carry them around as a burden, unable to see that it is time to release them and go on to the next idea. Giving them up is bittersweet, both a welcome release and a regret. This may represent the moment when a CEO passes the company he built on to his successor and goes into retirement, or when a woman realizes she can no longer personally run every aspect of the department she has built from scratch, or when a father realizes that he cannot and should not try to solve all his children's problems or direct them in how to live their lives now that they are adults. A person's ego and self-identity may be quite wrapped up in the previous cycle, and she has to make the transition to investing in a new cycle before the burdens can be willingly laid down.

Swords

A transition relating to ideas and attitudes, often more difficult or painful than others. Ideas, habits, and attitudes have a way of getting a very strong hold of us and our minds, and when it becomes necessary for a change to occur, it can be very difficult. We may struggle and struggle through the Eights and Nines before we are willing to do whatever is necessary to make the change, and even then, we may have to beat the old attitudes down hard before they finally lie down and give up the ghost. Or, it may come in a rush of surrender to the inevitable, giving ourselves up to the pain in a cathartic release that frees us to experience new ideas and ways of living our life.

Pentacles

Here we see Tens in their natural element of earth, representing all that we build in the material world and pass down from generation to generation. This may be the next generation of parents and children in the family. It can be material possessions such as homes or inheritance, cultural knowledge and traditions, or what we leave behind in our work to society to be built on by others. This card represents the time when we pass on what we have held to the next person or generation to hold and use. While we ourselves pass on, what we have created endures and makes up the fabric of family and society.

Astrological Associations

The following list provides the Golden Dawn astrological associations for the tarot. Alternatives methods can be developed, and may be specific to the deck you are using. One widely used alternative for court cards is also given.

Trumps

When the Golden Dawn originally developed their attributions, there were not enough astrological signs and known planets to cover all the trumps—they were three short. These three cards were assigned to three of the elements: air, water, and fire. Today these cards are typically attributed to the three additional planets that have been discovered since then: Uranus, Neptune, and Pluto.

> **0. The Fool**—Air (now Uranus)
>
> **1. The Magician**—Mercury
>
> **2. The High Priestess**—Moon
>
> **3. The Empress**—Venus
>
> **4. The Emperor**—Aries

5. The Hierophant—Taurus

6. The Lovers—Gemini

7. The Chariot—Cancer

8. Strength—Leo

9. The Hermit—Virgo

10. Wheel of Fortune—Jupiter

11. Justice—Libra

12. The Hanged Man—Water (now Neptune)

13. Death—Scorpio

14. Temperance—Sagittarius

15. The Devil—Capricorn

16. The Tower—Mars

17. The Star—Aquarius

18. The Moon—Pisces

19. The Sun—Sun

20. Judgment—Fire (now Pluto)

21. The World—Saturn

Court Cards (Golden Dawn)

King of Wands—20 degrees Scorpio to 20 degrees Sagittarius

Queen of Wands—20 degrees Pisces to 20 degrees Aries

Knight of Wands—20 degrees Cancer to 20 degrees Leo

King of Cups—20 degrees Aquarius to 20 degrees Pisces

Queen of Cups—20 degrees Gemini to 20 degrees Cancer

Knight of Cups—20 degrees Libra to 20 degrees Scorpio

King of Swords—20 degrees Taurus to 20 degrees Gemini

Queen of Swords—20 degrees Virgo to 20 degrees Libra

Knight of Swords—20 degrees Capricorn to 20 degrees Aquarius

King of Pentacles—20 degrees Leo to 20 degrees Virgo

Queen of Pentacles—20 degrees Sagittarius to 20 degrees Capricorn

Knight of Pentacles—20 degrees Aries to 20 degrees Taurus

Court Cards (Alternative)

Another method is to assign specific signs to the King, Queen, and Knight of each suit. The Pages are assigned the elemental energy of that suit. Using this approach, the cardinal signs are assigned to Queens, the fixed signs to Kings, and the mutable signs to Knights, as follows:

King of Wands—Leo (fixed fire)

Queen of Wands—Aries (cardinal fire)

Knight of Wands—Sagittarius (mutable fire)

Page of Wands—Elemental fire

King of Cups—Scorpio (fixed water)

Queen of Cups—Cancer (cardinal water)

Knight of Cups—Pisces (mutable water)

Page of Cups—Elemental water

King of Swords—Aquarius (fixed air)

Queen of Swords—Libra (cardinal air)

Knight of Swords—Gemini (mutable air)

Page of Swords—Elemental air

King of Pentacles—Taurus (fixed earth)

Queen of Pentacles—Capricorn (cardinal earth)

Knight of Pentacles—Virgo (mutable earth)

Page of Pentacles—Elemental earth

Cups

Ace—Water

Two—Venus in Cancer

Three—Mercury in Cancer

Four—Moon in Cancer

Five—Mars in Scorpio

Six—Sun in Scorpio

Seven—Venus in Scorpio

Eight—Saturn in Pisces

Nine—Jupiter in Pisces

Ten—Mars in Pisces

Wands

Ace—Fire

Two—Mars in Aries

Three—Sun in Aries

Four—Venus in Aries

Five—Saturn in Leo

Six—Jupiter in Leo

Seven—Mars in Leo

Eight—Mercury in Sagittarius

Nine—Moon in Sagittarius

Ten—Saturn in Sagittarius

Swords

Ace—Air

Two—Moon in Libra

Three—Saturn in Libra

Four—Jupiter in Libra

Five—Venus in Aquarius

Six—Mercury in Aquarius

Seven—Moon in Aquarius

Eight—Jupiter in Gemini

Nine—Mars in Gemini

Ten—Sun in Gemini

Pentacles

Ace—Earth

Two—Jupiter in Capricorn

Three—Mars in Capricorn

Four—Sun in Capricorn

Five—Mercury in Taurus

Six—Moon in Taurus

Seven—Saturn in Taurus

Eight—Sun in Virgo

Nine—Venus in Virgo

Ten—Mercury in Virgo

Elemental Associations

Fire
Wands
Kings

Air
Swords
Knights

Water
Cups
Queens

Earth
Pentacles
Pages/Princesses

Trumps

0. **The Fool**—Air (Uranus)

1. **The Magician**—Air (Mercury)

2. **The High Priestess**—Water (Moon)

3. **The Empress**—Earth (Venus)

4. **The Emperor**—Fire (Aries)

5. **The Hierophant**—Earth (Taurus)

6. **The Lovers**—Air (Gemini)

7. **The Chariot**—Water (Cancer)

8. **Strength**—Fire (Leo)

9. **The Hermit**—Earth (Virgo)

10. **The Wheel of Fortune**—Fire (Jupiter)

11. **Justice**—Air (Libra)

12. **The Hanged Man**—Water (Neptune)

13. **Death**—Water (Scorpio)

14. **Temperance**—Fire (Sagittarius)

15. **The Devil**—Earth (Capricorn)

16. **The Tower**—Fire (Mars)

17. **The Star**—Air (Aquarius)

18. **The Moon**—Water (Pisces)

19. **The Sun**—Fire (Sun)

20. **Judgment**—Fire or water (Pluto)

21. **The World**—Earth (Saturn)

Notes

1. Suit and court associations are those most commonly used. Some decks switch the air and fire associations, both in the suits and in the courts.

2. All court cards will have two elemental associations—one for the rank and one for the suit. For example, the Queen of Swords is known as the water aspect of air.

3. Elemental associations for the trumps are based on their astrological associations as given by the Golden Dawn. Astrological associations are given in parentheses. Alternative associations are possible and even likely, particularly when using pre-Golden Dawn decks. Trumps are also considered neutral by some authors, or as belonging to the element of spirit.

4. Prior to the discovery of certain outlying planets, several of the trumps were directly assigned to the elements rather than having astrological associations. These are also given here.

5. Though not shown here, I personally consider the Wheel of Fortune and the World to contain all four elements equally, and the Fool to be composed of pure spirit. Other personal modifications to trumps are possible, especially using older (e.g., Renaissance) associations, such as Mars/Aries with the Chariot, or Venus with the Lovers.

Glossary of Symbols

This appendix presents a glossary and some discussion of a wide variety of different types of symbols used on tarot cards, including colors, the elements and nature, numbers, plants and flowers, animals, celestial bodies, and built structures. It will serve as a convenient reference for tarot readers and students.

Colors

Tarot decks vary a great deal in their use of color symbolism. Sometimes the use of colors is purely aesthetic, while in other cases, such as the *Robin Wood* deck or decks using alchemical, magickal, or qabalistic color systems, colors are carefully chosen with specific meanings in mind.

White

White traditionally stands for innocence and purity, and is most often seen in white clothing or white flowers. The central figures in the High Priestess, Strength, and Temperance cards all wear white robes, representing their purity and virginity. White represents the source of all things and unity, since white light contains all colors. In the qabalistic Tree of Life, white is the color of the uppermost sephiroth, from which all creation emanates.

In the *Robin Wood* deck, white crystals at the tips of Wands are often used to symbolize clarity of thought and purpose. A white or silver color represents the light of the Moon, and the feminine principle associated with the Moon (yellow or gold being the sunny, masculine counterpart). White is also the symbol of cleansing and rebirth, and this is particularly emphasized in the traditional Death card. Death rides in on a white horse, symbolizing the purity of heart needed for this transition, and carries a flag of a white rose on a black background, symbolizing rebirth after a passage through darkness and the unknown. White has additional meanings when paired with red or black, discussed below.

White/Black

The combination of white and black has particular meaning in Western mysticism, the school of thought that greatly influenced the design of the *Rider-Waite-Smith* decks. Twin black and white pillars, such as can be found in the High Priestess, symbolize the feminine or receptive principle (black) and masculine or active principle (white) pillars of the Tree of Life. In this form, they represent absolutes, which do not exist in the real world unmingled, but only as archetypes.

The white/black pairing can also be seen in the Chariot. In the *Robin Wood* deck, the black/white passive/active pairing is emphasized by the yin/yang symbol above the unicorns (in *Rider-Waite-Smith* decks, these are usually black and white sphinxes). The creator of this deck, Robin Wood, has chosen to emphasize the feminine and masculine principles here by giving the unicorns silver and gold jewelry and horns, representing the light of the Moon and Sun, respectively. Notice that the horses are going in opposite directions, but are harnessed together. Part of the meaning of the Chariot has to do with integrating these two energies and getting them to work for you.

White/Red

The combination of white and red, particularly in flowers and clothing, is one often seen in the *Rider-Waite-Smith* decks, as well as many other decks. This combination of white and red can be viewed on a couple of different levels. First, white represents the passive principle and purity or innocence, while red represents the active principle and passions or lusts. This can be a bit confusing, because in the black/white pairing just discussed, white represents the masculine, while in the white/red pairing, white is normally associated with the feminine principle. The white/black appears on only a few cards—white/red is much more prevalent and is often used in cards where duality is part of the theme. The Magician shows his ability to use these opposite energies by wearing red robes over a white robe, and is surrounded by red roses and white lilies.

At a more esoteric level, red and white are key colors in alchemy, and this is one of the reasons for their use in the *Rider-Waite-Smith* tarots, as well as some earlier decks. In alchemy, red is again associated with the masculine elements, and white with the feminine. In the course of the Great Work (transforming lead to gold), the masculine and feminine elements are first separated and purified from baser materials, and then "married" together in the final step—the red (mercury) with the white (silver) to make gold. Red also represents blood, and white represents mother's milk, and in some versions of the Temperance card (e.g., *Wheel of Change*), you can see the two streams of blood and milk intermingling.

Black

When not paired with white, black simply means mystery, the unknown, and the dark. In the traditional decks, very few cards have prominent black, except Death and the Devil. In other decks, a black starry sky may indicate the greater cosmos, the universe, and the movement of the planets in relation to how they affect us here on earth.

Grey

Grey is also a little-used color in tarot, but where it is used it normally signifies gloom, stormy weather, and unhappiness. Robin Wood uses it to particularly good effect to indicate an unhealthy outlook on life (see the Seven of Swords and the Four of Pentacles). Notice particularly in the Four of Pentacles how the covetous man's world is grey and colorless, while outside his protective walls the city is gay and lively.

Red/Yellow/Blue (and Green)

Red, yellow, and blue are the three primary colors, and as such have an esoteric significance. These colors represent the first emanations from the white light or the origin of the universe, and are assigned to the three "spiritual" elements of fire (red), air (yellow) and water (blue). You may notice if you look through the *Rider-Waite-Smith* deck that these three colors predominate. The fourth and "mundane" element of earth is assigned to a secondary color, green. In general, the cool colors of green and blue represent the earth and water energies, which are attributed to passive, feminine, receptive qualities, while red and yellow are associated with the masculine, active qualities of fire and air. These color cues in a reading can give the reader a sense of which energies predominate in a situation.

These four colors may often be found in cards that combine the four elements in a ritual or magickal sense. The four quarters of the earth (and hence the circle) are represented by guardian angels, each associated with a specific elemental energy, which are called when forming the protective circle.

Red

As already noted, red is the color of fire, and represents action, passion, inspiration, energy, blood as a warm life-giving substance, Mercury, Mars, the suit of Wands (usually, although sometimes it may be Swords), and astrological fire signs. Red represents a passion for life, and also anger, lust, and other animal urges, which is one reason why the lion in the Strength card is sometimes colored red. The Empress sits on red drapes and pillows, a reference to menstruation and fertility. The Emperor is also a very red card, representing his strong will and masculinity, and his association with the astrological sign of Aries.

Orange

The Emperor is also one of the few cards with a lot of orange in it, in the steep mountains and sky behind his throne. This could be taken as a reference to difficult challenges, to be overcome by a force of will. In other decks, orange is simply one of the colors used to indicate fire and the suit of Wands.

Yellow

Yellow is associated with the element of air, and also with the masculine principle and sun energy. There is quite often a yellow rather than blue sky in the *Rider-Waite-Smith* deck, and the sun appears prominently, as in the Fool card. Yellow can be associated with the superconscious and the most direct connection to the higher spheres (hence its presence in the Fool). By comparison, red is the expression of the conscious mind and will, and blue the subconscious mind.

Green

Green is the color of the element of earth, and represents life, nature, abundance, and all growth. It is not widely used in older tarot decks, where nature is not represented in very many cards.

Blue

Blue is the color of the element of water, and the subconscious mind. Many cards with a deep blue sky or predominance of blue are associated with working through subconscious processes, including the High Priestess, the Hermit, the Star, the Moon, the Eight of Cups, and the Two of Swords. Anyone wearing blue clothing is likely to have an introspective frame of mind, or is making use of their subconscious in some way.

Purple

Purple is infrequently used in *Rider-Waite-Smith*, and generally represents luxury, opulence (King of Pentacles) or royalty (Emperor). One of my favorite connections between cards is the little purple tail of grapes that appears on the woman in the Devil card. These are the same grapes that appear in the King of Pentacles' robes, representing the chains of materialism that can bind you to the Devil if you let them (the man has a tail of fire, symbolizing his passions that get him in trouble).

Purple also has a strong association with psychic energy and mysteries, such as the purple veil draped behind Justice. Thus, purple is more widely used in some modern decks, such as the *Spiral* deck and *Daughters of the Moon*.

Pink/Rose

This is another color that is very seldom used in *Rider-Waite-Smith* decks, with one notable exception (Page of Cups). Pink usually shades into purple, and is most often seen with the suit of Cups, suggesting a psychic connection, but also a lighter shade of pleasant enjoyment. Pink sometimes reflects opulence or sensual pleasure, as in a lotus blossom (Ace of Cups).

Brown

In most decks, brown is also infrequently used, but invariably shows a connection to the earth or someone engaged in going about practical, everyday tasks. As such, it is most strongly represented in the suit of Pentacles (see the Eight of Pentacles).

Rainbows of Color

Rainbows and multicolored spectra are widely used in the *Robin Wood* deck, in a wide variety of manifestations: as crystals on the tips of Wands, rainbow cups (Eight of Cups), or multicolored Sword hilts, but they also appear in other decks (especially the Ten of Cups). Rainbows normally represent abundance, wishes come true, and happiness, such as in the Nine or Ten of Cups. In other contexts, they may represent a wide variety of resources to draw upon or to be protected, a variety of different problems with associated possible solutions, a depiction of the different conditions of life, or a celebration of diversity and an integration of the whole.

The Elements and Nature

Elemental Symbols

There are four symbols commonly used to represent the four elements, derived from alchemy:

Earth: Upside-down triangle with a horizontal bar $\bar{\nabla}$

Water: Upside-down triangle ∇

Air: Right-side-up triangle with a horizontal bar $\bar{\triangle}$

Fire: Right-side-up triangle $\triangle$

You can see all four symbols in the *Spiral* Chariot card, as emblems on the four pillars holding up the canopy of his chariot. This shows that in order to make this Chariot go, the driver has to not only be able to integrate and control his yin/yang energies (the Sphinxes), but also have command of the four elements. There is a larger downward-pointing triangle to the right, which indicates that the overall card is considered a water card, since it has the ruling sign of Cancer. This deck is one in which most of the symbols have been drawn right on the cards, particularly the trumps and court cards, and is useful as a reference deck for that reason. See, for example, the *Spiral* Empress—over her head from the left and going in a clockwise direction, we see the symbols for earth, the Hebrew letter corresponding to this card, the number of the card (III), the astrological symbol for Venus, and a miniature Tree of Life with the path corresponding to the Empress highlighted. The court cards also have these attributions; for example, on the King of Swords you can see the symbol for air, and a small symbol for Aquarius in the belt buckle.

Although these basic elemental symbols are used in many decks, Waite chose not to incorporate them into the *Rider-Waite-Smith* deck, perhaps preferring more arcane symbology. The only exception I have found is the Temperance card, which has rather obvious fire and sun symbols in it. The Charioteer wears a tunic covered with alchemical symbols for various elements, rather than the more straightforward symbols just pictured. Similarly, on the Wheel of Fortune card, we can see evidence of Waite's interest in alchemy by the four symbols on the middle ring of the Wheel. Starting in the east, or 3:00 position, and moving counterclockwise around the wheel, we have:

Sulfur: Expansion ♄

Mercury: Integration ☿

Salt: Contraction ⊖

Water: Dissolution ♒

The first three elements listed here represent three basic principles in alchemy from which all life is considered to be derived. These could be listed as the process of birth, life, and death, and can be considered to correspond to other three-part systems, like Maiden-Mother-Crone. However, there is a tension here between the number three and four. Like the Goddess cycle being of three parts but represented by a four-phase moon cycle, Waite felt it was appropriate to add a fourth principle—partly because it made his Wheel more aesthetically balanced, but also as a counterprinciple to Mercury's integration. Dissolution could be considered as that phase that takes place between death and rebirth, when the personality of the physical lifetime dissolves away, and only the higher self remains.

Moving from the esoteric to the more direct, some decks have represented the elements more directly on the cards, such as *Robin Wood.* For example, the World card in this deck has visual representations of the four elements in the four corners of the card, in the form of mountains, clouds, flames, and waves. Robin Wood's use of the elements in the four Knights cards is also wonderful—each of the Knights has a steed that is moving through the element in question, and is particularly adapted to that element. In the Knight of Cups, the Knight and his horse are riding into the sea, and his horse is really a mer-horse, with a mane of sea foam.

Natural Landscape

The natural world does not play a strong role in traditional tarot decks—it is more of a backdrop for people and their activities. This fits with the prevailing religious and cultural attitudes of the times, in which the natural world was largely considered to be present in order for man to exploit. These days there are several decks that have stronger nature elements, such as *Greenwood, Wheel of Change, Animal-Wise,* and various pagan/Celtic decks. *Legends: The Arthurian Tarot* is another deck in which the characters seem to live in the natural world, and where some of the court cards are replaced by animals. If you feel a strong pull toward the natural world, and miss it in the traditional decks, then you may want to explore some newer or alternative decks.

Sky

Try as I might, I have been unable to find a clear pattern associated with the color of the sky in the *Rider-Waite-Smith* decks and any specific meanings, except that yellow often appears on beneficial cards or those closely linked to the sun, with a very dark blue indicating cards that are dominated by night/moon energy. However, the weather is an indicator of what is going on: stormy weather is typically seen in cards like the Five of Swords and the Knight of Swords, where destructive and precipitous activity is occurring; gloomy clouds appear in cards like the Ten of Swords and the Three of Swords, indicating pain and suffering; and snow appears in the Five of Pentacles to emphasize the misery in this card. Perhaps the reason so much "weather" appears in the Swords cards is that the sky is part of air, which is the element associated with Swords. Therefore, the state of the sky represents in part the mental state of the querent.

Fluffy clouds, such as those from which the hands emerge in the Aces, generally seem to indicate mysterious or heavenly origins, and also appear in the Four of Cups (the fourth Cup being offered), the Seven of Cups (surrounding all the Cups), and the various flying creatures in the corners of the World card.

Water

Many cards have some form of water in them, and this is one important clue to what is going on in the card. Water generally represents the subconscious mind or the emotional state of the querent. If the water is calm, the emotions are calm. If they are turbulent, the emotional state may be distressed—sometimes only at a subconscious level. Decks may vary in the portrayal of the water. The Two of Cups and Two of Swords are cards in which the water is calm in some decks and stormy in others. This should be read however it appears in your deck, and is one of the examples of how decks can vary in their nuances of meaning by the portrayal of minor details.

One interesting example is in the Six of Swords. In some versions of this card, the water is more turbulent on one side of the boat than the other, indicating a passage from a stormy past to calmer waters. Note also that this apparent physical journey over water also stands for an emotional journey to a better state of mind. Also notice whether the water is still or flowing in your card—this can indicate whether this is a card of stability or whether there is motion. Flowing water is often associated with a link to memory and the past, passing through the present into the future.

Mountains, Cliffs

Mountains generally indicate challenges or obstacles. The prevalence of steep mountains in the background of the Emperor card shows his mastery at overcoming obstacles. There are mountains shown in the background of the Fool card, although the Fool himself stands on a plateau at the start of his journey. In the Hermit, we see that he has surmounted the obstacles and reached the top of the snowy peaks. Cliffs can indicate danger, as in the Fool card, or dangers and challenges successfully faced, such as in the Seven of Wands. Rolling hills and smaller cliffs may appear in cards where there is an element of challenge, but not as severe, such as the landscape in front of the Knight of Cups (note also the flowing stream). One thing to look out for is twin hills or peaks, particularly with paths leading up to them. These appear notably in the Temperance card, but also many other cards in a variety of decks. These twin hills are simply another form of the twin towers or gateways discussed later in this appendix, and usually represent a far-off goal that can be reached by working through the lessons of the trump.

Greenery

In the traditional *Rider-Waite-Smith* decks, greenery is used relatively sparingly, as a symbol rather than an integral part of the landscape. In the Empress card, it stands for fertility, abundance, and growth. The wooden wands in the suit of Wands are usually portrayed with buds, showing that they are not dead instruments, but sources of new growth, ideas, and change. This is also true of the tree from which the Hanged Man hangs, showing that his suspension is not stagnant; it results in inner growth. Another related symbol is plowed fields, appearing in the Death card and the Knight of Pentacles.

This represents a dormant state with the potential for new growth in the future—sowing the seeds of future change, and in the case of the Knight, material rewards and abundance.

Seasons

Various suits are associated with the seasons in some decks. This is possibly best illustrated in the *Ancestral Path* deck. In this deck, each suit is associated with a season and with one of the major cultures in the east, west, north, and south continents of the world. Note that the directional and seasonal correspondences in this deck differ from the Golden Dawn attributions.

Numbers

Numbers in the tarot are represented and used in many different ways. This discussion will focus mainly on the Major Arcana, because in the Minor Arcana the use of numbers is fairly obvious, and the numerological significance of these cards is discussed in appendix B. Each number is usually represented by suit symbols somewhere in the card (there are occasional additions to this, such as the infinity symbol in the Two of Pentacles card). In contrast, numbers are used in the Major Arcana to symbolize various esoteric concepts, and are usually worked into the drawing more subtly. This discussion refers to the *Universal Waite* version of the deck. Please note that many of these are religious and metaphysical symbols, and this discussion describes these symbols without endorsing or ascribing to these specific faiths or beliefs.

Zero

Only the Fool is numbered zero, and it is important to realize that in early tarot decks, trumps were not numbered at all. These 22 cards were usually referred to as 21 trumps plus the Fool, which stood outside the series of trumps, neither at the bottom nor the top, nor anywhere in between. It had its own special scoring rules in the game of tarocchi, as well. In fact, there is still disagreement about whether the Fool belongs at the beginning or the end, and perhaps the correct answer is both. As a Zero, the Fool represents a direct incarnation of the universal nothingness—true consciousness does not arise until the 1, or the Magician. The circular aspect of zero can be found in two other cards: 10, the Wheel of Fortune, and 21, the World. These three cards represent the beginning, middle, and end of the series of trumps and the Fool's journey. They form a never-ending cycle, circle, or spiral within which the dance of incarnation takes place. The circular nature of these cards suggests that one should not view the trumps as a linear progression, but rather as a repeating cycle or spiral.

One

Mirroring the Fool-Wheel-World cycle, we find that all the cards whose numbers reduce to one are the Magician, the Wheel of Fortune, and the Sun. The Wheel of Fortune, as mentioned before, is the pivot or turning point of the Major Arcana. The Magician and the Sun are the two cards that represent the conscious mind most directly; the Magician is the first spark of consciousness, and the Sun represents the final integration of consciousness with the other aspects of self. Here we have a sense of the first and second half of the Major Arcana being like mirrors of one another—the conscious self and the spiritual or shadow self that must become integrated into one.

Two

When discussing colors and landscape elements, we noted the ways in which the concepts of duality manifest in the Major Arcana. There are numerous pairings of masculine/feminine, yin/yang, positive/negative, passive/active, sun/moon, conscious/subconscious, and other concepts of duality represented by red/white and black/white pairings, twin towers or mountains, yin/yang symbols, and roses and lilies. In addition, there are cards like the Lovers and the Devil, where two people are prominent in the meaning of the card—in one case watched over by an angel, and in the other case by the Devil. Then there are cards such as Temperance and the Star, where water is being poured back and forth between vessels, and the central figure has one foot on land and one in the water. Twin keys in the Hierophant card represent the keys to heaven and earth—as above, so below. Duality is so integral a concept in the Major Arcana that it reinforces the idea that all things, including all tarot cards, have light and dark aspects to them.

Three

Three is a central concept in Western mysticism, and is used to represent a variety of similar but varying concepts, such as mind-body-spirit, father-son-holy ghost, the alchemical principles of expansion-integration-contraction, birth-life-death (also Maiden-Mother-Crone). In the Tree of Life, there are three realms above the material, through which one must climb to reach the Source. These are represented by the three primary elements, air, fire, and water, and the three primary colors, yellow, red, and blue. These also correspond to the three "mother" letters in Hebrew. These three higher realms or spheres are represented in the Hierophant card by the three crossbars on his wand of office and the three points on the highest level of his crown, not to mention the three tiers on the crown. Some authors believe the trumps were originally set up in groups of three, with one of the seven virtues in every third place (the game itself was set up for three players—if you remove the Fool, there are 21 trumps, divisible by three). Lastly, in the Judgment card, the families are being raised in groups of three—mother, father, child.

Four

Four is another central concept in numerology. There are four elements, four suits, four directions, four winds, four types of astrological signs, four letters in the mystical word of *taro,* or *rota.* All of these can be seen in the Wheel of Fortune and World cards, especially the Wheel of Fortune. Waite made this a central concept of his tarot deck, and doubled the four to make an eight-spoked Wheel. The name of God in Hebrew has three letters, one of which is repeated to make four, and these letters are seen along the wheel, interspersed with the mystical letters TARO. The four winged figures around the Wheel represent the four fixed astrological signs: Taurus the bull, Leo the lion, Scorpio the eagle, and Aquarius the man. Each is depicted with wings and reading a book, to show that knowledge is the way to the divine. These symbols are present in a slightly different form in the corners of the World card, tying together these two cards. The four pillars holding up the roof of the Charioteer's chariot are also a reference to the integration of the four elements, to supplement the yin/yang and other "integration of duality" symbols in this card.

Five

Five is the number of the pentacle, and the number of spirit, representing the fifth element. The tarot deck can be thought of as having five suits, the four suits representing the four elements, plus the trumps as a fifth suit of spirit. The only trump to show an obvious pentacle is the Devil, and his points downward, to represent the opposite of spiritual integration. The upright five-petaled white rose in the Death card is an alchemical symbol of the Rosicrucian Order, and is similar to the upright pentacle in that it represents the triumph of spirit over the baser elements, the purification of man in his longing and striving for God. One of the three tiers of the Hierophant's crown has five points, showing that he holds the key to these teachings.

Six

Six does not show up that often in the Major Arcana, and can be seen most clearly in the six-pointed Star of David that resides within the Hermit's lamp and gives light. The six-pointed star is an ancient symbol of balance between inward and outward flow of energy, male/female, fire/water (upward- and downward-pointing triangles), and other polar opposites. The Hermit achieves enlightenment through the perfect balance of these energies—note the similarities to our keywords for Sixes—this is an active, flowing balance rather than a static balance. This symbol is used to represent the heart chakra, and the sixth sephira, *Tephireth,* on the Tree of Life, which is the highest point on the Tree that we can reach in an incarnated form. Its paths to other sephiroth form a six-pointed star, and it is the only sephira we can reach that has a direct path to the Origin. All of these are concepts worthy of the Hermit as he seeks true enlightenment, and his is the last card in the first half of the trumps, before the Wheel turns and the rest of the cycle continues. Six-pointed stars also appear on the Empress' crown.

Seven

The third tier of the Hierophant's crown contains seven points, and this is a reference to the Seven Seals in the Book of Revelations. There are seven seals on the Book of God, which Jesus was given and began to open. As each seal is broken, more about God is revealed (hence, Revelations). Once the seventh seal is broken, Judgment will be upon us. Seven also has other meanings—three and four being the holiest numbers, 7 is 3 + 4, and so is considered a mystical or magickal number. At the time that the tarot was invented, there were seven known planets (counting the Sun and the Moon). There are seven days of the week (named after the seven principal Roman deities), Seven Wonders of the World, seven virtues and seven deadly sins, God made the world in seven days, King Solomon built his temple in seven days, seven liberal arts and sciences, and consequently many, many uses of the number seven in Masonry. It is interesting, then, that it does not appear more often in the tarot, since Waite was active in Freemasonry.

Eight

The number eight, as mentioned before, is derived by the doubling of the fours on the Wheel of Fortune, and is an important recurring symbol in Waite's tarot deck. The eight-spoked wheel has been repeated in many *Rider-Waite-Smith*-type decks, and Waite even wore a pendant that was an eight-spoked wheel as a reference to his tarot deck and the concepts embodied in this Wheel. The eight-spoked wheel originally appeared as decorations on the Fool's tunic, though poor line-drawing quality has obscured this symbol in many reproductions. We can see this appearing in other cards, most often in the form of eight-pointed stars (rather than the five-, six-, or seven-pointed stars that were more prevalent symbols then and now) in the Star and the Chariot. There are even eight eight-pointed stars in the Star card.

Here we will skip some numbers that do not appear symbolically in the tarot.

Twelve

The number twelve often appears in the tarot, and is nearly always a reference to the twelve astrological signs. Waite uses twelve less often than do many other deck authors, who often have a twelve-spoked Wheel of Fortune. However, if you look closely at the Charioteer's belt, you can see that it is made up of astrological symbols, and presumably it goes all the way around so that there would be twelve segments total (yet another example of how the Chariot represents mastery of every possible sphere). There are twelve flames on the Tree of Life behind the man in the Lovers. In Waite's tarot, you can see twelve stars on the Empress' crown, which represent her mastery over the twelve months of the year and the seasons, in her role as Mother Nature.

Twenty-Two

There are 22 letters of the Hebrew alphabet, each of which is also a number. Much has been made of this mystical system and the fact that there are also 22 trumps in the tarot, and 22 paths between the sephiroth on the Tree of Life. However, no one truly knows whether the trumps were designed to correspond to this mystical number or not. Some argue that in fact there were only 21 trumps, plus the Fool. However, the Golden Dawn firmly believed there was a correspondence, and it remains a topic of spirited discussion among tarot scholars.

Some tarot decks (such as *Spiral*) print the Hebrew letter considered to correspond to each trump on the cards, while others use a numbering system corresponding to the Hebrew numbers, which may be different from the typical numbers assigned to the trumps. The number 22 is also considered a "master number" in numerology, along with 11 and 33. This number has among its meanings alchemy and universal transformation, two concepts that have been closely linked with the progression of the Trumps.

Infinity

The sideways symbol eight appears on a few cards, and stands for infinity and endless repeating cycles. This symbol appears above the Magician, above the woman in the Strength card, and in the Two of Pentacles. I do not know why these two particular trumps were singled out to receive the infinity symbol, as an argument could be made that it would be appropriate for many of the trumps. Interestingly, in some of the early Italian deck designs, there were figures that wore a floppy hat with a wide brim, one end of which was turned up so that the rim followed a sideways figure eight or infinity symbol. No one actually knows whether the hat was designed after the symbol, or the symbol was added because of the hats, or whether there was actually any correlation between the two.

Plants and Flowers

Apples/Pears

Apples alone generally represent knowledge, as the Tree of Knowledge in the Garden of Eden was an apple tree. The knowledge is of a mystical nature, since if you slice open an apple, the seeds form a pentagram. Pears and apples are also shown together in certain *Rider-Waite-Smith* cards (Queen of Pentacles), and in this context generally symbolize fruitful abundance and nourishment.

Grapes

Seen in cards such as the Nine of Pentacles and the King of Pentacles, grapes symbolize abundance, prosperity, and celebration of the good life.

Holly

A symbol of the masculine, holly was used in pagan and Celtic cultures, and later incorporated into Christianity. It is not seen in *Rider-Waite-Smith,* but is used in many other decks.

Iris

Seen mainly in the Temperance card, growing by the side of the water, the iris symbolizes a message from the gods, or the inner guides. Iris was also the goddess of the rainbow, suggesting a spectrum of possibilities for the future, and the harmonious blending of all colors.

Ivy

A symbol of the feminine, ivy was used in pagan and Celtic cultures, and later incorporated into Christianity.

Laurel

Generally seen in the form of a wreath, laurel represents victory and accomplishments.

Lily, White

As discussed in the section on colors, white lilies are often used in tarot to symbolize purity of thought or action, innocence, chastity, clarity of thought, and the feminine/yin principle. They are often paired with red roses.

Lotus

The lotus is traditionally shown on the Ace of Cups, and may also be found in other Cups cards in some decks. The lotus symbolizes peace and purity, a flowering of the psychic self and opening upward toward higher consciousness.

Oak Leaves

Oak leaves symbolize strength, wisdom, age, kingly attributes, and the gateway into the Otherworld (pagan/Celtic).

Pomegranate

The pomegranate is seen on both the High Priestess and the Empress cards, and symbolizes female fertility and sexuality, the Goddess, secret knowledge, and rebirth.

Rose, Five-Petaled

The five-petaled rose is the symbol of the Rosicrucians, and symbolizes the four elements plus the fifth element of spirit, with the fifth point or petal pointing upward toward heaven, similar to an upright pentacle.

Rose, Red

The red rose is the rose of passion, courage, action, masculinity/yang, and blood. It is often paired with white lilies.

Rose, White

The white rose is the rose of transformation, and is usually a five-petaled rose. Its most prominent use is on the black flag carried by Death, as a symbol of what awaits once you pass through darkness, and the dissolution of self.

Squash, Garden Vegetables

These are symbols of the harvest. In the Three of Cups, they symbolize the abundance of the harvest and the celebration that comes with it, and in the Seven of Pentacles they symbolize a harvest yet to come, through one's own patient hard work.

Sunflower

The sunflower has long been used as a symbol of the Sun, and appears in cards related to the Sun, such as the Sun card itself, the Queen of Wands, and other fiery court cards. It symbolizes joy, vitality, and glowing energy.

Tree of Knowledge

The Tree of Knowledge appears in the Lovers card, usually on Eve's side. It symbolizes the conscious choice of knowledge, and the transformations and separations that inevitably follow.

Tree of Life

The Tree of Life can also be seen in the Lovers card, usually on Adam's side (with the flaming branches). It sometimes appears in the window of the church on the Five of Pentacles, as well. This is a reference to the qabala in modern decks.

Wheat

Wheat appears in the Empress card as a symbol of fertility, and her connection to the earth and nature. It symbolizes wholesomeness, life, nourishment, and the death/rebirth of the seasons and all living things.

Animals

Bat

Seen only in the bat's wings given to the Devil, the bat is a symbol of the subterranean dwelling of the Devil and the underworld, hidden and repressed desires, and our shadow selves.

Bird

Birds represent freedom, inspiration, and sometimes messengers related to the God/dess.

Bull

The bull is the symbol of Taurus, and is often seen on the King of Pentacles' throne. It is also one of the four astrological signs seen in the Wheel of Fortune and World cards. The bull stands for stability, strength, and power (and stubbornness).

Butterfly

The butterfly symbolizes transformation, freedom, and lightness of being. It is most often seen in the Death and Fool cards.

Cat

In most decks, the cat only appears in the Queen of Wands card, and symbolizes sensuality, playfulness, passion, and grace (with perhaps a bit of hedonism and haughtiness mixed in). The cat shares many of the qualities of the lion, but is tamer and domesticated.

Crayfish

In the Moon card, the crayfish rises up out of the collective unconscious, symbolized by the pool of water. The crayfish represents an unknown part of ourselves, part of our animal nature, primordial and a bit scary-looking, with a horny carapace. This unknown creature rises from the depths, and triggers the journey through the Moon card.

Dog

As seen in the Fool card, there are varying interpretations of the little white dog. Some say he is a faithful companion, blindly following the Fool out of love, willing to go wherever the Fool goes, while others say he is a messenger, trying to warn the Fool about the impending cliff. In the Moon card, the dog symbolizes the forces of civilization and restraint, as opposed to the wild, untamed nature of the wolf/jackal. These are the two extremes between which one must find the middle path.

Dove

The dove appears in the Ace of Cups, and is also the bird in the Star in some decks. It is a messenger of peace and of eternal love.

Dragon

The dragon is an ancient symbol of royalty and wisdom, and is often found on the King and Emperor cards.

Falcon

The falcon can be seen in the Nine of Pentacles, and represents intellect and clear sight, swiftness and freedom. It is sometimes hooded and restrained in this card to show that the woman in the card has chosen physical pleasures and abundance rather than independence and freedom.

Fish

The fish is a symbol of the element of water, and is also a symbol of Christianity and God's love.

Goat

The goat is the symbol of Capricorn, and the Devil wears goat's horns partly to symbolize the association of this card with Capricorn. The goat is also associated with the god Pan, playfulness, and trickster-like attributes, as well as perversity and black magic.

Horse

Horses are conveyances for the self, forces of nature or civilization that are harnessed, reined in, and brought under control. The Knights all ride horses to show that they have harnessed the elements of their suit, and are putting these energies to work in order to get somewhere.

Lion

The lion symbolizes the passionate, primal side of ourselves, our animal natures, as in the Strength card. In the context of court cards, it is a sign of nobility, pride, and courage. The lion is also the symbol of Leo, seen in the Wheel of Fortune and World cards.

Rabbit

A symbol of fertility, the rabbit is usually seen in the Queen of Pentacles card.

Ram

The ram is the symbol for Aries, and is thus found on the Emperor's throne. It is a symbol of virility, tenacity, and warlike nature (associated with Mars).

Salamander

The salamander is a creature mythically associated with fire, and is often seen decorating the clothing of Wands court cards.

Snake

The snake is a symbol of female wisdom and psychic abilities. It is the bringer of knowledge, as in the Garden of Eden. The snake swallowing its tail is a symbol of infinity and eternity—sometimes seen as the Magician's belt.

Sphinx

The sphinx is a mythical creature made up of the symbols of the four primary astrological signs: the lion, man, eagle, and bull. It is a gatekeeper and guardian of hidden mysteries.

Wolf/Jackal

The wolf (or jackal) appears in the Moon card, paired with the dog on either side of the central path. It represents our wild, untamed nature, excesses of passion, and uncontrolled emotion and desires, as well as violence and rapaciousness.

Celestial Bodies

Sun/Moon Pair

The Sun typically represents masculine or yang energy, while the Moon represents feminine or yin energy (except in a few cultures, where it is reversed!). Using this concept, the Sun and the Moon are equal—two sides of a coin, two complementary types of energy. This is one way of looking at the Sun and the Moon.

However, in the trump sequence, the Moon appears first and is typically considered a more problematic and difficult part of the journey than the Sun, in which, psychologically speaking, we have emerged from the underworld and our work with the shadow self, and are ready to make the transition to full integration. In this construct, the Sun is a later stage of the integration process than the Moon, which represents our long return through the underworld of the subconscious to the light.

This concept and associated Moon/Sun symbolism has its basis and origin in alchemy. There are three primary colors associated with alchemical processes: black, white, and yellow/red. The black represents the early stages of the alchemical transformation, in which the male and female elements are separated and recombined in various ways. They are reduced to ash, and undergo various other transformations which blacken the starting materials. These processes are represented by the Devil and the Tower. In the next stage, the black material is successively purified and whitened, which is represented by the Star and the Moon, and a white or silver color. Finally, this female material or silver/white stone is united with the golden seed or masculine principle to create the integrated self, represented by gold, or the philosopher's stone. This process is started in the Sun and culminates with the World.

Sun

An interesting additional detail is that the sun is represented in many decks with alternating straight and wavy rays. This is an ancient way of representing the sun known as the *philosopher's sun,* and illustrates the Sun as the source of light (straight rays) and heat (wavy rays)—illumination and warmth, the life-giving energies.

Moon

In *Rider-Waite-Smith,* the Moon has a somewhat golden color, which is not the color we would expect to be associated with the Moon. This illustrates the concept that the Moon reflects the light of the Sun, and the only light that shines on the underworld or subconscious is merely a reflection, which gives rise to distortions and illusions.

The falling drops from the Moon may be yet another alchemical reference to dew that was gathered by alchemists in the light of the full moon, and used to wash and purify the blackened material to silver. The dew, called *May Dew,* is collected at night from the air, and is milky in color. It is believed to be related to the milk and blood of alchemy, and so represents the feminine purifying and life-giving principle.

In some cards, the Moon is depicted as a larger circle with a smaller circle inside it, offset to one side. Robin Wood explains this as a symbolic representation of the "full moon in the arms of the new," an allusion to the ever changing phases of the moon and its changeable, yet predictable and cyclical nature.

Stars

In the Star card, the seven stars are references to the seven planets of ancient astronomy/astrology, and the seven alchemical operations and metals that they represent. The central eight-pointed star is a reference to the eight-spoked Wheel, which was one of Waite's central concepts for the tarot deck (see the "Numbers" section). However, the eight-pointed star goes back well beyond Waite to the *Tarot de Marseilles,* and may represent an older mystical tradition.

Built Structures

Houses/Castles

Castles appear in many *Rider-Waite-Smith* cards, and they are symbols of civilization, security, self-determination (as in the Ace of Wands), and stability. It is interesting how few actual houses appear, mostly on those cards that have a more humble status, such as the Six of Cups and the Ten of Wands. Perhaps this is because these cards were drawn in England, where castles abound and more of the country houses look like castles. A ruined castle appears in the background of the Eight of Wands, suggesting the passing of time and the change that comes to all things.

Towns

Larger towns appear in a few cards, such as the King of Pentacles and the Four of Pentacles. These are the cards most directly associated with commerce and money. There is also an entrance to a town in the Eight of Pentacles, suggesting an opportunity for trade and sale of one's work.

Inside Spaces

Only a very few cards depict interior scenes—again, these are all Pentacles, such as the Three and the Eight. These are the cards most associated with productive work.

Walls

Walls are another symbol of safety and security, appearing in the Sun, the Six of Pentacles, the King of Pentacles, and the Two of Wands. In some of these cases, the walls are protective—in the Six of Pentacles, they may hide something in the past that is walled off so that the past is seen in rose-colored nostalgia. In the Two of Wands, the person is standing behind their protective wall, safe and secure with what they already have. Their upcoming decision is whether to leave these protective walls and venture out into the world, not knowing what they will find there—the choice between safety and risk. In other decks, the man in the Four of Pentacles is walled in *(Robin Wood)* or even in a prison *(Spiral* deck).

Church

There are churches in a few cards, notably the Five of Pentacles and the Four of Swords, and a church is implied in the Hierophant. These are all cards about spiritual renewal. In the case of the Five of Pentacles, it is the way out of the physical deprivation being endured. Interestingly, the Three of Pentacles also appears to show a man working in a church—perhaps a message that spirituality can be found even in mundane, everyday tasks.

Tents

The tents in the Seven of Swords are the only ones in the deck, and to me they have always suggested a temporary habitation, probably related to a battlefield. This provides the moral ambiguity of the card: is the person stealing, or legitimately making life difficult for his enemies/oppressors? Or perhaps he is only making off with the spoils of war, belonging to nobody.

Towers

Many towers appear in the deck. Most notable are the twin towers depicted in Death and the Moon. These are both gateways—and these twin towers have the same symbolism as the twin mountains on other cards. In Death, the towers are far in the background, but as you look through them, the sun is rising, and it appears to actually be a different world. When you step through these towers, there is no returning whence you came. Also, a stream flows to the towers, and fills the space between them—the only path to these towers is to lose your ego in the subconscious, and follow the collective stream where it takes you.

The towers of the Moon are somewhat different. They are not so far off, and there is a path that leads to them; however, the path is very long and winding, and leads into a dark land that is more shadowed than the foreground. There are tiny windows in the tower, and you wonder if someone may be watching. These are almost like the eyes of the conscious mind, walled off—and we are walking in the subconscious, well below the towers and the thoughts going on above. Lastly, of course, there is the single tower depicted in the Tower card. This tower represents our ego, our material and intellectual constructs, our protective devices, and our arrogance, like the Tower of Babel. It has a large golden crown on top, which is the first to be blasted away, symbolizing the loss of our pride and the humility that comes with this card.

Pillars

Closely related to the towers is the symbolism of the pillars that appear in three Major Arcana cards: the High Priestess, the Hierophant, and Justice. Of these, two appear to be concrete (Hierophant and Justice), representing that these entities act in the physical or material world. The High Priestess has esoteric pillars, one black and one white, with lotus blossoms, linking her to the qabala, Freemasonry, and an existence on a more spiritual plane.

The High Priestess and Justice both have veils between their pillars, symbolizing their guardianship of hidden knowledge. The veil of the High Priestess contains references to the Empress (pomegranates), showing that even though she may be a virgin priestess, she contains the potential of all fertility and womanhood within her. Behind this veil is a vast sea, a reference to her realm of the subconscious and memory. The veil of Justice is purple, symbolizing her psychic ability to see with the third eye and her guardianship of universal karmic forces, which are not always apparent to our senses and knowledge. This is one reason the Justice of the Universe may be mysterious to us, since we cannot see all that is known to her. The pillars of the Hierophant appear to be walled in with concrete, suggesting that either there is nothing behind them, or that whatever is there is not accessible to mere mortals. The Hierophant holds the keys to heaven and earth, and perhaps there is a hidden keyhole behind his throne that we cannot see.

Thrones

The Kings and Queens, Emperor and Empress all have thrones, which is one reason the Kings and Queens are associated with these two trump cards. The thrones represent maturity and dominion over their chosen realm. There are often interesting details to be noted on the thrones, such as references to the elemental and astrological symbols of the cards, and other things, such as the King of Cups' throne being out in the middle of the water, yet floating easily, showing that he is perfectly at home in the element of water and emotions, and can create his own dry land at will.

Chariot

In this card, the charioteer has his own kind of throne, which is also made of concrete, but moves through an act of will. Without this will and a perfect understanding of his tools, the chariot would go nowhere. The four pillars of the chariot represent the four elements. The symbol on the front is quite amusing—a round peg in a round hole—everything in its proper place. Notice that the charioteer is actually encased within the concrete; he is part and parcel of this chariot, and it is not separable from him.

Ships

Several cards have ships sailing: the Three of Wands, the Two of Pentacles, the Six of Swords, sometimes the Page of Cups. In the Two of Pentacles and the Page of Cups, the ships are tossed on a stormy sea, suggesting that in the background of what is being decided, there are changes ahead and emotional turbulence. In the Six of Swords, a more orderly and positive journey is being made away from the troubles of the past, on a sea of calmer emotions. In the Three of Wands, we see a perfectly calm and glowing sea, with ships traveling in apparent prosperity and adventure. Yet we know that the travels that have led up to this positive juncture have not always been trouble-free, and that this is the reward for long hard work.

Bridges

Only one card has an obvious bridge: the Five of Cups. In this card, the man is away from his home and is brooding on his spilled cups. One imagines that he has journeyed way out here just for the purpose of brooding—possibly he does not want others to see him doing this. The river represents the emotions of the past, which are hard to cross. Yet there is a bridge, which implies that there is a path, even if it is not visible in the card. This person could choose to leave these spilled cups here, pick up the other two golden cups, find the path and cross the bridge, and return home.

Tombs

Last, but not least, two cards depict tombs: the Four of Swords and Judgment. While these cards do not have that much to do with each other, they are both cards of spirituality—one depicts a temporary but peaceful rest and opportunity for renewal, while the other represents a more permanent and joyful rebirth of the soul.

The Game of Tarocchi

The game of tarocchi (or *tarock/tarok,* as it is known in Germanic-speaking countries) is mostly played in Europe today, and rules for the game are difficult to find in English. I have done my best to translate here. Computer programs for desktop play are available on the internet, mostly in French. There are many varieties of the game, from historical to modern; the rules given here are for the most popular current French version, which you are likely to encounter if you buy a tarocchi program. French terms are indicated in italics. Rules for the historical game and other tarocchi variants can be found at the Card Games website, www.pagat.com. This is a very complex and fascinating game, and the strategy is quite difficult.

Deal

Seventy-two of the cards are dealt out to four players (there is also a three-person variant). The remaining six cards are placed in a kitty *(chien),* facedown. Cards should be organized by suit in the hand, in ascending order within the suit. Aces are low, and courts are high, in their usual order. The Major Arcana are treated as a fifth trump suit, with 1 (the Magician) low and 21 (the World) high. The Fool is unnumbered (it usually appears with a star in the corners), and can be placed either below 1 or above 21, as it has a different role from the other trumps.

Bids

Bidding starts with the person to the right of the dealer, and proceeds around the table to the right. There are five possible bids: Pass *(Passe)*, Take *(Prise)*, Guard *(Guarde)*, Guard Without the Kitty *(Guarde sans)*, and Guard Against the Kitty *(Guarde contre)*, in increasing order of difficulty and reward. If all the players pass, the hand is not played, the kitty is revealed, and the next hand is shuffled and dealt by the next person to the right. This can happen any number of times, until someone bids on a hand. If any player is dealt only the 1 of trumps (the Magician) and no other trumps (including the Fool), he immediately announces this, and the hand is not played, with the deal moving to the right as if everyone had passed.

If someone makes a bid other than Pass, anyone else who wants to bid must bid higher than the first person's bid. For example, if the second person bids Take, then the third person must bid Guard or above. If the third person bids Guard, then the fourth person must bid higher still. The person who bids the highest plays alone, trying to take as many tricks as possible, and everyone else plays as a team against him. The following are descriptions of the possible bids:

Take

The player takes the kitty and adds it to his hand, first showing it to all the other players. He must then discard six cards facedown, which will be added to his points at the end. He normally cannot discard Kings, the Fool, or trumps. If he has no choice but to discard trumps, he may not discard the 1, the 21, or the Fool, which have a special role in the game. If he discards trumps, he must show them to the other players first.

Guard

This bid is the same as Take, but the points for his hand are multiplied by two whether he wins or loses.

Guard Without the Kitty

The kitty remains facedown, and is not added to the player's hand. It is still turned over and counted up with his points at the end of the hand. The points for the hand are multiplied by four, whether he wins or loses.

Guard Against the Kitty

The kitty remains facedown, and is not added to the player's hand. It is turned over at the end, but the cards in it are added to the opposing players' point totals. The points for the hand are multiplied by six whether he wins or loses.

Announcements

During the first trick, there are various things that can be announced by the players, which affect the scoring. You must make an announcement on the first trick when it is your turn to play a card; otherwise the chance is lost and the scoring is done as usual. The extra points go to whomever wins the hand, not necessarily to the person who announces them. You are not required to make an announcement or reveal your cards. Possible announcements include:

Poignée

The player has ten trumps in his hand (worth 20 points).

Double Poignée

The player has thirteen trumps in his hand (worth 30 points).

Triple Poignée

The player has fifteen trumps in his hand (worth 40 points).

With any of these announcements, the player must reveal the number of trumps he is declaring to the other players, and only that many. He can only reveal the Fool as part of the number if there are no other trumps to reveal.

Grand Slam (chelem)

A Grand Slam may also be announced prior to play, indicating that the player expects to win all the tricks. If he does so, he earns an extra 400 points. If he fails, he loses 200 points. If a player wins all the tricks without announcing it in advance, he still earns an extra 200 points.

Play

The person to the right of the dealer leads the first trick, and can play any card other than a trump. Trumps cannot be led until one has been played to take a trick. Each player must play a card of the same suit as the one that was led. If a player does not have a card of the same suit, he must play a trump if he has one; otherwise he may play any card of any other suit. If he plays a trump, he must play a trump that is higher than any other trumps that have already been played, if he has one; otherwise he may play any trump.

The only exception to these rules involves the Fool. The Fool may be played at any time, regardless of what suit was led and what other cards the player may have in his hand. A player may lead with the Fool, and when doing so, the next player may play any suit (he is not required to play a trump), and that suit determines the leading suit of the hand from that point on.

If no trumps are played, the person playing the highest card of the suit that was led wins the hand. If trumps are played, the person playing the highest trump wins the hand. The Fool never takes a trick, except under very special circumstances (when the player has taken all the tricks in a Grand Slam, and is leading with the Fool in the last hand).

Whichever team wins the trick (either the one who bid highest, or the other three players together) takes the cards, and places them in their pile. However, if the Fool was played, the Fool is kept by whoever played it. If the one who played it is not the winner of the trick, a low-scoring card (see below) is transferred to the winner of the trick as a substitute.

The only exception to this (everything about the Fool is an exception!) is that in the last trick of the hand, the Fool is kept by the winner of the trick. Therefore it is preferable to play the Fool before the last trick, since it is worth extra points when scoring.

Also, if the 1 of trumps is played in the last trick, the team who wins the last trick receives an extra 10 points (*petit au bout*). Because of this, the 1 of trumps should only be saved for the last trick if you are certain that no one else has any trumps left.

Scoring

At the end of the hand, the kitty is added to the appropriate pile, and the cards are counted up. Cards are worth points as follows:

1 of trumps, 21 of trumps, the Fool: 4.5 points

Kings: 4.5 points

Queens: 3.5 points

Knights: 2.5 points

Pages: 1.5 points

All other cards (including 2–20 of trumps): 0.5 points

The person who bid highest compares the number of points he took to the number he needed to win the hand. The number needed to win a hand depends on the number of special cards (*bouts*) you take during the hand—these are the 1 of trumps, the 21 of trumps, and the Fool. The more you have, the fewer points you need to take to win the hand:

0 bouts: 56 points needed

1 bout: 51 points needed

2 bouts: 41 points needed

All 3 bouts: 36 points needed

As you can see, the number of bouts you have to start with strongly influences your chances of winning, and affects your bidding strategy. You can always expect to take tricks with the 21 of trumps, and in a well-played hand, you can usually take a trick with the 1 of trumps. And, you keep the Fool, as long as you play it before the last trick. Much of the bidding revolves around the number of these cards that each player has in his hand, as well as the high-ranking court cards.

Scoring is done as follows:

Step 1. The player who bid highest subtracts the number of points he needed to win the hand from the number he actually took. If the total is positive, he adds 25 points to the score. If the total is negative, an additional 25 points is subtracted (awarded to the other side). If he took the 1 of trumps on the last trick, he receives an additional 10 points; and if the other side took it, 10 points are subtracted from his score.

Step 2. The total from step 1 is multiplied by the amount associated with his bid. For example, if he bid Guard, it is multiplied by two, whether it is positive or negative.

Step 3. Points for any declared poignées are awarded. If the high bidder won his hand, then he receives the bonus scores for all the poignées. If he lost the hand, the bonus scores for the poignées are subtracted from his score. Similarly, the bonus points or loss for declaring or winning a Grand Slam are applied during this last step. All of these bonuses are added or subtracted *after* the multiplication in step 2.

Step 4. This final score affects all four of the players, as if each of the other three players had given this many points to the high bidder. If the high bidder wins the hand and his final score is positive, he receives three times as many points as the final score, and each of the other three players receives negative points equal to the final score. If he loses the hand and the final score is negative, he receives negative points equal to three times the final score, and each of the other players receives positive points equal to the final score.

Winning the Game

The game is normally played until one player wins by accumulating 1,000 points, or whatever alternate conditions are agreed upon by the players.

Glossary

Alchemy—A medieval science believed to be able to transmute base metals such as lead into gold, with philosophical and spiritual counterparts designed to purify the body and the spirit and achieve immortality and enlightenment.

Anima/animus—The inner self that resides in the unconscious; incorporates characteristics of the opposite sex.

Archetype—A universal idea or concept present in the collective unconscious of the brain, which everyone shares. An image linked with an emotion, serving as the prototype for more complex imagery and concepts in the conscious mind.

Astrological chart—A map of the sky showing the positions of the planets at the time you were born, or at the moment of any significant event or time and place that you are interested in. The chart is drawn as a circle divided into twelve houses, each of which has its own significance and meaning, and showing which astrological signs ruled or will rule the houses at that moment and the locations of the planets at that time.

Astrology—The study of the planets and their movements, and how they affect individuals and human affairs.

Celtic Cross—A ten-card tarot spread developed in the 1890s by a member or associate of the Golden Dawn. It was taught to first-level initiates of the Golden Dawn, and widely used thereafter, after publication by Arthur E. Waite in his *Pictorial Key to the Tarot*.

Collective unconscious—Part of the subconscious or unconscious mind that everyone is born with; natural biological patterns of the mind that are inherited, including archetypes, instincts, and collective memory.

Conscious—The uppermost portion of your mind and thoughts. The mental processes of which you are aware.

Court cards—The Page, Knight, Queen, and King of each suit. Some decks may use other names, such as Princes and Princesses, for certain court cards.

Deterministic—Spreads that imply fixed outcomes that cannot be changed. Spreads that are more definite and predictive than others.

Dignities—Elemental characteristics of tarot cards (i.e., associations with water, fire, earth, or air) that interact with one another to weaken or strengthen particular cards in a spread.

Divination—Any method used to seek information on future events or hidden knowledge not available through normal means, such as tarot, astrology, I Ching, runes, tea leaves, etc.

Ego—The conscious mind; your conscious perception of yourself.

Elements—The four classical elements of the Renaissance period: earth, air, fire, and water.

Golden Dawn—More properly, the Hermetic Order of the Golden Dawn. Founded in 1887 in London by Dr. William Westcott and Samuel MacGregor Mathers, it was a society dedicated to the teachings of the Western Mystical Tradition, including ceremonial magick, qabala, astrology, divination (including tarot), and alchemy. Several prominent tarotists were members of the Golden Dawn, including Arthur E. Waite, Aleister Crowley, and Pamela Colman Smith.

Keyword—A single word or phrase that represents the meaning of a tarot card.

Layout—See *Spread.*

Little white books (LWBs)—A small pamphlet included with many tarot decks that gives very brief descriptions and meanings for the tarot cards.

Major Arcana—The 22 trump cards; those cards not included in any of the four suits. The cards numbered 0 (the Fool) through 21 (the World).

Minor Arcana—The Ace through King cards of the four suits; i.e., court cards plus pips.

Moon sign—The astrological sign that the Moon is in at the moment of your birth.

Numerology—The study of numbers and their meanings.

Pips—The Ace through Ten cards of the four suits.

Qabala—A spelling often used to refer to a metaphysical version of the Jewish mystical tradition, or kabalah. See also *Tree of Life.*

Querent—A person who consults a tarot reader.

Retrograde—A period in which a planet appears to be moving backward in the sky and in an astrological chart (due to our vantage point from the earth).

Reversal—An upside-down card, often read differently than a right-side-up card.

Rider-Waite-Smith—Either the original tarot deck or a family of similar decks modeled after the *Rider Tarot* published in 1909. Rider refers to the publishing house, Arthur E. Waite was the author of the deck and associated book, and Pamela Colman Smith was the artist.

Rising sign—The astrological sign that is on the eastern horizon at the time of birth, and also rules the first house in one's astrological chart.

Shadow self—A part of our self or personality that is rejected by the conscious mind and is repressed. It still exists and affects our behavior, usually in negative ways, especially when we don't recognize these as traits of our own, and project them onto others.

Significator—A card that represents the querent in a tarot reading.

Spread—The physical arrangement of tarot cards laid out for a reading. Each card position normally has a specific meaning, though the cards can also be read freeform.

Subconscious—Mental processes that are buried, hidden, or suppressed. Thoughts, emotions, and motivations of which you are not aware, or only vaguely aware.

Sun sign—The astrological sign that the Sun was in at the moment of your birth.

Synchronicity—A "meaningful coincidence." The concept that the universe is linked by an underlying connection in time and space, and that seemingly random events (such as the fall of tarot cards in a spread) may reflect the state of the universe or actual events occurring at the same moment.

Tarocchi—A trick-taking card game for which the tarot deck was most likely originally invented, still played in many parts of Europe today (also known as *Tarock* in Germanic countries).

Transit—In astrology, a planet traveling through a part of the sky ruled by an astrological sign.

Tree of Life—A diagram representing the universe, or the creation of the universe, based on Jewish mystical tradition, or qabala. This diagram also represents the universe as it lives within us. The 22 paths on the Tree of Life have been related to the 22 Trumps, and the 10 nodes, or *sephiroth,* to the Ace through Ten cards of the tarot.

Trumps—The 22 cards of the Major Arcana; those cards not included in any of the four suits. The cards numbered 0 (the Fool) through 21 (the World).